Phraseology in Foreign Language Learning and Teaching

Phraseology in Foreign Language Learning and Teaching

Edited by

Fanny Meunier

Université Catholique de Louvain

Sylviane Granger

Université Catholique de Louvain

John Benjamins Publishing Company

Amsterdam / Philadelphia

TM The paper used in this publication meets the minimum requirements of American National Standard for Information Sciences — Permanence of Paper for Printed Library Materials, ANSI Z39.48-1984.

Library of Congress Cataloging-in-Publication Data

Phraseology in foreign language learning and teaching / edited by Fanny Meunier, Sylviane
    Granger.
    p. cm.
Includes bibliographical references and index.
1. Language and languages--Study and teaching. 2. Phraseology--Study and teaching. I.
    Meunier, Fanny. II. Granger, Sylviane, 1951-
P53.6123.P49   2008
401'.93--dc22   2007037810
ISBN 978 90 272 3244 1 (Hb; alk. paper)

John Benjamins Publishing Company • P.O. Box 36224 • 1020 ME Amsterdam • The Netherlands
John Benjamins North America • P.O. Box 27519 • Philadelphia PA 19118-0519 • USA

We wish to dedicate this volume
to the memory of John Sinclair,
who has played a key role in raising
the profile of phraseology and inspired
much of the work reported in the volume.

Table of contents

List of contributors

Averil Coxhead,
Massey University,
New Zealand

Nick C. Ellis,
University of Michigan,
United States of America

Tess Fitzpatrick,
University of Wales,
United Kingdom

Céline Gouverneur,
Université catholique de Louvain,
Belgium

Sylviane Granger,
Université catholique de Louvain,
Belgium

Susanne Handl,
Ludwig-Maximilians
Universität München,
Germany

Graeme Kennedy,
Victoria University of Wellington,
New Zealand

Fanny Meunier,
Université catholique de Louvain,
Belgium

JoAnne Neff van Aertselaer,
Universidad Complutense de Madrid,
Spain

John Osborne,
Université de Savoie,
France

Magali Paquot,
Université catholique de Louvain,
Belgium

Mojca Pecman,
Université Paris Diderot,
France

Dirk Siepmann,
Universität Osnabrück,
Germany

David Wible,
National Central University,
Taiwan

Alison Wray,
Cardiff University,
United Kingdom

Acknowledgements

We are indebted to the Communauté française de Belgique for funding the concerted action research project on 'Foreign Language Learning: Phraseology and Discourse' (N° 03/08–301) within the framework of which this volume and the conference that gave rise to it have been produced. We would also like to thank all the contributors to this volume for their diligence in keeping to deadlines and patience in complying with our editorial demands. We are indebted to the many reviewers who provided insightful comments on preliminary versions of the chapters, thereby improving the overall quality of the volume. Special thanks are due to Stéphanie Delier for her help in formatting the chapters and keeping track of the many versions of the files. Finally, we would like to express our gratitude to Kees Vaes at Benjamins for his trust, support and patience.

Phraseology

The periphery and the heart of language

Nick C. Ellis

> Good leaders make people feel that they're at the very heart of things, not at the
> periphery
> (Warren G. Bennis)

Words mean things in the context of other words. Out of context, the default meaning of the word *leader* might well be a person who leads or commands a group, organization, or country, or an organization or company that is the most advanced or successful in a particular area. In the context of marketing, instead, it often appears in the collocation "loss-leader," referring to a commodity offered at cost or below cost to attract customers. But in British English (more so than American English), the word *leader* can also refer to a leading article or editorial, a preface such as this. The collocation "leader comment" appears 37 times in the British National Corpus, all occurrences being found in the register of broadsheet newspapers reporting national affairs.

Leaders in our realization of the inseparability of lexis and linguistic context of usage were Firth, Fries, and Harris. Firth's words are engrained in our memories: "You shall know a word by the company it keeps" (Firth 1957). Quotations such as this become entrenched in our minds. Its meaning is at the core of Structuralist linguistics which explored language as a self-contained relational structure, whose elemental constructions derive their forms and functions from their distributions in texts and discourse. Fries, the founder of the English Language Institute at the University of Michigan, distinguished between lexical and structural meaning, with structural meaning concerning the patterns relating a particular arrangement of form classes to particular structural meanings. In this view, language acquisition is the learning of an inventory of patterns as arrangements of words with their associated structural meanings. Fries' (1952) *Structure of English* presented an analysis of these patterns, Roberts' (1956) *Patterns of English* was a textbook presentation of Fries' system for classroom use, and *English Pattern Practices, Establishing the Patterns as Habits* (Fries, Lado & the Staff of the Michigan English

Language Institute 1958) taught beginning and intermediate EFL students English as patterns using audiolingual drills. Harris (1955, 1968), founder of the first US linguistics department at the University of Pennsylvania, developed rigorous discovery procedures for phonemes and morphemes, based on the distributional properties of these units. For Harris too, form and information (grammar and semantics) were inseparable. He developed mathematical analyses of sequences or ntuples of word classes (plus invariant morphemes) in order to specify subsets of sentences that are formally alike. Operator Grammar, a mathematical theory of how language carries information, is the culmination of his lifelong continuation of this work. It proposes that each human language is a self-organizing system in which both the syntactic and semantic properties of a word are established purely in relation to other words, and that the patterns of a language are learned through exposure to usage in social participation (Harris 1982, 1991).

What in the 1950s were known as structural patterns would today also be referred to by other names – "constructions" or "phraseologisms". Constructions, a term used in Cognitive Linguistic circles, are form-meaning mappings, conventionalized in the speech community, and entrenched as language knowledge in the learner's mind. They are the symbolic units of language relating the defining properties of their morphological, syntactic, and lexical form with particular semantic, pragmatic, and discourse functions (Croft 2001; Goldberg 1995, 2003, 2006). The term phraseologism, more the currency of Corpus Linguistics, adds an additional statistical emphasis to its definition as the co-occurrence of a lexical item and one or more additional linguistic elements which functions as one semantic unit in a clause or sentence and whose frequency of co-occurrence is larger than expected on the basis of chance (Gries in press; Howarth 1998a).

Consider *lead* again. As a verb, the first meaning that comes to mind out of context is transitive – to cause an animal to go on by holding them with a hand or halter while moving forward. In conversation and fiction, the subject is usually animate, as is the object: in BNC fiction, people lead things like horses, men, and soldiers (Davies 2007). But in academic prose, where *lead* occurs roughly three times more often, 99% of full noun subjects are inanimate and abstract, and this "activity" verb commonly has a causative or facilitative sense (Biber et al. 1999). Its typical pattern then is [cause *leads to* effects]. It is a common structure in academic spoken language too (Simpson et al. 2002), where cause is some policy, process, decision or tendency, and effects can be abstract, like problems, good, victory, and conflict, or concrete like respiratory failure, or cell survival. In many ways it operates like the verb *cause*. But not in all ways. First, syntactically, *lead to* is not used with human subjects and does not appear in the passive. Second, semantically, *lead to* is less direct than *cause*, implying a series of steps between cause and effect. And third in terms of its semantic prosody (Louw 1993).

Consider the alternatives "tourism may cause economic improvement" vs. "tourism may lead to economic improvement". The latter seems more felicitous. *Cause* (something causes an accident/catastrophe/other negative event) has a negative semantic prosody or association (Hoey 2005). Its general tendency is to co-occur with negative expressions; its deep objects (or effects) are overwhelmingly negative and thus it acquires this "consistent aura of meaning" from these collocates. The generalization comes from usage – there are no defining aspects of the meaning of *cause* which entails that it will take negative rather than positive objects. But *lead to* does not have this semantic prosody – the split between positive and negative objects for *lead to* are approximately 50/50 (Johns 2007). And thus, of our two alternatives above, we prefer *lead to* in describing the positive outcomes of economic improvement. The patterns of *lead* illustrate quite clearly how patterns of usage become ingrained in the language, how repeated pairings of particular morphological, syntactic, and lexical form become associated with particular semantic, pragmatic, and discourse functions. High type frequency gives generalization (Bybee & Thompson 2000) – the greater the ratio of negative to positive objects, the greater the negative prosody (Ellis, Frey & Jalkanen 2007a). High token frequency leads to increasing entrenchment and idiomaticity (Bybee in press; Ellis 2002a), from the semi-productive 'lead [someone] up/down the garden path', to the idiomatic, 'lead the life of Riley' or 'you can lead a horse to water but you can't make him drink'. There is structural patterning at all levels of language.

Structuralism was the dominant approach in linguistics for the earlier part of the twentieth century. It was overtaken in the 1960s by Generative approaches. Harris' student, Chomsky (1965, 1981) abandoned construction-specific rules and developed the Principles-and-Parameters approach, the general grammatical rules and principles of Universal Grammar. Grammar became top-down and rule-governed, rather than bottom-up and emergent. Constructions were no longer interesting for such theories of syntax – instead they were epiphenomena arising from the interaction of more fundamental and universal principles. Chomsky (1981) classified grammatical phenomena into the 'core' of the grammar and a 'periphery', where the core phenomena were those describable by the parameterized principles of Universal Grammar, and peripheral phenomena were those marked elements and constructions that are not widespread. Grammar was modularized, encapsulated, divorced from performance, lexis, social usage, and the rest of cognition. Patterns, structures, constructions, formulas, phraseology, all were peripheral.

A ProQuest-CSA search through Social Science publications over the last 50 years identifies just 53 papers relating to *phraseology* in the 1960s and 199 in the 1970s.

But then something happened. There were 529 in the 80s, and 709 in the 90s. Which thinkers and what ideas brought phraseology back to the centre of things?

Within *Core Theories of Grammar*, the leaders were Fillmore, Goldberg, and Croft. Fillmore (1988; Fillmore, Kay, & O'Connor 1988) argued that far from being peripheral, constructions were in fact central to the grammar. A main tenet of this approach was that the grammatical mechanisms needed to account for the grammatical periphery can also be used to account for the core phenomena. Goldberg's (1995, 2003) Construction Grammar argues that all grammatical phenomena can be understood as learned pairings of form (from morphemes, words, idioms, to partially lexically filled and fully general phrasal patterns) and their associated semantic or discourse functions: "the network of constructions captures our grammatical knowledge in toto, i.e. It's constructions all the way down" (Goldberg 2006: 18). There are close relations here with Functional linguistic descriptions of the associations between particular lexico-grammatical patterns and their systemic functions (their propositional, interpersonal, and textual semantics) (Halliday 1985; Langacker 1987, 2000). Coming from a typological perspective, Croft's Radical Construction Grammar (2001; Croft & Cruise 2004) rejects the idea that syntactic categories and relations are universal and argues instead that they are both language- and construction-specific. What is universal is the ways that meanings map onto form.[1]

Fifty years after Firth, *Corpus Linguistic* analyses of large collections of text have affirmed that natural language makes considerable use of recurrent patterns of words and constructions. Lexical context is crucial to knowledge of word meaning and grammatical role. Sinclair (1991: 100) led here, summarizing the results of corpus investigations of such distributional regularities in the *Principle of Idiom*: "a language user has available to him or her a large number of semi-preconstructed phrases that constitute single choices, even though they might appear to be analyzable into segments," and suggested that for normal texts, the first mode of analysis to be applied is the idiom principle, as most of text is interpretable by this principle.[2] Kjellmer (1987: 140) reached a similar conclusion: "In all kinds of texts, collocations are indispensable elements with which our utterances are very largely made". Erman & Warren (2000) estimated that about half of fluent

---

1.   While there would be disagreement at the core, the growing recognition of constructions in language has prompted their analysis within generative approaches too (Culicover 1999; Jackendoff 1997).

2.   Note that linguistic constructions are not *either* memorized formulas or open constructions, instead this distinction is a matter of degree. The phenomenon is entirely graded, depending upon frequency of usage (Ellis 2002a).

native text is constructed according to the idiom principle.[3] Comparisons of written and spoken corpora suggest that phraseological units are even more frequent in spoken language (Biber et al. 1999; Brazil 1995; Leech 2000).

But there are other external forces motivating the revival too. Phraseology binds words, grammar, semantics, and social usage, and research in these areas provides further support. *Cognitive Linguistics* (Croft & Cruise 2004; Langacker 1987, 2000; Robinson & Ellis 2008b; Taylor 2002) shows how language draws on basic cognition, on perception, attention allocation, memory and categorization, that it cannot be separated from these as a distinct, modularized, self-governed entity, that knowledge of language is integrated with our general knowledge of the world, and that language use and language function interact with language structure. Thus Phraseology resonates with a wide range of research areas within Cognitive Linguistics and Cognitive Science more generally. Cognition, consciousness, experience, embodiment, brain, self, and human interaction, society, culture, and history are all inextricably intertwined in rich, complex, and dynamic ways in language, so an understanding of language is incomplete without them.

Usage-based theories of language acquisition (Barlow & Kemmer 2000) hold that we learn constructions while engaging in communication, the "interpersonal communicative and cognitive processes that everywhere and always shape language" (Slobin 1997). They have become increasingly influential in the study of child language acquisition. They have turned upside down again generative assumptions of innate language acquisition devices, the continuity hypothesis, and top-down, rule-governed, processing, bringing back data-driven, emergent accounts of linguistic systematicities. *Constructionist theories of child language acquisition* use dense longitudinal corpora to chart the emergence of creative linguistic competence from children's analyses of the utterances in their usage history and from their abstraction of regularities within them (Goldberg 1995, 2003, 2006; Tomasello 2003, 1998). Children typically begin with phrases and they are initially fairly conservative in extending the use of the particular verb within them to other structures. The usual developmental sequence is from formula to low-scope slot-and-frame pattern, to creative construction. They learn words from phrases as much as phrases from words. Each of the language subsystems develops hierarchically by repeated cycles of differentiation and integration: "Language, as a complex, hierarchical, behavioral structure with a lengthy course

---

3.   Note that idiomaticity is a graded phenomenon too. Think instead of a collocation-idiom continuum (Fernando 1996) with a variety of factors (their compositionality and syntactic, lexicosyntactic, and morphological flexibility) determining the degree of idiomaticity (Wulff submitted). Collocations and idioms are two poles of the very same thing, namely phraseological language.

of development . . . is rich in sequential dependencies: syllables and formulaic phrases before phonemes and features . . . , holophrases before words, words before simple sentences, simple sentences before lexical categories, lexical categories before complex sentences, and so on" (Studdert-Kennedy 1991: 10).

Psycholinguistic research demonstrates language users' exquisite sensitivity to the frequencies of occurrence of different constructions in the language input (Gernsbacher 1994) and to the contingencies of their mappings of form and meaning (MacWhinney 1987), and thus is clear testament of the influence of each usage event, and the processing of its component constructions, upon the learner's system. *Probabilistic and frequency-based theories* of language analyze how frequency and repetition affect and ultimately bring about form in language and how probabilistic knowledge drives language comprehension and production (Bod et al. 2003; Bybee & Hopper 2001; Ellis 2002a, 2002b; Hoey 2005; Jurafsky 2002; Jurafsky & Martin 2000). Collocations and formulaic sequences are processed more fluently than openly constructed language (Ellis, Frey & Jalkanen 2007a, 2007b; Ellis & Simpson-Vlach in preparation; Ellis, Simpson-Vlach & Maynard in preparation). *Cognitive theories of categorization and generalization* show how schematic constructions are abstracted over less schematic ones that are inferred inductively by the learner in acquisition (Harnad 1987; Lakoff 1987; Taylor 1998).

Phraseological analyses demonstrate that much of communication makes use of fixed expressions memorized as formulaic chunks, that language is rich in collocational and colligation restrictions and semantic prosodies, that the phrase is the basic level of language representation where form and meaning meet with greatest reliability, that formulaic sequences play a central role in child language acquisition, and that fluent language users have a vast repertoire of memorized language sequences (Ellis 1996; Granger & Meunier in press; Pawley & Syder 1983; Sinclair 1991, 2004; Wray 2002). The unit of language is "the phrase, the whole phrase, and nothing but the phrase" (Sinclair in press). The phrase is at the centre of language, and thus calls the attention of the broad range of language sciences.

What of the phrase in second language acquisition and instruction? What of those early theories of Fries and colleagues concerning phrases and other structural patterns? How have they fared over the last 50 years? In *SLA Description and Theory* they have cropped up repeatedly under various guises as holophrases (Corder 1973), prefabricated routines and patterns (Hakuta 1974), formulaic speech (Wong-Fillmore 1976), memorized sentences and lexicalized stems (Pawley & Syder 1983), lexical phrases (Nattinger 1980), formulas (R. Ellis 1994; McLaughlin 1995), chunks (Ellis 1996), and constructions (Ellis 2003, 2006). There has never been more interest in second language phraseology, as recent reviews in applied linguistics (Cowie 1998; Granger & Meunier in press; Schmitt

2004; Wray 2002) and cognitive linguistics (Gries & Wulff 2005; Robinson & Ellis 2008b) make clear. In *Testing*, the novice stages of adult language acquisition are characterized in the ACTFL Oral Proficiency guidelines as "relying heavily on learned phrases or recombinations of these" (American Council on the Teaching of Foreign Languages (ACTFL) 1999:8). Phraseology features centrally in special purposes tests, for example the International Civil Aviation Organization language proficiency requirements establish clear minimum proficiency level for native and non-native speaking flight crew members and air traffic controllers in the use of both plain language and ICAO phraseologies (Mathews 2004). Every genre of English for Academic Purposes and English for Special Purposes has its own phraseology, and learning to be effective in the genre involves learning this (Swales 1990). Lexicographers develop their learner dictionaries upon large corpora (Hunston & Francis 1996; Ooi 1998) and dictionaries focus upon examples of usage as much as definitions, or even more so. In *Instruction*, Nattinger & DeCarrico (1992) argue for the "lexical phrase" as the pedagogically applicable unit of pre-fabricated language, "for a great deal of the time anyway, language production consists of piecing together the ready-made units appropriate for a particular situation and ... comprehension relies on knowing which of these patterns to predict in these situations. Our teaching therefore would center on these patterns and the ways they can be pieced together, along with the ways they vary and the situations in which they occur" (Nattinger 1980:341) The Lexical Approach (Lewis 1993), similarly predicated upon the idiom principle, focuses instruction on relatively fixed expressions that occur frequently in spoken language. Corpora now play central roles in language teaching (Cobb 2007; Römer in press; Sinclair 1996). Phraseology is everywhere in current SLA research.

Yet, at the same time, there are many gaps in our understanding. Despite formulas being "one of the hallmarks of child second language development" (McLaughlin 1995) and, as the ACTFL guidelines demonstrate, their being central in novice adult learners' second language, advanced learners of second language have great difficulty with nativelike collocation and idiomaticity. Many grammatical sentences generated by language learners sound unnatural and foreign (Granger 1998; Howarth 1998b; Pawley & Syder 1983). This dissociation with proficiency suggests that the formulaic knowledge of the novice is different from that of the fluent language user, and is created differently. There are several consequences.

The first relates to explicit and implicit knowledge and their interface. Many of the novice's formulas are explicitly learned (N. C. Ellis 1994b) as wholes, fast mapped as declarative memories like other aspects of vocabulary (N. C. Ellis 1994a), whereas the graded statistical knowledge of sequences that underpins much of collocation knowledge is implicitly acquired from usage, with the system requiring hundreds of hours of usage for its appropriate tuning (Ellis 2002a, in press). The relations between explicit and implicit knowledge and their interface is as important for formulaic language as it is for other aspects of SLA (Ellis 2005), and the resolution of these issues lies at the core of second language instruction.

The second relates to language transfer. Languages lead their speakers to experience different 'thinking for speaking' and thus to construe experience in different ways (Slobin 1996). Learning another language involves learning how to construe the world like natives of the L2, 'rethinking for speaking' (Robinson & Ellis 2008a), and transfer affects L2 phraseology at numerous levels (Ellis 2007; Gass & Selinker 1983; Kellerman 1995; Odlin 1989; Neff van Aertselaer this volume; Paquot this volume).

The third relates to the ways in which schematic constructions are abstracted over less schematic ones inductively in acquisition, and how prototypicality of meaning and type and token frequency conspire in determining which formulaic patterns are learned first and how generalized productive schemata then emerge around them. Research suggests that category learning is optimized by an initial, low-variance sample centered upon prototypical exemplars. We learn about the category of birds, for example, better if we are first exposed to typical birds like sparrows, thrushes, and blackbirds, than if our initial experience is of diverse exemplars like ostriches, penguins, and humming-birds. This allows us to get a 'fix' on what accounts for most of the category members. Zipf's law describes how a few words in the language occur very often while many others occur rarely. Consequently, the more input of a language we get, the more salient the common words become. Goldberg (2006) proposes that Zipf's law applies within individual construction profiles too, so their learning as categories by children is optimized because there is one very high frequency exemplar that is also prototypical of their meaning (e.g., the [Subj V Obj Obl$_{path/loc}$] construction is exemplified in the children's speech by _put_ 31% of the time, _get_ 16%, _take_ 10%, and _do/pick_ 6%). This profile closely mirrored that of the mothers' speech to these children (with, e.g., _put_ appearing 38% of the time in this construction that was otherwise exemplified by 43 different verbs). These important insights have led us at least (Ellis in press; Ellis, Ferreira Junior & Ke in preparation; Robinson & Ellis 2008b) to consider how one cannot understand second language acquisition without considering the combined effects of form-meaning correspondences, construction types and tokens and their distributional properties, and prototypicality effects.

Phraseology 2005 (the "Many Faces of Phraseology") conference in Louvain in 2005 organized by Sylviane Granger and Fanny Meunier was an important landmark in that it was truly interdisciplinary, bringing together research specialists from the range of approaches which I have outlined in this preface. Only in the interactions of these fields will we understand second language acquisition and the instructional implications that ensue. The chapters that follow here, first discussed at that conference, concern these important themes of second language learning of formulaic language, its analysis in learner corpora, its limitations, its susceptibility to transfer, and, particularly, the types of support which might be given to learners through appropriate instructional methodologies, materials, digital resources, and dictionaries. They make it clear that phraseology pervades theoretical, empirical, and applied linguistics. Like blood in systemic circulation, it flows through heart and periphery, nourishing all.

Acknowledgement

I thank Stefanie Wulff for constructive comments on an earlier draft.

References

American Council on the Teaching of Foreign Languages (ACTFL) (1999). *ACTFL proficiency levels revised 1999*. Alexandria, VA: ACTFL.

Barlow, M. & S. Kemmer (eds.) (2000). *Usage based models of language*. Stanford, CA: CSLI.

Biber, D., S. Johansson, G. Leech, S. Conrad & E. Finegan (1999). *Longman grammar of spoken and written English*. Harlow: Pearson Education.

Bod, R., J. Hay & S. Jannedy (eds.) (2003). *Probabilistic linguistics*. Cambridge, MA: The MIT Press.

Brazil, D. (1995). *A grammar of speech*. Oxford: Oxford University Press.

Bybee, J. (in press). Mechanisms of change in grammaticalization: The role of frequency. In Janda, R. D. & B. D. Joseph (eds.), *Handbook of historical linguistics*. Oxford: Blackwell.

Bybee, J. & P. Hopper (eds.) (2001). *Frequency and the emergence of linguistic structure*. Amsterdam: John Benjamins.

Bybee, J. & S. Thompson (2000). Three frequency effects in syntax. *Berkeley Linguistic Society, 23*, 65–85.

Chomsky, N. (1965). *Aspects of the theory of syntax*. Cambridge, MA: The MIT Press.

Chomsky, N. (1981). *Lectures on government and binding*. Dordrecht: Foris.

Cobb, T. (2007). The compleat lexical tutor (v.4.5 03/06). For data-driven language learning on the web [Electronic Version] from http://132.208.224.131/.

Corder, S. P. (1973). *Introducing applied linguistics*. New York, NY: Penguin.

Cowie, A. P. (ed.) (1998). *Phraseology: Theory, analysis, and applications*. Oxford: Oxford University Press.

Croft, W. (2001). *Radical construction grammar: Syntactic theory in typological perspective*. Oxford: Oxford University Press.

Croft, W. & A. Cruise (2004). *Cognitive linguistics*. Cambridge: Cambridge University Press.

Culicover, P. W. (1999). *Syntactic nuts: Hard cases, syntactic theory, and language acquisition*. Oxford: Oxford University Press.

Davies, M. (2007). VIEW: Variation in English words and phrases, http://corpus.byu.edu/bnc/

Ellis, N. C. (1994a). Vocabulary acquisition: The implicit ins and outs of explicit cognitive mediation. In Ellis, N. C. (ed.) *Implicit and explicit learning of languages,* 211–282. San Diego, CA: Academic Press.

Ellis, N. C. (ed.) (1994b). *Implicit and explicit learning of languages.* San Diego, CA: Academic Press.

Ellis, N. C. (1996). Sequencing in SLA: Phonological memory, chunking, and points of order. *Studies in Second Language Acquisition, 18* (1), 91–126.

Ellis, N. C. (2002a). Frequency effects in language processing: A review with implications for theories of implicit and explicit language acquisition. *Studies in Second Language Acquisition, 24* (2), 143–188.

Ellis, N. C. (2002b). Reflections on frequency effects in language processing. *Studies in Second Language Acquisition, 24* (2), 297–339.

Ellis, N. C. (2003). Constructions, chunking, and connectionism: The emergence of second language structure. In Doughty, C. & M. H. Long (eds.) *Handbook of second language acquisition,* 63–103. Oxford: Blackwell.

Ellis, N. C. (2005). At the interface: Dynamic interactions of explicit and implicit language knowledge. *Studies in Second Language Acquisition, 27,* 305–352.

Ellis, N. C. (2006). Cognitive perspectives on SLA: The Associative Cognitive CREED. *AILA Review, 19,* 100–121.

Ellis, N. C. (2007) Learned attention in language acquisition: Blocking, salience, and cue competition. Paper presented at the EuroCogSci07, the Second European Cognitive Science Conference, May 23–27, Delphi, Greece.

Ellis, N. C. (in press). Optimizing the input: Frequency and sampling in usage-based and form-focussed learning. In Long, M. H. & C. Doughty (eds.) *Handbook of Second and Foreign Language Teaching.* Oxford: Blackwell.

Ellis, N. C., F. Ferreira Junior & J.-Y. Ke (in preparation). Form, function, and frequency: Zipfian family construction profiles in SLA.

Ellis, N. C., E. Frey & I. Jalkanen (2007a). The psycholinguistic reality of collocation and semantic prosody – Neighbourhoods of knowing (1): Lexical access. Paper presented at the Exploring the Lexis-Grammar interface, October 4–8, Hanover.

Ellis, N. C., E. Frey & I. Jalkanen (2007b). The psycholinguistic reality of collocation and semantic prosody – Neighbourhoods of knowing (2): Semantic access. Paper presented at the Symposium on Formulaic language, April 18–21, University of Wisconsin Milwaukee.

Ellis, N. C., & R. Simpson-Vlach (in preparation). Native and non-native processing of formulas and collocations: Psycholinguistic analyses.

Ellis, N. C., R. Simpson-Vlach & C. Maynard (in preparation). The processing of formulas in native and second-language speakers: Psycholinguistic and corpus determinants. *TESOL Quarterly.*

Ellis, R. (1994). *The study of second language acquisition.* Oxford: Oxford University Press.

Erman, B. & B. Warren (2000). The idiom principle and the open choice principle. *Text, 20,* 29–62.

Fernando, C. (1996). *Idioms and idiomaticity.* Oxford: Oxford University Press.

Fillmore, C. (1988). The mechanisms of construction grammar. *Berkeley Linguistics Society, 14,* 35–55.

Fillmore, C., P. Kay, & M. C. O'Connor (1988). Regularity and idiomaticity in grammatical constructions: the case of let alone. *Language, 64,* 501–538.

Firth, J. R. (1957). *A synopsis of linguistic theory, 1930–1955.* Oxford: Basil Blackwell.

Fries, C. C. (1952). *The structure of English*. New York, NY: Harcourt, Brace and Co.

Fries, C. C., R. Lado & the Staff of the Michigan English Language Institute. (1958). *English pattern practices: Establishing the patterns as habits*. Ann Arbor, MI: University of Michigan Press.

Gass, S. & L. Selinker (eds.) (1983). *Language transfer in language learning*. Rowley, MA: Newbury House.

Gernsbacher, M. A. (1994). *A handbook of psycholinguistics*. San Diego, CA: Academic Press.

Goldberg, A. E. (1995). *Constructions: A construction grammar approach to argument structure*. Chicago IL: University of Chicago Press.

Goldberg, A. E. (2003). Constructions: A new theoretical approach to language. *Trends in Cognitive Science, 7*, 219–224.

Goldberg, A. E. (2006). *Constructions at work: The nature of generalization in language*. Oxford: Oxford University Press.

Granger, S. (ed.) (1998). *Learner English on Computer*. London: Longman.

Granger, S. & F. Meunier (eds.) (in press). *Phraseology: An interdisciplinary perspective*. Amsterdam: John Benjamins.

Gries, S. T. (in press). Phraseology and linguistic theory: A brief survey. In Granger, S. & F. Meunier (eds.) *Phraseology: An interdisciplinary perspective*. Amsterdam: John Benjamins.

Gries, S. T. & S. Wulff (2005). Do foreign language learners also have constructions? Evidence from priming, sorting, and corpora. *Annual Review of Cognitive Linguistics, 3*, 182–200.

Hakuta, K. (1974). Prefabricated patterns and the emergence of structure in second language acquisition. *Language Learning, 24*, 287–298.

Halliday, M. A. K. (1985). *An introduction to functional grammar*. London: Arnold.

Harnad, S. (ed.) (1987). *Categorical perception: The groundwork of cognition*. New York, NY: Cambridge University Press.

Harris, Z. (1955). From phoneme to morpheme. *Language, 31*, 190–222.

Harris, Z. (1968). *Mathematical structures of language*. New York, NY: Wiley and Sons.

Harris, Z. (1982). *A grammar of English on mathematical principles*. New York, NY: John Wiley and Sons.

Harris, Z. (1991). *A theory of language and information: A mathematical approach*. Oxford: Oxford University Press.

Hoey, M. P. (2005). *Lexical priming: A new theory of words and language*. London: Routledge.

Howarth, P. (1998a). Phraseology and second language proficiency. *Applied Linguistics, 19* (1), 24–44.

Howarth, P. (1998b). The phraseology of learners' academic writing. In Cowie, A.P. (ed.) *Phraseology: Theory, Analysis, and Applications*, 161–186. Oxford: Oxford University Press.

Hunston, S. & G. Francis (1996). *Pattern grammar: A corpus driven approach to the lexical grammar of English*. Amsterdam: John Benjamins.

Jackendoff, R. (1997). Twistin' the night away. *Language, 73*, 543–559.

Johns, T. (2007, 5 July). Kibbitzer 24. Cause vs. lead to v. bring about, from http://www.eisu. bham.ac.uk/johnstf/revis024.htm

Jurafsky, D. (2002). Probabilistic modeling in psycholinguistics: Linguistic comprehension and production. In Bod, R., J. Hay & S. Jannedy (eds.) *Probabilistic Linguistics*, 39–96. Cambridge, MA: The MIT Press.

Jurafsky, D. & J. H. Martin (2000). *Speech and language processing: An introduction to natural language processing, speech recognition, and computational linguistics*. Englewood Cliffs, NJ: Prentice-Hall.

Kellerman, E. (1995). Crosslinguistic influence: Transfer to nowhere? *Annual Review of Applied Linguistics, 15*, 125–150.

Kjellmer, G. (1987). Aspects of English collocations. In Meijs, W. (ed.) *Corpus linguistics and beyond*, 133–140. Amsterdam: Rodopi.

Lakoff, G. (1987). *Women, fire, and dangerous things: What categories reveal about the mind.* Chicago, IL: University of Chicago Press.

Langacker, R. W. (1987). *Foundations of cognitive grammar: Vol. 1. Theoretical prerequisites.* Stanford, CA: Stanford University Press.

Langacker, R. W. (2000). A dynamic usage-based model. In Barlow, M. & S. Kemmer (eds.) *Usage-based models of language*, 1–63. Stanford, CA: CSLI.

Leech, L. (2000). Grammars of spoken English: New outcomes of corpus-oriented research. *Language Learning, 50*, 675–724.

Lewis, M. (1993). *The lexical approach: The state of ELT and the way forward.* Hove: Language Teaching Publications.

Louw, B. (1993). Irony in the Text or Insincerity in the Writer? The Diagnostic Potential of Semantic Prosodies. In Baker, M., G. Francis & E. Tognini-Bonelli (eds.) *Text and technology. In honour of John Sinclair*, 157–176. Amsterdam: John Benjamins.

MacWhinney, B. (ed.) (1987). *Mechanisms of language acquisition.* Hillsdale, NJ: Lawrence Erlbaum Associates.

Mathews, E. (2004). Language proficiency requirements of the international civil aviation organization. *Professional Communication Conference, IPCC 2004 Proceedings. International Volume, 29*, 266–270.

McLaughlin, B. (1995). Fostering second language development in young children: Principles and practices. *National Center For Research On Cultural Diversity And Second Language Learning: Educational practice report: 14*, from http://www.ncbe.gwu.edu/miscpubs/ncrcdsll/epr14.htm

Nattinger, J. R. (1980). A lexical phrase grammar for ESL. *TESOL Quarterly, 14*, 337–344.

Nattinger, J. R. & J. DeCarrico (1992). *Lexical phrases and language teaching.* Oxford: Oxford University Press.

Odlin, T. (1989). *Language transfer.* New York, NY: Cambridge University Press.

Ooi, V. B. Y. (1998). *Computer corpus lexicography.* Edinburgh: Edinburgh University Press.

Pawley, A., & F. H. Syder (1983). Two puzzles for linguistic theory: Nativelike selection and nativelike fluency. In Richards, J. C. & R. W. Schmidt (eds.) *Language and communication*, 191–225. London: Longman.

Roberts, P. (1956). *Patterns of English.* New York, NY: Harcourt, Brace & World.

Robinson, P. & N. C. Ellis (2008a). Conclusion: Cognitive linguistics, second language acquisition and L2 instruction—Issues for research. In Robinson, P. & N. C. Ellis (eds.) *A handbook of cognitive linguistics and SLA.* Mahwah, NJ: Lawrence Erlbaum.

Robinson, P. & N. C. Ellis (eds.) (2008b). *A handbook of cognitive linguistics and SLA.* London: Routledge.

Römer, U. (in press). Corpora and language teaching. In Lüdeling, A. & M. Kytö (eds.), *Korpuslinguistik – Corpus linguistics. An international handbook.* Berlin: Mouton de Gruyter.

Schmitt, N. (ed.) (2004). *Formulaic sequences.* Amsterdam: John Benjamins.

Simpson, R., S. Briggs, J. Ovens & J. M. Swales (2002). The Michigan corpus of academic spoken English. [Electronic Version]. *The Regents of the University of Michigan* from http://www.hti.umich.edu/m/micase.

Sinclair, J. (1991). *Corpus, concordance, collocation.* Oxford: Oxford University Press.

Sinclair, J. (2004). *Trust the text: Language, corpus and discourse.* London: Routledge.

Sinclair, J. (in press). The phrase, the whole phrase, and nothing but the phrase. In Granger, S. & F. Meunier (eds.) *Phraseology: An interdisciplinary perspective.* Amsterdam: John Benjamins.

Sinclair, J. (ed.) (1996). *How to use corpora in language teaching.* Amsterdam: John Benjamins.

Slobin, D. I. (1996). From "thought and language" to "thinking for speaking." In Gumperz, J. J. & S. C. Levinson (eds.) *Rethinking linguistic relativity, 70–96.* Cambridge: Cambridge University Press.

Slobin, D. I. (1997). The origins of grammaticizable notions: Beyond the individual mind. In Slobin, D. I. (ed.) *The crosslinguistic study of language acquisition,* Vol. 5, 265–323. Mahwah, NJ: Lawrence Erlbaum Associates.

Studdert-Kennedy, M. (1991). Language development from an evolutionary perspective. In Krasnegor, N. A., D. M. Rumbaugh, R. L. Schiefelbusch & M. Studdert-Kennedy (eds.) *Biological and behavioral determinants of language development,* 5–28. Mahwah, NJ: Lawrence Erlbaum Associates.

Swales, J. M. (1990). *Genre analysis: English in academic and research settings.* Cambridge: Cambridge University Press.

Taylor, J. R. (1998). Syntactic constructions as prototype categories. In Tomasello, M. (ed.) *The new psychology of language: Cognitive and functional approaches to language structure,* 177–202. Mahwah, NJ: Lawrence Erlbaum Associates.

Taylor, J. R. (2002). *Cognitive grammar.* Oxford: Oxford University Press.

Tomasello, M. (2003). *Constructing a language.* Boston, MA: Harvard University Press.

Tomasello, M. (ed.) (1998). *The new psychology of language: Cognitive and functional approaches to language structure.* Mahwah, NJ: Lawrence Erlbaum Associates.

Wong-Fillmore, L. (1976). *The second time around.* Stanford, CA: Stanford University.

Wray, A. (2002). *Formulaic language and the lexicon.* Cambridge: Cambridge University Press.

Wulff, S. (submitted). *Rethinking idiomaticity: A usage-based approach.*

Introduction

Sylviane Granger and Fanny Meunier

Phraseology in Language Learning and Teaching is one of the concrete outcomes of an interdisiciplinary conference on phraseology entitled 'Phraseology 2005. The Many Faces of Phraseology" organized in Louvain-la-Neuve in October 2005. The raison d'être of the conference, which brought together some 170 participants from a wide range of countries, was to look at phraseology from a wide range of perspectives. Three volumes emanated from the conference: a volume in French entitled *La phraséologie dans tous ses états* edited by Catherine Bolly, Jean René Klein and Béatrice Lamiroy (Cahiers de l'Institut de Linguistique de Louvain, Peeters, in press), and two volumes in English, one intended to highlight the multi-faceted nature of phraseology (*Phraseology: An Interdisciplinary Perspective*, edited by Sylviane Granger and Fanny Meunier (Benjamins in press) and the current volume, which, as the title suggests, investigates the role of phraseology in foreign language learning and teaching.

In the Preface, Nick Ellis offers an insightful overview of the place of phraseology within several linguistic approaches. He demonstrates that phraseology lies at the core of a wide range of research areas which all contribute to a better understanding of language, be it in terms of cognition, description, acquisition or teaching. The eleven chapters of the book each address a key issue raised by Ellis (p. 6): "What of the phrase in second-language acquisition and instruction"? The chapters are organized in three sections, each focusing on a specific perspective: Extracting and describing phraseological units, learning phraseological units, and recording and exploiting phraseological units. Although the articles have all been classified into one of these three sections, in accordance with their major focus, many in fact deal with two, and sometimes even three, perspectives. In the conclusion to the volume, the editors pull together the various threads running through the volume and identify key areas for further research.

Section I, *Extracting and describing phraseological units*, focuses on the key role played by native and learner corpora in the extraction and description of multiword units. Finding and extracting the relevant phraseological units to teach are two initial and crucial steps in informing language pedagogy. In the first chapter, Graeme Kennedy analyses the semantic preferences associated with eight high frequency verbs in the British National Corpus. He shows, among other things, that collocates are not arbitrary and that semantically close verbs may display different types of prosody. He then surveys the obstacles to integrating phraseology into the curriculum and suggests ways of overcoming them. Kennedy also addresses the relationship between explicit and implicit knowledge, an issue which as Ellis argues (p. 8) "lies at the core of second language instruction". The second chapter, by Susanne Handl, also deals with essential collocations for learners of English and examines the role of collocational direction and weight. Handl aims to find a method of selecting the most relevant collocations to be taught in an EFL context. Like Kennedy, she bases her study on the BNC and analyses high frequency verbs, but she uses different statistical measures to assess the degree of predictability of each constituent of the collocation. She argues that directionality of collocation constitutes an essential criterion for selecting which words must necessarily be taught with their typical collocates. In chapter three, John Osborne studies phraseology effects as a trigger for errors in L2 English. He works on two corpora of written productions by university level learners of English whose performance is predominantly target-like, and focuses on what he calls four 'simple' types of errors: omission of 3rd person -s, inappropriate adverb placement, pluralized adjectives, and plural use of mass nouns. Osborne aims to establish whether these errors are random instances of backsliding or whether there is some pattern to be found in the contexts in which they appear. Thanks to a clever use of automatic retrieval from part-of-speech tagged versions of the texts combined with manual weeding out of irrelevant occurrences, Osborne reveals clear phraseological error-inducing effects. Errors are shown to be the result of three processes: blending, bonding and burying. Chapters four and five focus on discourse issues. JoAnne Neff van Aertselaer contrasts interpersonal discourse phrases as used by novice and expert writers of argumentative texts of both English and Spanish. Novice writer texts produced by Spanish EFL and American university writers are first compared to a corpus of English editorials. Spanish editorials are then used to trace the transfer of interactional patterns in the Spanish EFL texts. This innovative four-way comparison enables Neff van Aertselaer to distinguish between three important types of factors: EFL developmental effects, novice writer features and L1-induced features. Magali Paquot's contribution to the analysis of discourse features lies in the area of exemplification in learner writing. Acknowledging the importance of phraseology in the expression of rhetorical functions in English for academic purposes (EAP), Paquot focuses on exemplification and more particularly on five key lexical items in native and non-native data: the two fixed conjuncts *for example* and *for instance,* the noun *example* and the verbs *il-*

lustrate and *exemplify*. She compares five subcorpora of the International Corpus of Learner English (ICLE) with corpora of the learners' L1. Her main objective is to distinguish crosslinguistic from L1-specific features and thereby contribute to a better understanding of the workings of transfer in phraseology.

The articles in Section II, *Learning phraseological units*, all deal with an oft-neglected yet essential dimension of phraseology in second/foreign language pedagogy: the learning aspect. The sixth chapter of the volume, written by Alison Wray and Tess Fitzpatrick, focuses on the key role of memorization in learning phraseology. Adopting a psycholinguistic approach, the authors analyze what we can learn from learners' deviations from memorized language. They argue that the use of memorized sentences is a liberating experience which promotes fluency and confidence, and that memorization could be used as a means of establishing the strengths and weaknesses of learners in relation to morphology, lexis and phraseology. In chapter seven, Averil Coxhead outlines some of the challenges of phraseology in EAP for teachers, researchers, and students. Like the authors of chapters one and two, Coxhead addresses the question of what we should teach but her focus is mainly on the how. She describes several ways of answering the what question (for instance by providing a new Academic Formulas list to complement the existing Academic Wordlist). As for the how, she stresses the importance of three psychological conditions (noticing, retrieval and generation) and provides useful and novel information on the reasons why learners tend to avoid using formulaic sequences, notably lack of confidence and fear of being accused of plagiarism. In the next chapter, David Wible tackles the issue of how second language learners can come to master multiword expressions and the facilitating role that digital language input can play. He addresses the limitations of lexical representations in traditional dictionaries, shows that whilst electronic dictionaries solve some of these problems, their treatment of multi-word units remains largely inadequate. Wible argues that as the target language input that second language learners are exposed to is increasingly digital in nature, this digital turn should have implications for the learning of multiword expressions. And given that recognizing that strings of words form chunks is a key problem for learners, he suggests a contextual view of word identity and presents types of digital resources and tools that can foster learners' mastery of multiword expressions.

Section III, *Recording and exploiting phraseological units*, focuses on pedagogical tools, i.e. reference tools such as monolingual and bilingual dictionaries as well as textbooks. Chapters nine and ten both deal with phraseology in dictionaries. Dirk Siepmann analyses current learners' dictionaries and shows that they still tend to focus on traditional non-compositional idioms whilst disregarding compositional routine formulae that have been shown to be much more frequent in both writing and speech. Errors found in a corpus of German learner writing highlight the types of problems that learners have and that should be addressed by learners' dictionaries. Siepmann also gives arguments in favour of an onomasiological phraseological dictionary that allows learners to start from a given meaning and find the range of words and phrases that express it. In chapter ten, Mojca Pecman tackles the problems in the compilation, formalisation and presentation of bilingual phraseology and offers some possible solutions. Like Neff van Aerstelear and Paquot in Section II, Pecman focuses on variable multiword units typical of EAP vocabulary but this time from the perspective of bilingual lexicography. After outlining the difficulties in processing bilingual lexicography, she presents an innovative writing aid tool which offers users a flexible approach to collocations: one semasiological, allowing them to access the data from their form and one onomasiological, providing an access key to the same data from their meaning. In the last chapter of Section III, Céline Gouverneur assesses the place of phraseology in a new pedagogically annotated corpus of textbook material, the TeMa corpus. She focuses on the presentation of the high frequency verbs *make* and *take* and demonstrates, among other things, that textbooks offer a very limited range of vocabulary exercises devoted to the phraseological uses of the two verbs and that there is very little overlap in different textbook series as regards selection of the phraseological patterns they include.

In the conclusion, the editors take stock of the work devoted to phraseology in language learning and teaching and identify major avenues for future theoretical and applied work in the field. The challenges they identify include, among other things, redefining the role of grammar within a phraseologically-oriented approach to teaching, substantiating the processing and use of phraseology in L2 (more particularly in an instructed context), and incorporating phraseology into teacher training.

Extracting and describing phraseological units

Phraseology and language pedagogy

Semantic preference associated with English verbs in the British National Corpus

Graeme Kennedy

The key role of phraseology in language acquisition and use has been recognised by a number of distinguished linguists during the twentieth century. Research in cognitive science has shown that frequency of occurrence and frequency of experience establishes words and collocations as units of learning, and becomes a determinant in their use. This chapter first describes the distribution of phraseology associated with a number of very high frequency lexical verbs in the British National Corpus, and explores the extent to which the collocates of particular verbs tend to reflect underlying semantic preference and grammatical processes. Collocations associated with the verbs *enjoy, give, receive, start, begin, stop, end,* and *finish* are analysed. Frequency of occurrence and the extent of collocational bonding as revealed by the Mutual Information measure are used in the study to identify collocational relations. The chapter then explores why, in light of the evidence from corpora on the nature and pervasiveness of phraseology, there has not been a more explicit and prominent place in language pedagogy for the learning of multi-word units.

1. Introduction

In a study of grammatical and semantic associations between adverbs of degree and the adjectives and participles they modify in the British National Corpus (BNC), apparent synonyms such as *completely* and *totally* were shown to each bond strongly (as defined by Mutual Information values) with different adjectives and participles having different grammatical and semantic characteristics (Kennedy 2003). Partington (2004: 146–149) also reports on an earlier study of the collocational behaviour of degree adverbs in the Cobuild corpus. *Completely* tends to be associated with words having negative semantic prosody (Louw 1993), involving 'abolition' or 'destruction' (e.g., *eradicated, gutted, lifeless, wrecked, de-*

stroyed, eliminated, overgrown); 23 percent of the most strongly bonded collocations containing *completely* have a negative prefix (e.g. *untrue, disoriented, insane,
irrelevant*); 10 percent have an *out-* or *over-* prefix (e.g. *outclassed* or *overgrown*);
78 percent of the collocates have an *-ed* suffix (e.g. *completely unsuited, completely
unprepared*). *Totally* also tends to be associated especially with words having negative semantic prosody. Some have intrinsic negative polarity (e.g. *lacking, alien,
pissed off*); 65 percent of the adjectives have a negative prefix (e.g. *unsuited, illeg-
ible, inadequate, disproportionate*); 45 percent of the collocates have an *-ed* suffix.
Among the 40 most strongly bonded collocations, *totally* has four times as many
words with an *un-* prefix (16) as does *completely* (4). Adverbs of degree thus tend
to be associated with particular adjectives, each having certain grammatical and
semantic properties.

The present chapter extends to a different grammatical area the approach
taken in Kennedy (2003) by describing salient characteristics of the content word
collocates associated with a number of very high frequency English lexical verbs
in the BNC. In the second part of the chapter brief consideration is given to why
phraseological phenomena have tended to be neglected in language pedagogy.

2.   The phraseology of high frequency verbs

About one word in every ten used by speakers or writers of English is a lexical
verb. The chapter examines eight of the most frequent of these verbs, all occurring
between 120 and 1284 times per million words in the 100-million-word BNC. The
verbs to be considered are the following (with the number of tokens per million
words shown in parenthesis): *enjoy* (146), *give* (1284), *receive* (247), *start* (414),
begin (440), *stop* (255), *end* (158), *finish* (120).

The purpose of this research is to explore whether collocations involving lexical verbs are arbitrarily-constituted, multi-word units with idiomatic status based
on their form, along the lines of what Biber et al. (1999:990) characterised as
"lexical bundles" (which) "are simply sequences of word forms that commonly go
together in natural discourse", or whether the collocates of particular verbs are not
arbitrary but tend to have common features of form and meaning.

2.1   Retrieval of significant collocations

The analysis is based on the whole BNC. The collocates of the eight lemmatised
verbs were first identified and analysed using the BNCWeb interface developed by
Lehmann et al. (2002). Since verb predicates were the main focus of the analysis,

and as Sinclair et al. (1970:8) demonstrated in the OSTI report, frequently-oc-curring words predict better to the right than to the left, the concordances used for identifying the collocations in the present study were based on a window size of +1 to +4. For each of the eight verbs, two separate analyses were undertaken: (i) the frequency of a word as a collocate of the verb, and (ii) Mutual Informa-tion (MI) values (Church & Hanks 1990). The MI value is used to compare the actual frequency of co-occurrence of two words with the predicted frequency of co-occurrence of the two words if each were randomly distributed in the corpus. Although the MI value tends to highlight collocations containing very low fre-quency words, it is nevertheless one useful indication of the strength of associa-tion between two (or more) words within the phrase. The results of the analysis are shown in Tables 1 to 8. Each table shows results separately for frequency and MI values. Part (a) of each table shows the 80 most frequent content word col-locates of the eight verbs, listed in rank order. Part (b) of each table shows the 80 content word collocates with the highest MI values occurring in eight or more texts of the corpus. The cut-off criterion of eight texts was to reduce the likelihood of the data being distorted by very rare, strongly-bonded collocations occurring in very few texts.

Only content word collocates of the eight verbs were included in the study to avoid the analysis being cluttered with very high frequency collocations such as *enjoy his*, or *give to*. The main categories of function words omitted from the anal-ysis included personal and possessive pronouns, cardinal numbers, determiners, prepositions, adverbial particles, conjunctions, modals, comparative *more* and *less, not, no, have, be,* and *do*. One disadvantage of the decision to omit colloca-tions containing function words was that high frequency multi-word units such as phrasal verbs were not part of this analysis.

2.2   Eight verbs under the microscope

This section describes the frequency of occurrence, extent of collocational bond-ing and types of collocational relations of the eight high frequency verbs listed above.

2.2.1 *Enjoy*
The 156th most frequent lexical verb in the BNC is ENJOY. It occurs 146 times per million words. Table 1a shows that *enjoy* collocates most frequently with *life*, (occurring 244 times) and that the speakers and writers recorded in the BNC also frequently associate ENJOY with *themselves, himself, yourself, myself, herself, our-selves, people, together, sex, company, meeting,* and *relationships*.

Table 1. ENJOY in the BNC

(a) Collocates by frequency						(b) Collocates by MI value					
1	life	244	41	going	53	1	immensely	6,9	41	benefits	4,3
2	themselves	204	42	here	52	2	yourselves	6,6	42	reputation	4,3
3	himself	168	43	meal	50	3	comforts	6,5	43	delicious	4,3
4	good	160	44	ourselves	50	4	hugely	6,4	44	holiday	4,3
5	so	157	45	watching	49	5	pleasures	6,2	45	monopoly	4,3
6	yourself	154	46	minute	49	6	fruits	6,2	46	joke	4,2
7	company	149	47	music	49	7	vogue	6	47	autonomy	4,2
8	myself	128	48	making	48	8	leisurely	6	48	themselves	4,1
9	success	101	49	great	48	9	popularity	6	49	boom	4,1
10	very	100	50	meeting	48	10	delights	5,6	50	warmth	4,1
11	herself	99	51	best	47	11	privileges	5,6	51	ride	4,1
12	work	98	52	other	47	12	spectacle	5,6	52	privilege	4
13	working	97	53	only	47	13	hospitality	5,5	53	renaissance	4
14	support	94	54	view	47	14	scenery	5,3	54	watching	4
15	day	84	55	last	45	15	prestige	5,2	55	chat	3,9
16	full	83	56	relationship	44	16	sunshine	5,2	56	dancing	3,9
17	playing	81	57	considerable	44	17	immunity	5,2	57	cooking	3,9
18	reading	81	58	job	44	18	thrill	5,2	58	playing	3,9
19	having	81	59	things	43	19	enormously	5,2	59	success	3,9
20	benefits	78	60	drink	43	20	gardening	5	60	reading	3,9
21	freedom	78	61	popularity	42	21	lifestyle	5	61	trips	3,9
22	holiday	76	62	views	42	22	skiing	4,9	62	holidays	3,9
23	experience	73	63	then	42	23	revival	4,9	63	colourful	3,8
24	time	68	64	power	42	24	yourself	4,9	64	status	3,8
25	such	68	65	long	42	25	relaxing	4,9	65	retirement	3,8
26	status	66	66	part	39	26	sensation	4,8	66	spell	3,8
27	too	66	67	now	39	27	fame	4,7	67	taste	3,8
28	people	65	68	immensely	38	28	freedom	4,7	68	lively	3,8
29	new	65	69	better	38	29	sights	4,7	69	countryside	3,8
30	own	62	70	seeing	37	30	outdoor	4,6	70	trip	3,8
31	evening	61	71	position	37	31	meal	4,6	71	superb	3,7
32	same	60	72	Christmas	37	32	luxury	4,6	72	singing	3,7
33	high	59	73	special	37	33	prosperity	4,5	73	sex	3,7
34	food	57	74	reputation	37	34	patronage	4,5	74	entertainment	3,7
35	game	57	75	looking	36	35	oneself	4,5	75	surroundings	3,7
36	first	55	76	way	36	36	ourselves	4,5	76	finest	3,6
37	years	55	77	fruits	36	37	advantages	4,4	77	leisure	3,6
38	together	55	78	protection	35	38	myself	4,4	78	herself	3,6
39	sex	54	79	moment	35	39	rewards	4,3	79	performances	3,6
40	little	54	80	even	35	40	privileged	4,3	80	friendship	3,6

The MI values in Table 1b similarly show that ENJOY is strongly bonded with reflexive pronouns, (including *yourselves, yourself, oneself, ourselves, myself, themselves,* and *herself*), and with a variety of pleasurable sensations. For example, *comforts, pleasures, popularity, delights, privileges, hospitality, scenery, sunshine, prestige, fame, freedom, luxury, prosperity, holidays, jokes, warmth, success, trips, retirement, countryside, sex, entertainment, leisure, performances,* and *friendship*.

Table 1 also shows that a large number of the collocates of ENJOY, whether identified by frequency of occurrence or MI, are words ending in *-ing*. According to the BNC the British enjoy (by frequency) *working, playing, reading, having, going, watching, making, meeting, seeing,* and *looking*. By MI they enjoy *gardening, skiing, relaxing, watching, dancing, cooking, playing, reading,* and *singing*. Many of these activities are enjoyed *immensely, hugely,* or *enormously*. Overall, the objects of ENJOY are typically positive things which reveal the British to be active enjoyers of a wide range of activities. It is perhaps worth noting, however, that in materials prepared for learners of English, ENJOY is often associated with food and with somewhat passive activities such as *watching*.

2.2.2 *Give*

Table 2 shows the words associated with GIVE, the tenth most frequent lexical verb in the BNC. The rank order frequency listing in Table 2a shows that apart from the words *money* and *people* in lines 14 and 19, GIVE is particularly associated with abstract entities (e.g. *give rise, give way, give opportunities*). But above all, GIVE seems to be associated most frequently with 'communication nouns'. The British give *information, evidence, advice, details, notice, ideas, indication, account, answers, help, pleasure, reasons, examples, permission, warning, address, ring,* and *orders*.

When we turn from collocations as defined by frequency of occurrence, in Table 2a, to collocations as defined by the strength of the bond between GIVE and its collocates in Table 2b, it can be seen that many of the collocates also have something to do with communication. (e.g. *thumbs-up, thumbs-down, go-ahead, carte-blanche, all-clear, send-off, impression, indication, assurances, clue, absolution, wink, encouragement, impromptu, permission, nudge, dispensation, ovation, salute, advice*) and that most of these are nouns.

Although it is not shown in Table 2, there is also a marked difference between GIVE and GAVE in the collocates they bond with. The 40 strongest MI values for GAVE include these bizarre behaviours: *yelp, snort, shrug, grunt, gasp, sigh, gurgle, whoop, whimper, chuckle, squeal, groan, shudder, shriek, grimace, laugh* and *shiver*. None of these collocates of GAVE occur as strong MI collocates of GIVE. That is, we are more likely to find, *"He gave a chuckle or a grimace"* than we are to find *"He'll give a chuckle or a grimace"*.

Table 2. GIVE in the BNC

(a) Collocates by frequency						(b) Collocates by MI value					
1	rise	1975	41	account	424	1	thumbs-up	7	41	derisive	4,9
2	chance	1486	42	great	422	2	thumbs-down	6,9	42	absolution	4,9
3	time	1455	43	attention	411	3	go-ahead	6,7	43	birth	4,8
4	way	1439	44	best	406	4	carte-blanche	6,7	44	lurch	4,8
5	opportunity	1094	45	answer	399	5	credence	6,7	45	wholehearted	4,7
6	information	1071	46	other	396	6	once-over	6,6	46	jolt	4,7
7	good	994	47	help	389	7	all-clear	6,4	47	chance	4,7
8	impression	981	48	job	389	8	shrift	6,2	48	alms	4,7
9	new	920	49	life	366	9	fillip	6,1	49	ultimatum	4,7
10	evidence	911	50	better	366	10	send-off	6	50	wink	4,7
11	little	907	51	work	364	11	mirthless	5,8	51	facelift	4,6
12	advice	872	52	pleasure	355	12	intravenously	5,8	52	gasp	4,6
13	support	809	53	credit	348	13	yelp	5,8	53	encouragement	4,6
14	money	792	54	clear	346	14	creeps	5,8	54	opportunity	4,6
15	name	755	55	extra	346	15	rueful	5,7	55	chuckle	4,6
16	back	721	56	hand	340	16	impression	5,7	56	cursory	4,6
17	details	708	57	reasons	339	17	snort	5,7	57	much-needed	4,6
18	right	707	58	confidence	338	18	hug	5,6	58	withering	4,6
19	people	671	59	example	335	19	indication	5,6	59	inkling	4,5
20	birth	661	60	different	329	20	sidelong	5,6	60	impromptu	4,5
21	very	598	61	same	327	21	prominence	5,5	61	berth	4,5
22	notice	597	62	children	325	22	shrug	5,5	62	permission	4,5
23	idea	589	63	permission	325	23	leeway	5,5	63	nudge	4,5
24	first	576	64	warning	323	24	rein	5,4	64	dispensation	4,4
25	such	554	65	special	317	25	rise	5,4	65	fright	4,4
26	something	549	66	small	315	26	nod	5,4	66	toss	4,4
27	look	524	67	consideration	306	27	impetus	5,4	67	grounding	4,4
28	full	522	68	then	305	28	cuddle	5,4	68	whimper	4,4
29	number	513	69	just	302	29	assurances	5,3	69	clout	4,4
30	access	508	70	hope	301	30	orally	5,2	70	assurance	4,4
31	thought	507	71	further	300	31	grunt	5,2	71	boost	4,3
32	indication	506	72	choice	299	32	insight	5,1	72	indigestion	4,3
33	only	492	73	address	293	33	clue	5,1	73	ovation	4,3
34	power	486	74	enough	292	34	wry	5,1	74	salute	4,3
35	so	473	75	himself	282	35	succour	5,1	75	damn	4,2
36	priority	464	76	laugh	281	36	sight	5,1	76	kiss	4,2
37	smile	458	77	ring	280	37	foretaste	5	77	undivided	4,2
38	free	435	78	sense	279	38	priority	4,9	78	shudder	4,2
39	greater	434	79	lift	275	39	vent	4,9	79	advice	4,2
40	effect	426	80	orders	273	40	clues	4,9	80	laugh	4,1

2.2.3 *Receive*

Table 3 shows the 80 most frequent collocates, and the 80 most strongly bonded collocates of RECEIVE, which is the 76th most frequent lexical verb in the BNC.

Whether measured by frequency or strength of bonding, it is clear that among the semantic associates of RECEIVE there are many nouns associated with 'money'. By frequency, we receive *money, payment, income, free, benefits, grant, funding, payments, pay, compensation, pension, financial, cash, allowance, grants, cheque,* and *share.* By MI, the money words include *rebate, voucher, refund, cheque, allowance, remuneration, royalty, dividends, payment, grants, compensation, vouchers, invoice, subsidy,* and *royalties.*

BNC speakers and writers also refer a lot to the receiving of accolades in one form or another. By frequency, they RECEIVE *awards, approval, recognition, certificate,* and *prize.* By MI value, they receive *knighthood, rapturous, acclaim, commendation, OBE, accolade, ovation, MBE, honorary, doctorate, Nobel, medal, acknowledgement, awards,* and *homage.* These collocates may, of course, reveal as much about the construction of the corpus as they do about the use of English in Britain.

Table 3 also reveals that while concrete entities (such as *letters, copy, report, reply, message, form, notice, telegram*) are received there is also a very strong association between RECEIVE and abstract 'communication nouns', including, for example, *support, attention, treatment, information, training, help, care, advice, assistance, aid, response, complaints, assent, absolution, notification, assurance, transmissions, representations, apologies, threats, invitation, requests, summons, attention, confirmation, reply, tuition, forgiveness, publicity, treatment, coverage, endorsement, invitations.* The MI values for RECEIVE also show that there are strong associations with medically related words such as *transfusions, injections, doses,* and *placebo.* We tend to *receive medicine* but not *breakfast* or *lunch.*

2.2.4 *Start*

The verb START is the 37th most frequent lexical verb in the BNC. About 25 percent of the collocates of START identified by frequency in Table 4a end in *-ing.* Forty-nine out of the 80 most strongly bonding MI collocates of START (61 percent) are similarly words ending in *-ing.*

One semantic characteristic of some of the collocates associated with START is a sense of 'loss of control' or 'violent and disturbed behaviour'. Table 4b shows that the MI values associated with START include *scratch, yelling, crumble, crying, unravel, giggle, coughing, shouting, banging, messing about, screaming, moaning, rolling, cry, laughing, howling, snatching, throwing, shooting, charging, hitting, fires, complaining, worrying, laugh, cough, knocking, firing, scream.*

Table 3. RECEIVE in the BNC

(a) Collocates by frequency

1	support	421	41	boost	89			
2	attention	415	42	message	88			
3	letter	381	43	payments	87			
4	treatment	311	44	pay	86			
5	information	278	45	compensation	86			
6	training	195	46	form	86			
7	benefit	190	47	special	86			
8	money	177	48	bottle	85			
9	percent	173	49	pension	85			
10	letters	170	50	government	82			
11	award	163	51	financial	82			
12	help	161	52	service	81			
13	payment	157	53	welcome	80			
14	little	146	54	calls	80			
15	care	144	55	response	77			
16	education	140	56	cash	77			
17	income	139	57	complaints	76			
18	copy	139	58	additional	75			
19	full	135	59	aid	74			
20	new	133	60	good	74			
21	report	132	61	last	74			
22	reply	129	62	approval	73			
23	free	127	63	news	72			
24	such	125	64	reports	71			
25	call	115	65	recognition	71			
26	year	107	66	allowance	71			
27	number	107	67	notice	69			
28	million	106	68	sparkling	68			
29	advice	105	69	certificate	68			
30	benefits	105	70	grants	67			
31	so	105	71	gift	67			
32	grant	101	72	death	66			
33	royal	99	73	sentences	66			
34	same	99	74	publicity	65			
35	other	98	75	cheque	65			
36	further	96	76	phone	64			
37	very	94	77	share	64			
38	assistance	93	78	extra	63			
39	sentence	91	79	votes	63			
40	funding	90	80	prize	63			

(b) Collocates by MI value

1	shrift	7,5	41	allowance	5,2
2	assent	7,4	42	remuneration	5,2
3	absolution	7,2	43	transfusion	5,2
4	knighthood	7,1	44	requests	5,2
5	rapturous	6,9	45	royalty	5,2
6	custodial	6,9	46	summons	5,2
7	transfusions	6,9	47	attention	5,1
8	acclaim	6,9	48	dividends	5,1
9	notification	6,8	49	confirmation	5,1
10	commendation	6,8	50	reply	5,1
11	OBE	6,8	51	doses	5,1
12	accolade	6,7	52	payment	5,1
13	rebate	6,7	53	letter	5
14	ovation	6,6	54	tuition	5
15	MBE	6,6	55	complaints	5
16	assurances	6,4	56	reinforcement	5
17	transmissions	6,4	57	grants	5
18	telegram	6,4	58	compensation	5
19	honorary	6,4	59	vouchers	4,9
20	doctorate	6,3	60	forgiveness	4,9
21	sacrament	6,3	61	invoice	4,9
22	placebo	6,3	62	publicity	4,9
23	invalidity	6,2	63	treatment	4,9
24	scant	6,1	64	acknowledgement	4,9
25	Nobel	6	65	coverage	4,9
26	medal	6	66	endorsement	4,8
27	communion	6	67	awards	4,8
28	setback	5,8	68	invitations	4,8
29	voucher	5,7	69	subsidy	4,8
30	jolt	5,7	70	impetus	4,8
31	refund	5,6	71	royalties	4,8
32	boost	5,6	72	copy	4,8
33	representations	5,6	73	injection	4,8
34	supplementary	5,5	74	certificate	4,7
35	apology	5,3	75	sentences	4,7
36	threats	5,3	76	gift	4,7
37	invitation	5,3	77	replies	4,7
38	disproportionate	5,3	78	homage	4,7
39	cheque	5,2	79	dose	4,7
40	injections	5,2	80	letters	4,7

Table 4. START in the BNC

(a) Collocates by frequency

1	again	1173	41	feel	135
2	work	671	42	using	129
3	new	530	43	think	127
4	then	332	44	take	127
5	get	285	45	coming	126
6	life	285	46	week	123
7	talking	281	47	saying	123
8	own	268	48	career	122
9	now	262	49	end	121
10	next	260	50	way	121
11	back	257	51	ago	118
12	going	256	52	writing	115
13	here	245	53	run	115
14	first	243	54	walk	113
15	looking	237	55	engine	113
16	getting	230	56	today	112
17	thinking	222	57	scratch	111
18	so	222	58	right	110
19	making	217	59	fire	109
20	doing	216	60	asking	108
21	year	216	61	tomorrow	106
22	early	207	62	car	106
23	business	205	63	small	102
24	working	203	64	move	102
25	day	197	65	come	102
26	go	186	66	same	102
27	school	184	67	people	102
28	just	175	68	process	100
29	make	168	69	training	99
30	do	166	70	running	98
31	look	163	71	soon	95
32	time	155	72	only	93
33	playing	153	73	cry	89
34	well	152	74	building	88
35	something	152	75	crying	88
36	last	150	76	game	87
37	very	148	77	beginning	87
38	years	143	78	long	86
39	things	142	79	morning	85
40	taking	139	80	family	85

(b) Collocates by MI value

1	afresh	7,4	41	packing	4
2	scratch	6,4	42	climb	4
3	premise	5,8	43	repairing	4
4	rehearsing	5,6	44	throwing	4
5	yelling	5,5	45	talking	3,9
6	crumble	5,2	46	shake	3,9
7	anew	5,1	47	barking	3,9
8	crying	5	48	rebuilding	3,9
9	earnest	5	49	again	3,8
10	unravel	5	50	violently	3,8
11	giggle	4,9	51	shooting	3,8
12	shipping	4,8	52	singing	3,6
13	coughing	4,7	53	charging	3,6
14	rehearsals	4,7	54	hitting	3,6
15	shouting	4,6	55	noon	3,6
16	digging	4,5	56	asking	3,6
17	fade	4,5	57	thinking	3,6
18	banging	4,5	58	pouring	3,6
19	messing	4,4	59	fires	3,5
20	screaming	4,4	60	complaining	3,5
21	moaning	4,3	61	worrying	3,5
22	rolling	4,3	62	laugh	3,5
23	cry	4,3	63	career	3,5
24	laughing	4,3	64	chatting	3,4
25	ringing	4,3	65	cough	3,4
26	weep	4,3	66	smoking	3,4
27	howling	4,2	67	knocking	3,4
28	basics	4,2	68	emerge	3,4
29	scratching	4,2	69	firing	3,3
30	circulate	4,2	70	knitting	3,3
31	experimenting	4,1	71	playing	3,3
32	downhill	4,1	72	filming	3,3
33	collecting	4,1	73	rumour	3,3
34	counting	4,1	74	pulling	3,3
35	raining	4	75	drilling	3,3
36	descend	4	76	arriving	3,2
37	finishes	4	77	scream	3,2
38	straightaway	4	78	dancing	3,2
39	behaving	4	79	laying	3,2
40	engine	4	80	questioning	3,2

Although not included with the present data, some of the most strongly bonded collocates of the verb *send* as identified by the MI value also have something to do with being 'out of control'. e.g. *shivers, shockwaves, scurrying, plummeting, sprawling, reeling, shiver, crashing, hurtling, soaring, ripples, tumbling, packing, spiralling, plunging, swirling, spinning, waves, rushing,* and *flying.* Many of these collocates of *send* also have an *-ing* suffix.

2.2.5 Begin
The 32nd most frequent lexical verb in the BNC is BEGIN, which may seem to be a verb roughly synonymous with START. The BNC reveals, however, that START and BEGIN tend to keep different company.

Only one word, *working,* out of the 80 most frequent collocates of BEGIN in Table 5a has an *-ing* suffix, and only three of the MI collocates in Table 5 (b) end in *-ing.*) The MI collocates of BEGIN also include some disturbed, negative, or unwelcome behaviours, e.g. *tremble, sob, tire, weep, snore, wail, pacing, hum, mutter, cry, twitch, scream, shiver, moan.* Many of the MI collocates of BEGIN seem to be verbs associated with 'involuntary deterioration' (e.g. *wane, tremble, subside, disintegrate, crumble, seep, falter, dwindle, fade, waver, droop, sob, tire, weep, darken, deteriorate, evaporate, wail, unravel, mutter, weaken, sag, fray, dissolve, shake, cry, trickle, twitch, melt, ache, buckle, scream, shiver, drift, moan*). It is the involuntary nature of many of the collocates of BEGIN which seems to set them apart from START.

2.2.6 Stop
The 73rd most frequent lexical verb in the BNC is STOP, which has some things in common with its apparent antonym, START, in that it tends to precede verbs or gerunds. Table 6 shows that 67 out of the 80 most strongly bonded MI collocates of STOP end in *-ing.* As defined by frequency, 31 out of the top 80 collocates also end in *-ing.* However, it is what the British (as revealed by the BNC) STOP doing that is particularly interesting.

Table 6b shows that there is a strong tendency to stop doing unpleasant, irritating, negative, or frustrating things. e.g. *whingeing, fussing, fooling, mucking about, fretting, crying, whining, worrying, pacing, chattering, smoking, moaning, messing about, interrupting, giggling, bleeding, biting, frowning, banging, blaming, scratching, coughing, teasing, leaking, wasting, shaking, interfering, beating, speeding, slipping, stealing, hitting, hurting, dumping, arguing, shouting, kicking, escaping, struggling, trembling, fighting, staring, complaining.* Other words which do not quite bond strongly enough with STOP to be included in the top 80 include *snivelling, fidgeting, sniffing, nagging, panicking,* and *quarrelling.*

Table 5. BEGIN in the BNC

(a) Collocates by frequency					(b) Collocates by MI value				
1	feel	588	41	process	125	1	unbutton	7,9	41	mutter	5,2
2	again	547	42	long	122	2	unfasten	7,7	42	lighten	5,2
3	work	426	43	go	118	3	wane	7,4	43	weaken	5,2
4	take	396	44	last	118	4	tremble	7,1	44	caress	5,2
5	think	390	45	speak	117	5	earnest	7,1	45	sag	5,1
6	look	365	46	lose	116	6	subside	7	46	restlessly	5
7	see	359	47	own	115	7	disintegrate	6,8	47	annoy	5
8	get	332	48	find	115	8	crumble	6,7	48	fray	5
9	make	320	49	play	113	9	seep	6,7	49	dissolve	5
10	move	275	50	so	113	10	falter	6,5	50	shake	5
11	wonder	254	51	laugh	112	11	dwindle	6,5	51	cry	5
12	new	239	52	next	112	12	fade	6,3	52	trickle	5
13	appear	208	53	late	112	13	abate	6,3	53	twitch	5
14	life	200	54	just	107	14	thicken	6,2	54	swell	4,9
15	early	195	55	ago	103	15	waver	6,2	55	climb	4,9
16	show	191	56	series	102	16	droop	6,2	56	realise	4,9
17	understand	190	57	use	101	17	circulate	6,1	57	withdrawing	4,8
18	fall	180	58	time	100	18	sob	6,1	58	melt	4,8
19	career	178	59	climb	99	19	vibrate	6	59	experimenting	4,8
20	emerge	175	60	working	99	20	unpack	6	60	wonder	4,7
21	walk	169	61	slowly	99	21	hesitantly	6	61	sing	4,7
22	then	159	62	day	97	22	tire	6	62	thump	4,7
23	first	156	63	read	94	23	weep	5,9	63	shipping	4,7
24	develop	154	64	question	93	24	undress	5,9	64	ache	4,7
25	run	152	65	form	92	25	snore	5,9	65	reap	4,6
26	talk	147	66	build	91	26	emerge	5,8	66	stir	4,6
27	very	147	67	themselves	90	27	recite	5,8	67	sway	4,6
28	cry	147	68	write	90	28	sprout	5,7	68	soar	4,5
29	years	145	69	only	89	29	darken	5,7	69	buckle	4,5
30	way	144	70	now	86	30	deteriorate	5,6	70	scream	4,5
31	change	141	71	tell	83	31	unfold	5,6	71	shiver	4,5
32	grow	141	72	sing	82	32	evaporate	5,6	72	loom	4,5
33	year	139	73	himself	82	33	creep	5,6	73	crawl	4,4
34	away	138	74	study	81	34	diverge	5,5	74	drift	4,4
35	rise	136	75	something	81	35	descend	5,5	75	chew	4,4
36	earnest	132	76	together	80	36	disperse	5,4	76	laugh	4,4
37	come	130	77	enjoy	80	37	wail	5,4	77	moan	4,3
38	end	127	78	put	80	38	unravel	5,3	78	resent	4,3
39	turn	126	79	campaign	79	39	pacing	5,3	79	descent	4,3
40	realise	126	80	slow	79	40	hum	5,3	80	bite	4,3

Table 6. STOP in the BNC

(a) Collocates by frequency						(b) Collocates by MI value					
1	short	262	41	moment	78	1	whingeing	7,2	41	half-way	4,5
2	now	253	42	turned	78	2	fussing	6,8	42	beating	4,5
3	going	235	43	door	75	3	fooling	6,7	43	speeding	4,4
4	talking	212	44	police	75	4	mucking	6,7	44	slipping	4,4
5	so	187	45	get	73	5	fretting	6,4	45	stealing	4,4
6	getting	180	46	moving	72	6	abruptly	6,4	46	admire	4,4
7	car	178	47	eating	69	7	tracks	6,3	47	hitting	4,4
8	people	171	48	fighting	67	8	crying	6,3	48	hurting	4,4
9	then	169	49	falling	67	9	whining	6	49	dumping	4,3
10	working	147	50	things	64	10	worrying	6	50	arguing	4,3
11	just	144	51	too	64	11	pacing	5,9	51	shouting	4,3
12	taking	139	52	round	64	12	rot	5,9	52	kicking	4,3
13	think	135	53	speaking	63	13	raining	5,9	53	eating	4,3
14	work	134	54	way	62	14	chattering	5,9	54	talking	4,2
15	smoking	134	55	other	59	15	smoking	5,7	55	drinking	4,2
16	said	134	56	seeing	59	16	loving	5,5	56	sliding	4,2
17	here	132	57	press	58	17	moaning	5,5	57	believing	4,1
18	again	132	58	months	58	18	breathing	5,5	58	escaping	4,1
19	tracks	131	59	first	57	19	messing	5,4	59	leak	4,1
20	thinking	129	60	loving	57	20	interrupting	5,4	60	chat	4,1
21	looked	127	61	happening	56	21	behaving	5,3	61	firing	4,1
22	crying	125	62	drinking	55	22	giggling	5,3	62	falling	4,1
23	dead	124	63	right	55	23	laughing	5,2	63	momentarily	4,1
24	using	124	64	traffic	55	24	bouncing	5,2	64	smiling	4
25	time	119	65	still	52	25	bleeding	5,1	65	short	3,9
26	outside	117	66	go	52	26	biting	5,1	66	wandering	3,9
27	playing	116	67	start	52	27	ringing	5,1	67	swinging	3,9
28	back	115	68	immediately	51	28	frowning	5	68	happening	3,9
29	making	109	69	giving	51	29	banging	5	69	struggling	3,9
30	look	103	70	got	49	30	blaming	5	70	trembling	3,8
31	trying	99	71	put	49	31	scratching	4,9	71	halfway	3,8
32	looking	96	72	growing	48	32	coughing	4,9	72	fighting	3,8
33	breathing	90	73	feeling	47	33	pretending	4,9	73	spinning	3,8
34	abruptly	86	74	see	47	34	teasing	4,8	74	drying	3,7
35	coming	85	75	night	47	35	medication	4,8	75	issuing	3,7
36	suddenly	85	76	take	47	36	leaking	4,8	76	searched	3,7
37	only	84	77	saying	46	37	altogether	4,8	77	staring	3,7
38	running	83	78	asking	46	38	wasting	4,7	78	complaining	3,7
39	worrying	80	79	long	46	39	shaking	4,7	79	singing	3,7
40	laughing	79	80	watch	46	40	interfering	4,6	80	speaking	3,7

2.2.7 *End*

The tendency of *STOP* to be associated with negative polarity is much more marked than is the case with its apparent synonyms *END* and *FINISH*.

Tables 6 and 7 show that whereas *STOP* tends to precede verbs, *END*, the 129th most frequent lexical verb in the BNC, tends to precede nouns. We tend to *END* big, unpleasant processes which have negative affect, including *war, conflict, siege, stalemate, boycott, monopoly, rebellion, nightmare, violence, chaos, hunger, uncertainty, discrimination, isolation, strike, fighting, affair, killing, occupation, suffering, struggle, crisis. End in* is also associated with generally negative things such as *tears, divorce, disaster, failure, death, tragedy, conflict, prison, stalemate, deadlock, defeat, controversy, chaos,* and *poverty*.

2.2.8 *Finish*

The 175th most frequent lexical verb in the BNC, *FINISH*, is associated with different words than *END*. Whereas *END* is associated with big or global events such as *wars, nightmares, conflict, violence* and *suffering,* Table 8 shows that *FINISH* is associated with more mundane or small-scale activities or events.

By frequency, the British *FINISH work, jobs, meals, tea, eating, coffee, book, drink, school, breakfast, training, lunch, story, week, game, morning, business, dinner, race, bottle, task* and *tour.* Table 8b shows that the MI values associated with *FINISH* also tend to be less spectacular or global, including *unpacking, apprenticeship, meal, eating, dressing, speaking, breakfast, coffee, tea, drinks, lunch, reading, bottle, cleaning, poem, washing, job, beer, painting, dinner, cooking, conversation, tour, session, wine, race, tomorrow, song, task, novel, tonight, game, book, glass, work, letter, training, afternoon.* Thus, although *STOP, END* and *FINISH* might have much in common semantically, it seems that these verbs are not strongly associated with the same words.

2.3 Semantic prosody and semantic preference

This analysis of words associated with high frequency verbs in the BNC suggests that whether we identify phraseology by means of frequency of occurrence, or through strength of bonding, multi-word units need not be seen just as 'idiomatic' sequences of word forms that are arbitrarily bundled together. The analysis demonstrates that high frequency lexical verbs tend to be associated with other words having particular grammatical features or belonging to particular semantic domains. We have seen that at least for some collocational associations, there seem to be underlying grammatical patterns or templates into which particular collocations tend to fit. Thus, *start* and *stop* are characteristically followed by a

Table 7. END in the BNC

(a) Collocates by frequency						(b) Collocates by MI value					
1	war	147	41	losing	33	1	stalemate	6,9	41	fighting	3,2
2	here	130	42	strike	33	2	abruptly	6,5	42	era	3,2
3	day	110	43	speculation	32	3	peacefully	6,2	43	affair	3,2
4	years	93	44	began	32	4	deadlock	6,2	44	killing	3,2
5	last	75	45	working	32	5	farce	5,7	45	note	3,1
6	year	75	46	way	32	6	divorce	5,4	46	session	3
7	life	73	47	night	32	7	boycott	5,1	47	occupation	3
8	days	72	48	long	32	8	speculation	5,1	48	conflict	3
9	career	67	49	making	31	9	siege	5	49	staying	2,9
10	just	65	50	week	31	10	marrying	5	50	civil	2,9
11	about	64	51	political	31	11	disaster	5	51	prison	2,8
12	death	61	52	such	31	12	tragedy	5	52	draw	2,8
13	only	60	53	tragedy	30	13	monopoly	4,7	53	conversation	2,8
14	abruptly	59	54	fighting	29	14	tears	4,7	54	ban	2,8
15	run	59	55	draw	28	15	wars	4,6	55	buying	2,8
16	tears	57	56	playing	28	16	flourish	4,4	56	marriage	2,7
17	so	57	57	marriage	28	17	paying	4,1	57	season	2,7
18	getting	56	58	court	28	18	happily	4,1	58	relationship	2,6
19	same	50	59	point	27	19	losing	4	59	death	2,5
20	divorce	49	60	points	27	20	career	4	60	spending	2,5
21	note	49	61	new	27	21	costing	4	61	agreement	2,4
22	disaster	49	62	now	27	22	hunger	3,9	62	poverty	2,4
23	paying	44	63	almost	26	23	rebellion	3,9	63	victory	2,4
24	very	44	64	conflict	26	24	nightmare	3,8	64	getting	2,4
25	failure	43	65	right	26	25	controversy	3,7	65	run	2,3
26	saying	43	66	own	26	26	defeat	3,7	66	playing	2,3
27	relationship	42	67	defeat	26	27	violence	3,7	67	eating	2,3
28	going	42	68	monopoly	24	28	chaos	3,6	68	testing	2,2
29	first	41	69	hopes	24	29	uncertainty	3,6	69	suffering	2,2
30	users	40	70	wars	24	30	discrimination	3,6	70	badly	2,2
31	agreement	40	71	said	24	31	isolation	3,5	71	doing	2,2
32	yesterday	40	72	feeling	24	32	bang	3,5	72	brief	2,2
33	season	39	73	prison	24	33	users	3,5	73	struggle	2,2
34	violence	39	74	state	23	34	reign	3,4	74	winning	2,1
35	months	38	75	even	23	35	strike	3,4	75	saying	2,1
36	early	38	76	today	22	36	hopes	3,4	76	crisis	2,1
37	time	36	77	people	22	37	failure	3,3	77	sentence	2
38	civil	36	78	date	22	38	dispute	3,3	78	days	2
39	looking	34	79	different	22	39	scoring	3,3	79	properly	2
40	then	33	80	together	22	40	war	3,3	80	row	2

Table 8. FINISH in the BNC

	(a) Collocates by frequency								(b) Collocates by MI value						
1	now	167	41	lunch	32		1	unpacking	8,4	41	race	2,8
2	work	160	42	other	30		2	apprenticeship	5,8	42	strongly	2,7
3	then	141	43	past	29		3	lengths	5,7	43	points	2,7
4	first	129	44	story	29		4	packing	5,5	44	top	2,7
5	last	120	45	week	29		5	meal	5,1	45	tomorrow	2,6
6	yet	113	46	lengths	28		6	eating	5	46	song	2,6
7	job	91	47	very	28		7	dressing	4,7	47	telling	2,6
8	so	83	48	clear	27		8	sentence	4,6	48	begun	2,6
9	about	80	49	sat	27		9	shots	4,5	49	sat	2,6
10	just	77	50	game	27		10	speaking	4,4	50	paying	2,5
11	time	77	51	o'clock	26		11	breakfast	4,3	51	task	2,5
12	top	68	52	writing	25		12	coffee	4,3	52	putting	2,5
13	here	67	53	morning	25		13	tea	4,2	53	finished	2,5
14	meal	61	54	quickly	25		14	drinks	3,9	54	playing	2,5
15	said	61	55	left	25		15	lunch	3,9	55	overall	2,4
16	tea	60	56	right	25		16	o'clock	3,8	56	writing	2,4
17	reading	60	57	today	24		17	drink	3,8	57	story	2,4
18	only	60	58	side	24		18	reading	3,8	58	novel	2,4
19	sentence	58	59	long	24		19	bottle	3,8	59	bottom	2,4
20	day	56	60	business	24		20	cleaning	3,6	60	quickly	2,3
21	eating	56	61	playing	24		21	seconds	3,6	61	tonight	2,3
22	year	53	62	talking	24		22	poem	3,5	62	score	2,3
23	coffee	51	63	tomorrow	23		23	washing	3,4	63	talking	2,2
24	course	49	64	next	23		24	shooting	3,3	64	game	2,2
25	speaking	49	65	started	23		25	job	3,3	65	book	2,2
26	book	45	66	career	23		26	beer	3,3	66	glass	2,1
27	drink	45	67	got	22		27	painting	3,3	67	work	2,1
28	season	42	68	hours	22		28	season	3,2	68	saying	2,1
29	early	42	69	joint	22		29	dinner	3,2	69	equal	2,1
30	place	41	70	years	22		30	cooking	3,1	70	products	2
31	end	39	71	dinner	22		31	tape	3	71	last	2
32	school	39	72	new	22		32	yet	3	72	Saturday	1,9
33	well	39	73	night	22		33	Friday	3	73	letter	1,9
34	points	38	74	making	22		34	conversation	3	74	training	1,9
35	breakfast	35	75	race	22		35	tour	3	75	afternoon	1,9
36	put	33	76	bottle	22		36	session	2,9	76	style	1,8
37	go	33	77	point	21		37	preparing	2,9	77	Christmas	1,7
38	training	32	78	task	21		38	joint	2,9	78	goods	1,7
39	saying	32	79	tour	21		39	career	2,9	79	started	1,7
40	went	32	80	letter	21		40	wine	2,8	80	evening	1,7

word ending in -ing whereas the semantically related words *begin* and *end* are less commonly associated with words ending in -ing. Semantically-related words can prefer to keep quite different company. This applies whether we are considering antonyms such as *begin* and *end*, or synonyms such as *start* and *begin*, or related types in the same lemma. We *give support* rather than **make support*; we *give a sigh, a grunt,* or *a whimper* rather than **do a sigh, a grunt* or *a whimper*, because 'words describing human behaviour' in English tend to be associated with *give* rather than *make* or *do*.

The types of phraseological phenomena exemplified in this analysis of the BNC have been discussed by others, most recently by Partington (2004). In earlier studies by Sinclair (1987), and Louw (1993) the phenomenon of 'semantic prosody' was described. Verbs such as *happen* or *set in*, for example, were characterised as having negative semantic prosody, being associated with words representing unpleasant events or entities. Stubbs (2001:65) however, suggested that a somewhat wider semantic framework could be employed, by characterising as 'semantic preference', "the relation, not between individual words, but between a lemma or word-form and a set of semantically related words" such as the relation between *large* and words associated with quantification, or the semantic preference of *undergo* to be associated with medical procedures which are not sought. Partington (2004) suggests that semantic prosody may be viewed as a sub-category of semantic preference.

3.   Phraseology and language pedagogy: concluding remarks

Multi-word units give meaning to text and are part of what we learn when we learn a language. However, the nature and role of phraseology in language pedagogy has tended to be neglected over the last few decades. This may seem surprising because, as Sinclair et al. (1970:ix) acknowledged in the OSTI report, "the idea of collocation first emerged in the work of language teachers between the two world wars, particularly that of Harold Palmer in Japan". As early as 1933 Palmer suggested that "a collocation is a succession of two or more words that must be learned as an integral whole and not pieced together from its component parts" (1933:i); "There is a vast and little-charted linguistic territory lying between (but sometimes overlapping) the respective fields of the lexicographer and the grammarian" (1933:11); "A mere selection of common collocations is found to contain thousands of examples – and therefore to exceed by far the popular estimate of the number of single words contained in an everyday vocabulary…" (1933:13). Palmer's language teaching methodology involved urging his Japanese students to learn large numbers of collocations by heart as if they were single lexemes.

More recently, Firth (1957), Sinclair et al. (1970), Hakuta (1974), Halliday & Hassan (1976), Wong Fillmore (1976), Nattinger (1980), Peters (1983), Pawley & Syder (1983) and Wray (2002) are among those who have kept reminding us of the formulaic nature of much of our speech behaviour, and that learning a language involves learning many multi-word sequences.

In this light, we might be forgiven for thinking it would be obvious that in addition to providing insights which contribute to the description of a language and how it is used, modern corpus-based research would have the potential to contribute considerably to language pedagogy, not only through direct applications of distributional information to curriculum content, but also by informing teachers about the nature of language learning. Further, as Nesselhauf (2005: 237) has suggested, up to a third of the collocations used by learners of English tend to be sources of error, and length of exposure to English in English-speaking countries has a more positive effect on learning collocations than the number of years a learner has had of classroom instruction. Work on phraseology in relation to language learning has tended to emphasise the form and the arbitrary nature of collocations, ranging from the description of so-called proverbial sequences of words (e.g. *Make hay while the sun shines*), to descriptions of lexicalised compounds such as, *civil war,* and *ill-gotten gains,* and so-called 'idiomatic' sequences such as *heavy rain* (rather than *thick rain*).

If we may be permitted to speculate as to why phraseology has not featured more prominently in language pedagogy we may consider the following:

i.   Since Palmer's 1933 list of several thousand English collocations, subjectively identified, there has not been a reliable way of establishing what constitutes the multi-word units in a language, and what principles may govern their composition. The development of computer corpus-based analysis has of course made it easier to identify recurring multi-word units.

ii.   There has been a persistent tension among language teachers in many parts of the world over the last 50 years between form-focused and message-focused approaches to language pedagogy. Analysis of phraseology has tended to favour pedagogical approaches based on form. It is relatively easy with computer assistance to discover many tokens of a particular structure such as the following, for example: *at the__ of the__ (e.g. at the end of the day)*. There is however, no obvious semantic coherence here, and therefore little to engage the motivation of learners.

The availability of corpus-based descriptions of phraseology focusing especially on form came at the very time that language teaching theory and practice was favouring a focus on messages and function, through 'communicative language teaching', taking account of advances in sociolinguistics, discourse analysis and pragmatics as the basis for curricula and classroom practice. Calls for balance between pedagogical focus on form and meaning have in turn contributed to the modern emphasis on descriptive grammar and on vocabulary teaching, seen in the application of lexical grammar, and in the multi-word lexical approach of Lewis (1993) and others. Too great an emphasis, however, on multi-word frameworks from a formal perspective, can lead to overlooking the kinds of semantic relationships associated with phraseology identified in the first part of this chapter.

iii. There is no tried and true 'method' for teaching phraseology. Distributional information from a corpus is not necessarily a reliable guide for inclusion in a language learner's curriculum, especially if native speaker norms are used. A learner-directed phraseology curriculum could be ideal, however, if it could relate the items to be learned to what the learner might be motivated to say or write (see Wray & Fitzpatrick, this volume). With regard to methodology, it has been suggested by some enthusiastic protagonists that data-driven learning of phraseology based on the analysis of corpora by learners themselves could encourage learner autonomy, in some way suggesting that language learners could be made to be like aspiring descriptive linguists, discovering the facts about a language, and that the interactional driver of communicative language teaching could be by-passed, with the teacher's job reduced to being a facilitator. Some learners have been encouraged to explore the company words keep by having the key word highlighted in context through simplified concordancing. Unfortunately apart from the fact that it is difficult to keep all but the most highly motivated learners sitting in front of a screen looking at unrelated lines of text, it is simply unrealistic to expect a return to teaching languages as unapplied systems. In addition to being influenced by descriptions of grammar and lexis, language teaching curriculum development is also driven by error analysis (as developed in learner corpora), and by needs analysis. Further, it is not necessarily efficient to have to discover the differences in use between *tall, high, upright* and *vertical* through a corpus, when the differences are made explicit in good dictionaries.

iv. Although teachers have long recognised that there are different kinds of learning involved in language learning, the relative weight given to each has not always been clear. Some language learning is implicit and some is explicit. As Kirsner (1994) and Ellis (1994) have argued, it seems that phraseology is learned especially through implicit learning by unconsciously meeting multi-word sequences repeatedly in context. The more we encounter these multi-word units, the more fluent we become in retrieving and producing them (Bybee & Hopper 2001). Explicit learning, on the other hand, is learning with awareness. In English, for example, it might include that there are regular -s noun plurals and -ed past tense morphemes, or that adjectives and nouns have gender agreement in French. Instruction on the code and on how to use it to perform speech acts is part of explicit learning. However, it is obviously impossible to make explicit the whole complex grammatical, lexical and pragmatic system of a language.

The focus of explicit teaching and learning should be the items of a language which are frequent and useful. Few learners of English will ever have been told explicitly that in English we say *thank you very much*, but not **thank you much*; that if we say *I completely forgot to ring you* it is probably less likely to seem offhand or insulting than if we say *I forgot to ring you*; that we are more likely to see *a heavily-laden truck* than *a laden truck*. Learning such phraseology has largely been left to implicit learning which occurs when the focus of pedagogy is on messages rather than form.

While recognizing that it is not easy to teach explicitly the kind of phraseological complexity revealed by the corpus, the challenge for language teachers is how to devise methodologies which maximize the opportunities for implicit learning, for learners to get enough experience of multi-word units in use in order to internalise them. It should be clear from Tables 1–8 that some of the collocations which contain the strongest bonds, as measured by the MI score, are in fact not frequent, and should not be a pedagogical priority. Frequent collocations (e.g. *very good, enjoy life, give rise, send back, start again, find a way, stop talking, lose weight, at the moment*), can find a place in explicit teaching and learning in a curriculum, while infrequent collocations such as *finding solace* or *losing momentum* should be left to implicit learning, part of a hidden curriculum of both collocational forms and semantic preference. From a pedagogical viewpoint, it is, of course the most frequently-occurring collocations which normally need to be learned first. Some explicit instruction in using frequently-occurring collocations taught as vocabulary is therefore almost certainly worthwhile.

v.   There is much about phraseology that linguists do not yet understand. For example, how much of language use is formulaic? What are the best ways of teaching phraseology, as compared with learning it through exposure? It is all too easy for linguists who are not deeply involved in language teaching to assume that phraseology should be part of the explicit curriculum. There is a need, however, for more research evidence to support the inclusion of phraseology in the explicit curriculum. One particular irony is that among English teachers at least, phraseology has often been condemned as 'cliché' when formulaic, prefabricated multi-word units are produced by native speakers, whereas the ability to use such multi-word sequences is simultaneously recognised as a mark of fluency if applied to second or foreign language learners.

vi. Corpus-based research has particularly challenged language educators to work out how to maximize the exposure needed for learners to acquire multi-word sequences that cannot easily be taught explicitly. The encouragement of autonomous language learning, especially through reading, is obviously very important to help maximize exposure to language in use. It may be that reading of all kinds, including literary works, may make an overdue return for greater attention in language pedagogy, for reading does provide the kind of exposure which facilitates implicit learning. In addition to this contribution to language teaching practice, research in phraseology can also contribute to language acquisition theory by revealing something of the semantic complexity of languages and the cognitive processes which lie behind language learning and use, and which enable us to become fluent language users.

Developing capacity in corpus-based research has already provided rich opportunities for researchers to undertake descriptions of languages for pedagogical purposes. There have already been advances in lexicography from corpus-based research, leading to new kinds of dictionaries. There is room for more. For example, a dictionary of the 2000 most frequent words in English (or in particular genres of English) showing the linguistic ecology of each of the headwords more fully than has hitherto been possible could be a useful project for language pedagogy and for revealing new insights about language use and human cognition.

References

Biber, D., S. Johansson, G. Leech, S. Conrad & E. Finegan (1999). *Longman grammar of spoken and written English*. London: Longman.

Bybee, J. & P. Hopper (eds.) (2001). *Frequency and the emergence of linguistic structure*. Amsterdam: John Benjamins.

Church, K. & P. Hanks (1990). Word association norms, mutual information, and lexicography. *Computational Linguistics, 16*, 22–29.

Ellis, N. (ed.) (1994). *Implicit and explicit learning of languages*. London: Academic Press.

Firth, J. (1957). *Papers in linguistics, 1934–1951*. London: Oxford University Press.

Hakuta, K. (1974). Prefabricated patterns and the emergence of structure in second language acquisition. *Language Learning*, 24, 287–298.

Halliday, M. & R. Hasan (1976). *Cohesion in English*. London: Longman.

Kennedy, G. (2003). Amplifier collocations in the British National Corpus: Implications for English language teaching. *TESOL Quarterly, 37*, 467–487.

Kirsner, K. (1994). Second language vocabulary learning: The role of implicit processes. In Ellis, N. (ed.) *Implicit and explicit learning of languages*, 283–311. London: Academic Press.

Lehmann, H.-M., P. Schneider & S. Hoffmann (2002). *BNCWeb*. Zurich: University of Zurich. Available from http://escorp.unizh.ch/.

Lewis, M. (1993). *The lexical approach: The state of ELT and a way forward*. London: Language Teaching Publications.

Louw, B. (1993). Irony in the text or insincerity in the writer? The diagnostic potential of semantic prosodies. In Baker, M., G. Francis & E. Tognini-Bonelli (eds.) *Text and technology: In honour of John Sinclair, 157–176*. Amsterdam: John Benjamins.

Nattinger, J. (1980). A lexical phrase grammar for ESL. *TESOL Quarterly, 14*, 337–344.

Nesselhauf, N. (2005). *Collocations in a learner corpus*. Amsterdam: John Benjamins.

Palmer, H.E. (1933). *Second interim report on English collocations*. Tokyo: Kaitakusha.

Partington, A. (2004). "Utterly content in each other's company". Semantic prosody and semantic preference. *International Journal of Corpus Linguistics, 9* (1), 131–156.

Pawley, A. & F. Syder (1983). Two puzzles for linguistic theory: Nativelike selection and nativelike fluency. In Richards, J. & R. Schmidt (eds.) *Language and communication*, 191–226. London: Longman.

Peters, A. (1983). *The units of language acquisition*. Cambridge: Cambridge University Press.

Sinclair, J. (1987). *Looking up*. London: Collins.

Sinclair, J., S. Jones & R. Daley (1970). *English collocation studies: The OSTI Report.* (edited by Ramesh Krishnamurthy 2004) London: Continuum.

Stubbs, M. (2001). *Words and phrases*. Oxford: Blackwell.

Wong-Fillmore, L. (1976). The Second Time Around. PhD dissertation, Stanford University.

Wray, A. (2002). *Formulaic language and the lexicon*. Cambridge: Cambridge University Press.

Essential collocations for learners of English

The role of collocational direction and weight

Susanne Handl

This chapter points into a new direction for defining and classifying collocations, taking into account the needs of advanced learners of English. After a brief review of the common practice in representing collocations in dictionaries, the theoretical framework for the study is introduced. Most definitions are based on the claim that collocations constitute a gradable phenomenon. What is often not accounted for is the fact that their scalar characteristic lies in a set of three gradable criteria. This assumption is taken up to develop the multidimensional classification as an alternative to traditional methods. In this perspective collocations are understood as a product of two elements which can both have different positions on the lexical, the semantic and the statistical dimension. Within the core area of these dimensions, the quality of the relation between the two partners can be determined according to the role they play in the collocation, either a stronger or a weaker one. Thus collocations are not considered as uniform lexical combinations, but as directional relationships with the partners exerting different degrees of attraction, which can be used as a classifying feature for lexicography. The paper ends with a tentative proposal for an application of this notion of collocational direction and weight in learners' dictionaries.

1.   Introduction

'Collocation' is a traditional term that has long been used for syntagmatic lexical relations in a language.[1] But, especially since the advent of computerised corpora for linguistic research, the analysis of collocations has become more and more prominent. Any corpus tool offers collocation queries and in every concordance

---

1.   Although commonly ascribed to J. R. Firth, the term 'collocation' was actually used in the 1950s by H. E. Palmer and still earlier (in 1917) by Otto Jespersen (cf. Mitchell 1971: 35; Bartsch 2004: 30).

line word combinations can be investigated in their co-occurrences and context. The examples below[2] are taken from an in-depth corpus study in the *British National Corpus* (BNC) that forms the basis for the new approach to collocation described in this chapter.

(1) [B03] *... technology, and even in the **foreseeable future**, this is simply not possible.*

[KDO] *... next time they can **roll the dice** if they get it.*

[A04] *... artists working in several media have **a wide range** of references.*

[AHX] *... believes the ruling will work against dyslexic children with **special** educational **needs**.*

[A03] *... approach to school art instruction is to **draw attention** to the types ...*

[ECE] *... reflects the influence of cultural and social factors as it was **totally unacceptable** for women to smoke when ...*

The major aim of the study was to find a systematic procedure for selecting collocations from authentic language and displaying them in dictionaries aimed at non-native speakers of English. A look at available learner dictionaries reveals a variety of ways of representing collocations. Although the recent editions all explicitly mention collocation as an important area for learners, they do not usually explain how they have decided whether to include a potential collocation in the dictionary or how collocations are to be presented in an entry. Comparing older editions with the later, corpus-based, ones, reveals a considerable increase in the number of useful collocations presented. However, a learner often has to perform a double look-up before they find the correct collocation, and is often left in the dark about the status of the collocation, since they also occur in example sentences without a special mark. This method is implicitly justified in the Macmillan English Dictionary (MED[3]) as a way to save space: but how is the learner to know if a co-occurrence in an example sentence is just a chance combination or a recurrent collocation that is worth remembering? The latest edition of the traditional Longman Dictionary of Contemporary English (LDOCE), on the other hand, claims to consistently highlight collocations in bold or list them in separate collocation boxes (a method the MED also uses sporadically).

---

2. The letters and numbers in square brackets indicate the source texts in the BNC. Examples of usage from the BNC were obtained under the terms of the BNC End User Licence. Copyright in the individual texts cited resides with the original IPR holders. For information and licensing conditions relating to the BNC, see the web site at http://www.natcorp.ox.ac.uk

3. Cf. the foreword by Michael Hoey (2002: viii).

look up s.v.	found in **MED**	found in **LDOCE**	collocates in **OCD**
future	no mention of the collocate, only similar ones in bold type within sense 1: ***near/not-too-distant/immediate~***	in bold type within sense 1a): ***near/immediate/foreseeable/not too distant ~***	*foreseeable/immediate//near/not-too-distant/remote ~*
foreseeable	in bold type at the end of the entry: ***for/in the ~ future***	in bold type as sense 1 and sense 2: ***for/in the ~ future***	no entry
need (N)	in an example sentence for a sub-sense: ***sb's needs:*** *People with mental health problems have special ~s*	after sense 8: reference to extra entry SPECIAL NEEDS	*basic, essential, fundamental/particular, special, specific ~ ,...*
special	no mention of the collocate, but extra dictionary entry for ~ ***needs*** as compound noun	no mention of the collocate, but extra dictionary entry for ~ ***needs*** as compound noun	no entry
unacceptable	in an extra box "words frequently used with": ***completely, quite, simply, totally, utterly, wholly***	in example sentence: *I found her attitude totally ~*	*completely, quite, simply, totally, utterly, wholly/inherently ~*
totally	no mention of the collocate	in bold type within the entry: ~ ***unacceptable/ unneccessary/unsuitable*** *etc.*	no entry

Figure 1. Examples of the representation of collocations in dictionaries

Both dictionaries rely on large corpora, but they do not explain their method of extracting collocations, although the MED does mention that their data extraction is based on *Word Sketch* (a program developed at the University of Brighton by Adam Kilgarriff, see http://www.sketchengine.co.uk/). So it seems that, although statistical measures are used for uncovering collocations, there is still no consistent approach to deciding on the relevance and status of a collocation. A simple comparison of the entries for some of the collocations listed in (1) should illustrate this. In Figure 1, I have listed the results of a search in the MED and the LDOCE[4] for each word in the target collocations, thus imitating the process a

---

4. MED and LDOCE are chosen as representatives for the most recent development in lexicography, not as individual cases. The phenomenon could be illustrated with any of the other

learner goes through when searching for the correct collocation to use in a text. As a reference source, I used the Oxford Collocations Dictionary for Students of English (OCD).

Although this is only a random sample, and the dictionaries used are up-to-date and based on authentic language, it is evident that the practice applied to collocations differs. Either the sets of collocates for a lexeme do not correspond in the dictionaries (e.g. for *totally*) or the same collocation is treated differently within a single dictionary. This is the case for *special needs* in the MED, which, on the one hand, assigns lemma status to the collocation, but, on the other hand, lists it only as an example of a sub-sense of the noun *need*. Thus, it is mainly a matter of chance whether learners arrive at the collocation they are looking for, depending on the dictionary they use, or which of the collocational constituents they use as the starting point for their search.

Obviously a learners' dictionary cannot be expected to contain the same number of collocations as a collocation dictionary. A learners' dictionary addresses multiple needs, its major purpose being to clarify all the senses of a word. The actual use of the word is a secondary consideration that can often only be partly taken into account because of the complexity of usage and lack of space. Collocation here has a dual function: from a decoding perspective, it helps to clarify the meaning, where definitions alone are not enough (cf. *foreseeable*); and for encoding, it leads the learner towards a native-like usage of words. This twofold character requires collocations to be listed systematically under both constituents, at least with cross-references, or in a special list at the end of the dictionary. The qualitative aspect of the entries should make it obvious to learners whether the word combinations they encounter are recurrent in the language and, as such, worth acquiring actively. Thus, what is needed is a method of finding out which collocations are most relevant to non-native speakers, and a method of showing their importance to learners.

Before this is tackled in later sections of this article, there is the problem of defining and classifying collocation adequately. Reviewing the relevant literature gives the impression that the classification of the phenomenon is still an unsolved puzzle, influenced by various views on the reason, function and representation of collocations as habitual lexical co-occurrences in a language.

The aim of this chapter is to work out a multi-layered conception of habitual co-occurrences of words, based on the assumption that the classification problems mainly arise from the status of collocation as a product of two elements characterised by the varying nature of the relation between the collocational partners.

---

common dictionaries for advanced learners. The second edition of the MED (2007) unfortunately could not be taken into account for this paper.

Fixed expressions (i.e. idioms), where the elements taken together form their own unit of meaning, are not considered in this approach. Although they represent a significant part of language, for learners they are problematic mainly from a decoding perspective, and as such are usually adequately captured in idiom dictionaries. For everyday conversation and standard writing tasks, however, collocation is much more important, since the incorrect use of a word in the context immediately unmasks the non-native speaker. Avoiding idioms in language production only leads to a more sober style, it is not as revealing as mistakes in the use of collocations. The following examples, taken from the results of an Internet search, illustrate the actual usage of the idiom *to rain cats and dogs* and its collocational counterpart in different writing styles. Sample (2) comes from the review of a blues band, sample (3) from a news report on an accident.

(2)   *It was raining cats and dogs in Dublin all day long ...* (www.irishblues.com/reviews/hollywoodslim.html)

(3)   *At the time of the accident, it was raining heavily and ...* (news.bbc.co.uk/2/hi/uk_news/wales/2673685.stm)

The query in the UK-part of the search engine Yahoo (www.uk.search.yahoo.com) shows that the collocation is much more frequent than the idiom. It returned 396 hits for the string *"was raining cats and dogs"*, compared to 1,300 for *"was raining heavily"*, whilst an unusual combination like *"was raining strongly"* only occurred twice. One was from an online diary by a German tourist in Rome, and the other from a report on red rain, where *strongly* was a premodifier to the adjective *red*.

Collocation is the centre of interest here, because it is a pervasive, but, at the same time, elusive phenomenon in language. Unlike idioms, it is difficult to delimit the scope of collocation. Therefore, after setting the scene with the most important definitions and classifications used so far, I will illustrate the essential criteria for collocation on the basis of which my multi-dimensional view is constructed. Each dimension in the model is presented with a few examples from the corpus study, with special emphasis on the frequency-based, statistical approach, smoothing the way for an account of collocational direction and weight. The final section provides a short conclusion and perspectives for future research.

2.   Basic framework

The starting point for this article is the unclear state of classification in collocation research. Not only have syntagmatic lexical relations been approached from different linguistic perspectives, there is – within the realm of contextualism, where the notion of collocation is commonly rooted – a wide range of definitions and ty-pologies as well (Sinclair 1966; Cowie 1978; Hausmann 1984; Benson et al. 1986; Carter 1987; Schmid 2003). In the larger area of phraseology, however, it seems that collocation has not been at the centre of research. Gläser (1986), for example, gives an extensive account of the structure and meaning of phraseological units such as idioms or proverbs, but she only dedicates five pages to the phenomenon of collocation (1986: 38–43). This may be because a collocation is considered to be largely compositional, so the decoding of a word combination does not pose any problems, since the meaning of the whole is just the sum of the meaning of its parts. From a typological point of view, however, it has to be acknowledged that collocation is not a homogeneous phenomenon, but a notion encompass-ing various types of word combination. And from the encoding perspective, the compositional view is highly problematic; in order to sound like a native speaker, you have to be sure about which company a word normally keeps. So linguists either disagree about the concept of collocation or tend to disregard it. Sometimes this notion is even exploited for other linguistic purposes, such as the study of sociolects, register and style, learner language and meaning analysis (cf. Halliday & Hasan 1976; Stubbs 1995; Lipka 2002; Nesselhauf 2004).

This great interest in collocation as a tool of analysis can also be seen as evi-dence for the assumption that it is an integral part of any language, and as such, of paramount importance to learners. Especially when they are trying to achieve native-like fluency, learners must be provided with a more objective and intui-tive access to collocations. Dictionaries should give explicit information about their status and relevance, so that learners are constantly reminded of their role, which should eventually lead to the acquisition of collocational knowledge by learning vocabulary, not as isolated items, but as items in collocation. This is the ultimate aim, but first the elusiveness of the collocation concept has to be dealt with. Therefore, I will try to devise a more comprehensive classification based on necessary and gradable criteria. A very short overview of the most important classifications and definitions so far will serve as the basis for a new approach to collocation.

2.1   Definitions and classifications

The classic and most basic definition of word co-occurrences is, of course, J.R. Firth's (1957) "You shall know a word by the company it keeps". Firth is generally considered the father of collocation. Many other definitions followed, but they can all be more or less assigned to four major categories.

The first group consists of text-oriented definitions like the one by Sinclair (1991), who sees collocation as "the occurrence of two or more words within a short space of each other in a text" (1991:170).[5] Although this seems trivial at first glance, it is the basic tenet for recognising collocations, the one on which all classifications have to be based, since without text syntagmatic relations would not exist.

Other definitions emphasise the associative nature of collocation: Firth points out that it is an order of mutual expectancy (cf. Palmer 1968:181). There is a certain associative bond between two words that collocate. Aitchison (2003:91) assigns an even greater role to collocations, when she says that "[w]ord meaning is probably learned by noting the words which come alongside". Sinclair (1991:109ff.) goes one step further in postulating the idiom principle of language, which holds that for a large part of text production we use semi-preconstructed phrases that we choose simultaneously when speaking or writing. His example here is *of course*, which is not the result of combining the words *of* and *course*, but the outcome of a single choice. Using the term 'semi-' in the explanation of this principle allows for a certain variation in the preconstruction of phrases. An expression like *of course* would be a fully preconstructed item, whereas classical collocations like *hard + work/luck/facts* are less fixed. This illustrates the fact that syntagmatic lexical relations are a gradable phenomenon of language. So, the idiom principle does not only apply to compounds that almost have the status of separate lexemes, or to idioms with their non-compositional meaning, but also to looser combinations of words that are simply activated together, such as:

(4)   *to pay attention*
       a clear conscience
       closely tied to.

A third type of definition is mainly statistically oriented. The question is whether the co-occurrence of two words only occurs by chance or whether it reappears with greater than random probability (cf. Halliday 1961; Sinclair 1966). This is the major definition used as a basis for all corpus linguistic studies of collocation, and it also plays an important role in my analysis.

The last group of definitions can be mainly seen as a counter-position to the statistical definition. It could be called the semantic type, since researchers like Hausmann (1979, 1984, 1985), Benson (1985), Benson et al. (1991) and Klotz (2000) try to put the relation between co-occurring words down to aspects of meaning. This leads to a distinction between the *basis* and the *collocator* – later

---

5. See also Halliday & Hasan (1976) and Hoey (1991).

renamed the autosemantic and synsemantic components (Hausmann 1997)[6] –
for the two elements of a collocation, and to a typology of lexical collocations using semantic features to determine the *collocator*. Thus the verb in *reach a verdict*
is assigned the meaning [CREATION], whereas [ACTIVATION] is the feature
present in *fly a kite* (Benson 1985: 191). The driving force behind this approach is
a lexicographic description of collocations.

These four categories are only tentative groupings, and it has to be noted that
a definition can, of course, be assigned to more than one type. The variety of definitions entails a variety of classifications, since classification systems depend on
the point of view taken towards collocation and on the criteria used. Again, four
major groups of approaches, that sometimes overlap or merge into one another,
can be distinguished. First, there are the binary classifications, where collocation is simply contrasted with free combination without further subdivision or
specification (cf. Firth 1957; Sinclair 1966; Greenbaum 1970). Second, there are
typological classifications with fixed classes that theoretically should have neatly
defined labels – although in reality this does not always work – such as free construction vs. collocation vs. idiom (Weinreich 1969; Heid 1994), or collocation
vs. co-creation vs. counter-creation (Hausmann 1984). Then, there is the most
convincing type of gradual classification, where collocation is seen as a stretch on
the continuum between free word combinations and fully fixed idioms or compounds (cf. Cowie 1978; Benson et al. 1986; Carter 1987). Finally there is a proposal by Schmid (2003) to classify collocations as a prototypical category with the
most typical examples in the centre and more peripheral members at the edges.
The problem with this type of classification is that not only is the collocation itself
a gradual phenomenon, but the criteria used to determine a collocation can also
be gradual. So it may be helpful to have a more detailed look at the criteria commonly used to describe and delimit collocation.

2.2   Criteria

As with the classifications involved, collocational criteria also present a very diverse picture. The different definitions are based on various sets of criteria applied
to lexical co-occurrences to a major or minor degree. Basically, two main types of
criteria can be distinguished: prerequisites and continua.

---

6. Although Hausmann recognises that collocation is an oriented relation, he allocates the
roles of basis and collocator simply on semantic grounds. He does not consider frequencies in
real language, which is the method employed in this study.

The prerequisites are conditions that have to be fulfilled in order to be able to talk of collocations at all. They can also be seen as the defining criteria, in contrast to the classifying criteria. The indispensable criterion for defining a collocation is, of course, the co-occurrence of two or more words (cf. Sinclair 1966; Stubbs 1995; Moon 1998). This could be considered too obvious to mention, but, as a prerequisite, it has logical consequences for the potential areas that provide material for collocations. It means that the words in question must be open to combination; they must belong, for example, to the same register or text type (cf. Lipka 2002: 184f.), since otherwise they will usually not occur together. As a second criterion, they also have to occur in a common context (cf. Sinclair 1966; Carter 1987; Hoey 1991) or, to be more precise, in a common co-text.[7] This does not, however, imply that they necessarily have to be part of the same sentence or the same clause. It is often possible for the elements of a collocation to be separated by intervening linguistic material as in this famous example by Greenbaum (1970: 11) with the collocational components *collect* and *stamps*:

(5) a.   *They <u>collect</u> many things, but chiefly <u>stamps</u>.*
     b.   *They <u>collect</u> many things, but [they] chiefly [collect] <u>stamps</u>.*

The only condition that has to be fulfilled is that the syntactical relation between the constituents in question allows a reconstruction of an adjacent collocation as given in (5b). Example (6) shows a text sample, taken from a report on the internet, where *stamp* and *collect* do not form a collocation; rather, *collect* collocates with *revenue*.

(6)   *The first adhesive postage <u>stamp</u> was used in Great Britain in 1840. At the time, the British post office was having trouble <u>collecting</u> <u>revenue</u>.*
      (Jim Watson on http://pages.ebay.co.uk/community/library/catindex-stamps-hist.html)

Continua are more difficult criteria, in that they are themselves gradable. They do not simply apply or not apply, rather they are applicable to varying degrees to different kinds of collocations. The first continuum is semantic transparency, which can be seen as the counterpart to idiomaticity. It is largely responsible for the distinction between collocations and idioms, although a clear boundary has not been determined (cf. Carter 1987; Fernando 1996). So, in terms of prototype theory, we are dealing with two categories with fuzzy boundaries, depending on the degree of semantic transparency a word combination exhibits. This also has

---

7.   This also implies co-occurrence in the same text, as mentioned by Sinclair (1991) in his text-oriented definition.

to do with the notion of compositionality, the quality normally ascribed to col-locations. Taking a closer look at regularly co-occurring words, it is clear that they cannot be divided into one group where the meaning of a larger expression is simply the sum of its parts, and another group that conveys a meaning totally independent of the semantic components of its elements (cf. Carter 1987:63f.). With real examples, there is always something in-between. A recurring word combination can acquire a new meaning. This can be either a feeble connotation, as in the case of the phrasal verb *to set in*, which according to Sinclair (1994:21) usually refers to something unpleasant. Or it can be a completely new denotation, acquired from the frequency of its usage in this combination or in a specific con-text. This holds for the verb *to run*, which has its literal meaning 'move quickly' in the combination *to run a race*, but has a new denotation 'to organise or control' in *to run a farm* (cf. Gläser 1986:43). So, depending on the semantic contribution an element makes to the meaning of the whole expression, there are different degrees of transparency or opacity[8] (for an in-depth discussion of the notion of non-com-positionality, see Svensson in press).

Another criterion that is scaled on a continuum is the so-called collocational range, which is simply the number of potential collocates a node (i.e. the word being analysed) can take. Thus, a node can have a very restricted, or a rather wide range. The larger the list of potential combinatory partners is, the less typical it is as a collocation. A combination with a very restricted range, on the other hand, is either an idiom or a complex lexeme. The examples with the verb *to face* in (7) show a narrowing of the collocational range, and its consequences. (7a) clearly has the status of collocation because of its collocational range, whereas (7b) is a sort of transition area, and (7c) only has one possible collocate and must be as-signed to the class of idioms (cf. Aisenstadt 1979:71f.).

(7) a. *to face* + *the facts/truth/problems/reality* etc.
     b. *to face* + *charges/counts*
     c. *to face* + *the music*

What also becomes evident here is a further complication for the classification, namely the fact that the criteria are interdependent. There seems to be a paral-lel between collocational ranges and semantic transparency. In more restricted ranges, like (7b) and (7c), there is a growing tendency towards semantic opacity in at least one of the elements.

---

8. The syntactic-fixedness of word co-occurrences could, of course, be added here. However, to my mind this is more properly considered a criterion for subclassifying idioms, and is not of great help for the concept of collocation.

The third gradable criterion is the essential one for corpus linguistic studies of collocation, namely frequency. Especially in recent decades, as corpus research has become more and more prominent, collocation studies have increasingly been frequency-based (cf. Sinclair 1991; Tognini-Bonelli 2001; Hunston 2002; Stubbs 2002; Bartsch 2004). The study presented here is also frequency-based, and I assume that the question of whether or not two words frequently co-occur is of prime importance in deciding on the relevance of that collocation for learners of a language. But one has to be careful, because frequency alone is not a reliable criterion. Further statistical aspects which take questions of probability and inter-relation between the elements into account also have to be incorporated. Taken together, these two continua (collocational range and frequency) can be used to derive a fundamental criterion for collocations which is observable and easy to grasp, namely the predictability or mutual expectancy of words. Predictability is a cognitive or psychological feature which is decisive for collocations. This can easily be experienced in association tests, or even in everyday conversation, when a hearer feels that s/he is able to continue an utterance begun by a speaker. Native speakers often only become aware of collocations when they are used creatively or inappropriately in a text: you immediately stumble over such unusual expressions when reading or hearing them. So, the observability of this criterion is usually restricted to artificial experimental situations or depends on chance. But with the help of large data sets and corpus linguistic methods, the role that predictability plays can be at least approximately measured.

Based on these criteria, I have developed a multi-dimensional classification, where each item can be positioned at different points along the dimensions, thus incorporating all the characteristics of a collocation instead of highlighting only one feature. This integrative method has also been used in other approaches. For example, Barkema (1996) criticises traditional terminology and claims that, for the classification of idioms,

> [...] a well-defined model is required that distinguishes between various descrip-
> tive dimensions and at the same time pays heed to the scalar nature of the differ-
> ent types of characteristics.   (Barkema 1996:154)

3.   A multi-dimensional framework

3.1   A detailed view of the three dimensions

The continua described above were used to establish three dimensions, each rang-ing from minimum to maximum on one criterion. For this learner-oriented ap-

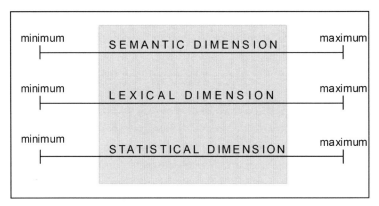

Figure 2. A multi-dimensional classification

proach, the extreme points on the scale were excluded from the area of collocation, since they outline the border zone between a collocation and an idiom or compound, on the one hand, and free ad-hoc combination, on the other. Instead, a core area was determined, which contains the most obvious and clear examples, and I concentrated on this area of prototypical collocations because it makes up a large part of the syntagmatic relations that cannot easily be assigned to hard and fast categories. Still within the collocational area, it is possible to grade word co-occurrences along these dimensions, thus characterising more or less typical examples for the concept of collocation. Figure 2 gives an idea of the three dimensions.

The first dimension is based on the variation of the semantic contribution of one element to the whole expression. By comparing the meanings of isolated items with those of the items within the combination the collocation can be positioned along the continuum. If the meaning inside the combination is the same as the meaning outside (e.g., in *to run a race*) the expression is maximally transparent and is positioned towards the free-combination endpoint of the dimension. If knowing the meanings outside the combination does not help in understanding the whole expression (e.g. in *to run the gauntlet* or *to face the music*), this is a semantically opaque idiom.

The lexical dimension is guided by the size of the collocational range. In a corpus query, the range of a node word can be determined by retrieving the list of all the co-occurring lexical items from its concordance. A typical collocation may consist of elements chosen from a restricted set of lexical items, i.e. from a small collocational range. There may be alternative combinations for similar meanings (as in (8a)), or completely different collocations built with the same node (as in (8b)).

(8)   a.   *in the near/not-too-distant/immediate/foreseeable*   +   *future*
      b.   *uncertain/painful/bright*   +   *future*

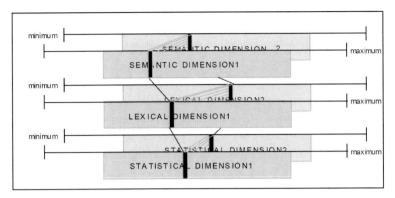

Figure 3. A collocational profile

The endpoints of the scale are again reserved for idioms and compounds in the case of very small ranges, and for free combinations if there is a large range.

The last continuum in the model, the statistical dimension, shows a similar distribution of collocation, idiom/compound and free co-occurrence. While the latter two hold the extreme positions, determined by either the highest or the lowest statistical scores, collocation occupies the core area of the dimension. As well as the probability measures normally used in large corpora, the decisive criterion is the relation between the independent frequencies of the single items and the frequency of their combination.

As each collocational partner has its own overall frequency in the corpus, two different scores for the collocation can be determined depending on which constituent is chosen. The resulting collocational factor (see Section 3.2 below) describes the impact a lexical item has on the collocation it occurs in. This gives rise to the general observation that collocations cannot be allocated to the three dimensions described here as single spots; rather the dimensional classification has to be effected for each collocational partner separately. This doubling of the classification holds not only for the statistical dimension, but also for both the semantic and the lexical dimensions, so that we end up with an even more complex picture of collocation. The criteria of semantic transparency or contribution, collocational range and frequency have to be considered for each element of a collocation, so that it can be assigned its own position; and the position of the whole collocation is then a collocational profile defined by the single positions on each dimension. Figure 3 provides an illustration of the three dimensions, doubled for two-word collocations.

3.2   The statistical dimension as a starting point for a revised account
of collocation

The new classification of collocation described in this article results from a large-scale corpus analysis of syntagmatic lexical relations in the *British National Corpus*. The aim was to devise a method of determining the scope of relevant collocation for advanced learners of English. I ran 250 highly frequent words as the nodes for analysis through the *BNC*, each returning 200 statistically significant collocates. Available significance scores[9] in corpora integrate the question of random co-occurrence into various association measures. Irrespective of which kind of measure is chosen, they all share the assumption that collocation is not just a random co-occurrence, but a unit made up of elements that have a certain connection to each other. According to this, a word combination is judged to be significant if its partners co-occur more often than they would if the words in the corpus were distributed by chance.

These scores, do not, however, distinguish between the collocational partners in terms of relevance. The mutual dependency expressed is hypothesised to be a constant and balanced relationship, i.e. the score is the same for each constituent of a collocation (cf. Berry-Rogghe 1973; Barnbrook 1996; McEnery & Wilson 1996; Kennedy 1998; Hunston 2002; Meyer 2002). But the undisputed criterion of predictability suggests that the status of the elements in a collocation must be unequal, or, at least, that each constituent has a certain force to predict the other one. In order to capture this unequal status of the partners in a collocation, I propose a new score that relates the frequency of the single item (i.e. all occurrences of the word) to the frequency of the item within the collocation (i.e. its occurrences in the combination in question). This automatically leads to the development of two different factors for each collocation, one for each partner. The so-called collocational factor (CF) is calculated as a ratio between the frequency of the collocation ($F_{combined}$) and the frequency of the independent word ($F_{isolated}$). The formula is given in Figure 4.

In the corpus analysis, the method produces a spreadsheet, as shown in Figure 5, which lists every node with its collocate, their part-of-speech tags, the various frequencies, a probability measure, in this case the Z score, that is incorporated in the collocational factor, and the CFs for each of the partners.

---

9.   The most widely used tests are t-tests, chi-squared, MI (mutual information) scores and Z scores (for details see, for example, Barnbrook 1996; McEnery & Wilson 1996 and Hunston 2002). Z scores were chosen for this study mainly because of their ease of use and the fact that they tend to return the intuitively most significant words as top collocates, with few hapaxes, and only a small set of function words.

$$CF_{(a)} = \frac{F \text{ combined}_{(a+b)}}{F \text{ isolated}_{(a)}}$$

Figure 4. The Collocational Factor

CF(n)	NODE	TAG	F isolated (n)	F com- bined	Z-score	F isolated (c)	COLLOCATE	TAG	CF(c)
6,059.79	minister	SUBST	30,176	9,976	18,330	11,959	prime	ADJ	15,290.58
1,435.64	report	SUBST	32,157	3,816	12,098	3,772	video-taped	ADJ	12,239.12
658.52	steel	SUBST	4,022	290	9,133	307	stainless	ADJ	8,627.26
458.18	punishment	SUBST	2,449	141	7,958	157	corporal	ADJ	7,146.99
1,919.05	pool	SUBST	5,544	975	10,912	1,762	swimming	SUBST	6,038.14
1,104.31	bean	SUBST	1,827	228	8,849	445	baked	ADJ	4,533.87
137.07	basket	SUBST	1,715	45	5,224	53	wastepaper	SUBST	4,435.47
198.62	chalk	SUBST	916	34	5,351	54	belemnite	SUBST	3,369.15
451.68	punishment	SUBST	2,449	176	6,285	392	capital	ADJ	2,821.84
74.03	future	SUBST	15,382	289	3,940	427	foreseeable	ADJ	2,666.65

Figure 5.　Collocational spreadsheet

The examples given here illustrate the upper endpoint of the statistical dimension containing compounds and more typical collocations.[10] The word *prime* occurs almost 12,000 times in the *BNC* ($F_{isolated(c)}$), and almost 10,000 of these occurrences ($F_{combined}$) are with the word *minister*. So, the relation between these two frequencies, expressed in the CF(c) for *prime*, which is more than twice the CF(n) for *minister*, tells us something about the role the word plays in the collocation. In this case, *prime* is the stronger partner, since it occurs almost exclusively together with *minister*. The word *minister*, on the other hand, occurs to a higher degree outside the combination. Thus, *prime* has more collocational weight than its partner, it guides the collocation and attracts the weaker component, *minister*. This directional aspect is ignored by traditional association measures such as the Z score, where one and the same number characterises both collocational constituents.

Two general observations about the behaviour of the collocational factor can be made: A low-frequent word, for example, that is accompanied in all, or almost all, of its rare occurrences by a mid- or high-frequency word, has a very high CF. This means that the word cannot exist without its collocation, a fact which is obviously important to know for a learner. The more frequent word in this scenario, however, has a low CF. It takes part in many other combinations, and its collocational behaviour is not that fixed. On the doubled statistical dimension of the

---

10. In the course of the analysis it turned out that a strict delineation between collocations and compounds was not easy to achieve. Moreover, from the learner's point of view, such a distinction is not helpful. So for the sake of clarity, compounds are seen as a subgroup of collocations, defined by high CFs.

collocational profile in Figure 3, such a collocation would therefore be assigned to two distant positions, i.e. partner 1 would tend towards the maximum, and partner 2, the one with the low CF, towards the minimum endpoint of the scale.

For a systematic account of collocations based on a large-scale corpus analysis, this collocational factor constitutes the primary criterion, as it offers a method to reduce the number of potential collocations by excluding co-occurrences that show a statistical tendency towards one or the other extreme of the continuum. Findings from the other two dimensions can then be integrated to form a complete picture of the core area of collocation.

3.3   The semantic and lexical dimensions as supporters

Starting with the results of the statistical analysis, the positions of potential collocations on the lexical and semantic dimension can be worked out. This means that the first step is the allocation of recurring word combinations to the extremes or to the collocational area on the statistical dimension, and this provides the data for a more qualitative analysis of the semantic contribution and collocational range to derive a collocational profile for each partner.

To illustrate this, I selected three examples from the statistical analysis to judge according to the other two dimensions. These are shown in Figure 6, with their frequencies and their CFs.

A collocational range, as mentioned in Section 2.2, consists of the most significant collocates, excluding function words, proper nouns and numbers. The size of a collocational range depends, of course, on where the boundary between important and unimportant collocations is set. In this case, I chose a CF of 0.74 worked out on the large-scale corpus analysis which is the basis of the present article (Handl in preparation).

Looking at the collocational range of *foreseeable future*, which has a high CF for the first partner and a very low one for the second, a very special behaviour on the lexical dimension can be seen for the two partners. In the *BNC*, *future* has a collocational range of 32, whereas *foreseeable* has an extremely restricted range of 1, i.e. *foreseeable* only occurs with *future* (besides the function words *for*

CF(n)	NODE	F isolated (n)	F combined	F isolated (c)	COLLOCATE	CF(c)
0.92	**future**	15,382	14	15	**foreseeable**	951
474	**attention**	13,582	1,789	21,706	**draw**	296
1,281	**wide**	16,143	3,278	20,166	**range**	1,025

Figure 6. Three selected collocations

and *the*). The lexeme *future*, on the other hand, also includes in its collocational range partners like *near, uncertain, secure, bright, immediate, distant* etc. On the lexical dimension, *foreseeable future* would therefore have a tendency towards the minimum endpoint of the scale for the first word. However, judged on the second component, the combination would be considered a typical collocation.

The lexical dimension of *draw attention* (with CFs of 296 and 474) shows another picture. Both partners have medium collocational ranges, with 48 for *attention* and 60 for *draw*. Other co-occurring items for *attention* are *pay, attract, focus, turn, receive, give, rivet* as well as *particular, direct, special, urgent* etc. *Draw*, on the other hand, often combines with *conclusion, distinction, inference, analogy*, but also with *breath, curtain, sword* and *line, graph, diagram* or *near, closer, heavily*. The range shows that there is much more variation for both partners; neither tends towards the outer reaches of the dimension, and they thus belong to the core of collocation.

The same applies to the example *wide range* which, having two very similar CFs, also has two rather large sets of possible collocates. For *wide*, there are 115 lexemes, including *variety, area, context, choice, issue, audience, implication, gap, definition*, as well as *world, mouth, eye, smile* and *open, awake, deep, long* etc. The noun *range* has a list of 76 with lexemes like *whole, broad, full, narrow, limited, extensive, vast*, as well as *extend, encompass, cover, include*, and *temperature, frequency, service, option, goods, material* etc.

On the whole, it seems that the findings from the lexical dimension support the results of a statistical analysis, although a more detailed investigation is still necessary, especially in the case of the large collocational ranges belonging to polysemous lexemes. This holds for the verb *draw* in the examples above, where the 60 possible collocates can be assigned to various categories of meanings. There are abstract collocations with *draw* in the abstract sense of 'compare two things', 'get particular reaction' or 'make somebody notice', and more concrete ones in 'create a picture' or 'pull something'. On the semantic dimension, combinations with *draw* in the latter sense would be positioned outside the area of collocation, since the semantic contribution is high, whereas the semantic contribution to the former group, including *draw attention*, is minor, so that the result is a less transparent collocation, belonging to the core area on this dimension. In the other two examples, I would suggest borderline positions, tending towards the free end of the spectrum, but for a definite answer a thorough semantic analysis would be needed – a task which still involves a lot of manual work, and the intuition of the researcher. So, even in this more objective, statistically oriented classification, semantics involves a degree of subjectivity.

4.   The role of direction and weight

Having established collocation as a multidimensional relationship between two lexical items with a certain internal structure, we can go on to investigate in more detail the different structural types. It is assumed that the relevance of a collocation for the vocabulary of advanced learners can be deduced from its positioning on the three dimensions, i.e. from its collocational profile. The decisive step, however, is the statistical analysis of the collocational factors of the partners, since this functions as a vehicle for predictability, to my mind, the criterion that provides the most valuable insight into native-speaker usage. This can be completed with information from the lexical dimension, which is also fundamental for the lexicographic description of collocations. Section 4.1 below will highlight the conclusions that can be drawn from collocational factors, their relation within a collocation (i.e. the collocational attraction), and their role in determining words in a language that are very apt to produce collocations, which should therefore be included in the vocabulary of advanced learners.

4.1   Collocational direction

In 1991, Sinclair proposed a formal distinction between upward and downward collocates, on the one hand, and neutral collocates, on the other,[11] thus implying that collocations have a certain direction, depending on the relationship between their overall frequencies in a corpus. Following his suggestion, but replacing raw frequencies by the collocational factor, we can postulate two groups that show a different collocational behaviour, based on the collocational weight of the partners. The higher a CF, the more weight is given to the respective lexeme. Seen from the point of view of producing a collocation, this is the stronger, or collocationally more important, partner. A lexeme with a lower CF does not contribute as much to the collocation; it is more independent, taking part in various word combinations, so that its role in the collocation in question is a minor one. The two types of collocations arising from the concept of collocational weight are illustrated in Figure 7, with examples from the *BNC*.

The directional class contains collocations where one partner is clearly leading the combination, so that a direction from one partner to the other can easily be detected. In Figure 7, the collocationally stronger lexemes are those on the

---

11. Upward collocates are those that occur more often than the node. Downward collocates are less frequent. The neutral ones belong to "a buffer area of (plus or minus) 15 per cent of the frequency of the node word" (Sinclair 1991: 116). This means that the direction depends on the question of which of the collocational partners is seen as the node.

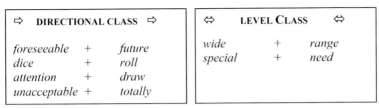

⇨ DIRECTIONAL CLASS ⇨		⇔ LEVEL CLASS ⇔	
foreseeable +	*future*	*wide* +	*range*
dice +	*roll*	*special* +	*need*
attention +	*draw*		
unacceptable +	*totally*		

Figure 7. Two types of collocations

left – those with the higher CF. If the collocational weight of two partners is very similar, or almost identical, and a definite direction cannot be recognised, I propose to speak of a level class.

So, if a native speaker hears or reads *foreseeable* or *attention*, they immediately associate *future* or *draw*, but not necessarily vice versa, or at least not with the same speed and result. This assumption is supported by the findings from the lexical dimension (cf. Section 3.2). However in a level class, on encountering *wide* the language user will think of *range*, and vice versa. The strength of an association depends on the collocational factors, i.e. a level collocation can be tightly linked if it has two high CFs, but only has a loose connection if both the CFs are low.

For non-native speakers of English, the classification of collocations in a directional class suggests that an active acquisition and the anchoring of the collocation in the mental lexicon should proceed in the same direction as the CF i.e. they should learn the stronger lexemes such as *foreseeable* or *dice* with their typical collocates *future* or *roll*. This is, for instance, important for the selection and usage of vocabulary in a textbook. In a dictionary, it seems reasonable to have a cross-reference from the entry of the weaker partner to the collocational entry under the stronger partner.

4.2   Collocational attraction

Looking at directional collocation in more detail, it becomes evident that the stronger partner exerts a certain attraction. To illustrate how this works, imagine the collocation as a seesaw with the collocational partners at either end. The stronger partner, i.e. the one with the higher collocational weight makes the seesaw go down, so that the lighter partner slides towards the heavier one. In Figure 8, ball **a** stands for the collocationally stronger partner that attracts **b**. Thus, the partners *foreseeable*, *dice*, *attention* and *unacceptable* attract *future*, *roll*, *draw* and *totally* respectively. In the case of *wide range* and *special need*, the collocational weight of the two partners is similar, and the seesaw is more or less balanced. The strength of attraction, i.e. the question of how fast and how far the seesaw goes

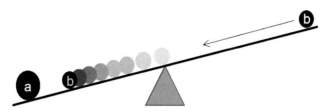

Figure 8. Collocational attraction

down, can be deduced from the difference between the collocational factors of the partners.

Again, the collocational attraction is an aspect that dictionaries could incorporate into their entries, thus informing the learners about the collocational status of a lexeme. It is more important to remember a lexeme that binds many words into strong collocations than one that only has very weak collocations.

The whole concept of collocation as a structured relationship between two partners logically leads to the need to redefine collocation as an extended linguistic unit that is characterised by the quality and strength of the link of the constituents (cf. Sinclair 1996 and Stubbs 2002). It also stresses the role of each partner as either a collocation-builder or a collocation-supporter, which is especially relevant for the description of collocations in a non-native context. Lexeme **a**, in Figure 8, would be a collocation-builder, the active partner with more collocational weight, whereas a collocation-supporter (lexeme **b** in the diagram) plays a more minor role in the collocation, being pulled by its partner.

5.   Conclusion

The new approach to the phenomenon of collocation taken in this chapter is multi-layered in two respects: first, collocations can be classified on three dimensions, with the help of the criteria of semantic transparency, collocational range and related frequency; second, there is the doubling of layers, because of the fact that collocation is always made up of (at least) two constituents that each exhibit a distinctive behaviour on these dimensions.

It is with the help of the collocational factor responsible for the statistical dimension that a systematic picture of the internal structure of collocations can be drawn. This is determined by the collocational weight of the partners, the collocational direction, and the attraction within the collocation. Findings from the lexical and semantic dimensions support the notion of collocation as an extended lexical unit. For a refined representation of collocations in learners' dictionaries,

> **node**■ ■ ▪·· ··▪ ■ ■**collocate**
> = a very low CAT + low attraction for both partners
>
> **node**■ ■**collocate**
> = a very high CAT + strong attraction for both partners
>
> **node**■ ■ ▪·· ■**collocate**
> = a very high CAT for the collocate, a very low CAT for the node
>   + collocation is guided by the word exerting the stronger attraction

Figure 9. CAT-dots for a learners' dictionary

this means that a lexical entry should also provide information about the collocational behaviour of the lexeme in question. On the one hand, this is information about how productive the lexeme is in building collocations, which could be called the collocational index; on the other hand, the collocational partners that belong to the lexeme could appear in the entry with CAT-dots (square dots representing the Collocational Attraction), indicating the strength of attraction, and the quality of the link between the partners. Figure 9 gives a brief illustration of the different types of entry. Depending on the level of the collocational factors, there are either some square dots, decreasing in size, as in the first line; or there are only two large dots. The more dots a collocation has, the weaker is the attraction, whereas if there are only two, as in the second example, the attraction is strong for both partners. A directional link can also be indicated as in the last example, where there is a low CAT for the node and a high CAT for the collocate.

This is just a tentative proposal for a possible application of the results from the statistical dimension of the present study, which would support advanced learners, especially in the production of language. The lexical and semantic dimensions would be more likely to be used by lexicographers to decide which collocations should be included in the dictionary and to which sense they apply. In this context it seems promising to carry out the dimensional analysis not only for lemmas but also for word forms, in order to account for the preference of a word for specific patterns. The advantage of the collocational factor for the statistical dimension lies in the fact that it turns the abstract notion of predictability into a measurable one, thus providing learners with reliable information about native-speaker usage. On the whole, it seems that a systematic analysis and representation of syntagmatic relations in lexicography is necessary not only to achieve a comprehensive picture of collocations, but also to facilitate an intuitive access to this essential area of English for language learners.

Acknowledgement

I would like to thank my colleagues and friends Wolfgang Falkner, Leonhard Lipka (both LMU Munich) and Eva-Maria Graf (University of Klagenfurt) for helpful comments on earlier drafts of this chapter. I am equally grateful to the participants at the conference Phraseology 2005 in Louvain-la-Neuve for questions and new ideas. Special thanks go to Eileen Carty for invaluable native-speaker advice.

References

Aisenstadt, E. (1979). Collocability restrictions in dictionaries. In Hartmann, R.R.K (ed.) *Dictionaries and their users*, 71–74. Exeter: University of Exeter.

Aitchison, J. (2003). *Words in the mind*. Oxford: Blackwell.

Barkema, H. (1996). Idiomaticity and terminology: A multi-dimensional descriptive model. *Studia Linguistica, 50* (2), 125–160.

Barnbrook, G. (1996). *Language and computers. A practical introduction to the computer analysis of language*. Edinburgh: Edinburgh University Press.

Bartsch, S. (2004). *Structural and functional properties of collocations in English*. Tübingen: Narr.

Benson, M. (1985). A combinatory dictionary of English. *Dictionaries: Journal of the Dictionary Society of North America, 7*, 189–200.

Benson, M., E. Benson & R. Ilson (1986). *The lexicographic description of English*. Amsterdam: John Benjamins.

Benson, M., E. Benson, R. Ilson & R. Young (1991). *Using the BBI: A workbook with exercises for the BBI Combinatory Dictionary of English*. Amsterdam: John Benjamins.

Berry-Rogghe, G.L.M. (1973). The computation of collocations and their relevance in lexical studies. In Aitken, A.J., R.W. Bailey & N. Hamilton-Smith (eds.) *The computer and literary studies*, 103–112. Edinburgh: Edinburgh University Press.

Carter, R. (1987). *Vocabulary: Applied linguistic perspectives*. London: Allen & Unwin.

Cowie, A.P. (1978). The place of illustrative material and collocations in the design of a learner's dictionary. In Strevens, P. (ed.) *In honour of A.S. Hornby*, 127–139. Oxford: Oxford University Press.

Fernando, C. (1996). *Idioms and idiomaticity*. Oxford: Oxford University Press.

Firth, J. R. (1957). *Papers in linguistics 1934 –1951*. London.

Gläser, R. (1986). *Phraseologie der englischen Sprache*. Tübingen: Niemeyer.

Greenbaum, S. (1970). *Verb-intensifier collocations in English*. The Hague: Mouton.

Halliday, M.A.K. (1961). Categories of the theory of grammar. *Word, 17*, 241–292.

Halliday, M.A.K & R. Hasan (1976). *Cohesion in English*. London: Longman.

Handl, S. (in preparation). *Collocation – Convenience food for the learner: A corpus-based, EFL-oriented study of syntagmatic lexical relations*.

Hausmann, F. J. (1979). Un dictionnaire de collocations est-il possible? *Travaux de Linguistique et de Litérature, 17* (1), 187–195.

Hausmann, F. J. (1984). Wortschatzlernen ist Kollokationslernen. Zum Lehren und Lernen französischer Wortverbindungen. *Praxis des neusprachlichen Unterrichts, 31,* 395–406.

Hausmann, F. J. (1985). Kollokationen im deutschen Wörterbuch. Ein Beitrag zur Theorie des lexikographischen Beispiels. In Bergenholtz, H. & J. Mugdan (eds.) *Lexikographie und Grammatik,* 118–129. Tübingen: Niemeyer.

Hausmann, F. J. (1997). Semiotaxis und Wörterbuch. In Konerding, K.P. & A. Lehr (eds.) *Linguistische Theorie und lexikographische Praxis,* 19–23. Tübingen: Niemeyer.

Heid, U. (1994). On ways words work together – topics in lexical combinatorics. In Martin, W., W. Meijs, M. Moerland, E. ten Pas, P. van Sterkenburg, P. Vossen (eds.) *EURALEX 1994. Proceedings. Papers submitted to the 6th EURALEX International Congress on Lexicography in Amsterdam, the Netherlands,* 226–257.

Hoey, M. (1991). *Patterns of lexis in text.* Oxford: Oxford University Press.

Hunston, S. (2002). *Corpora in applied linguistics.* Cambridge: Cambridge University Press.

Kennedy, G. (1998). *An introduction to corpus linguistics.* London: Longman.

Klotz, M. (2000). *Grammatik und Lexik. Studien zur Syntagmatik englischer Verben.* Tübingen: Stauffenburg.

Lipka, L. (2002). *English lexicology.* Tübingen: Gunter Narr.

McEnery, T. & A. Wilson (1996). *Corpus linguistics.* Edinburgh: Edinburgh University Press.

Meyer, C. (2002). *English corpus linguistics: An introduction.* Cambridge: Cambridge University Press.

Mitchell, T.F. (1971). Linguistic 'goings-on': Collocations and other lexical matters arising on the syntagmatic record. *Archivum Linguisticum, II* (ns), 35–69.

Moon, R. (1998). *Fixed expressions and idioms in English.* Oxford: Clarendon Press.

Nesselhauf, N. (2004). *Collocations in a learner vorpus.* Amsterdam: John Benjamins.

Palmer, F.R. (1968). *Selected papers of J.R. Firth, 1952–59.* London: Longman.

Schmid, H.-J. (2003). Collocation: Hard to pin down, but bloody useful. *Zeitschrift für Anglistik und Amerikanistik, 51* (3), 235–258.

Sinclair, J. (1966). Beginning the study of lexis. In Bazell, C.E., J.C. Catford, M.A.K Halliday & R.H. Robins (eds.) *In memory of J.R. Firth,* 148–162. London: Longman.

Sinclair, J. (1991). *Corpus, concordance, collocation.* Oxford: Oxford University Press.

Sinclair, J. (1994). Trust the text. In Coulthard, M. (ed.) *Advances in written text analysis,* 12–25. London: Routledge.

Sinclair, J.(1996). The search for units of meaning. *Textus, 9,* 75–106.

Stubbs, M. (1995). Collocations and semantic profiles: On the cause of trouble with quantitative studies. *Functions of Language, 2* (1), 23–55.

Stubbs, M. (2002). *Words and phrases: Corpus studies of lexical semantics.* Oxford: Blackwell.

Svensson, M. (in press). A very complex criterion of fixedness: Non-compositionality. In S. Granger & F. Meunier (eds.) *Phraseology: An interdisciplinary perspective.* Amsterdam: John Benjamins.

Tognini-Bonelli, E. (2001). *Corpus linguistics at work.* Amsterdam: John Benjamins.

Weinreich, U. (1969). Problems in the analysis of idioms. In Puhvel, J. (ed.) *Substance and structure of language,* 23–81. Berkeley, CA: University of California Press.

Dictionaries

LDOCE: *Longman dictionary of contemporary English* (2005) ed. by D. Summers. 5th edn with Writing Assistant. Harlow: Pearson Education.

MED: *Macmillan English dictionary for advanced learners* (2002) ed. by M. Rundell. Oxford: Macmillan Education.

OCD: *Oxford collocations dictionary for students of English* (2002). ed. J. Crowther. Oxford: Oxford University Press.

Corpus

The British National Corpus, version 2 (BNC World). 2001. Distributed by Oxford University Computing Services on behalf of the BNC Consortium. URL: http://www.natcorp.ox.ac. uk/

Phraseology effects as a trigger for errors in L2 English

The case of more advanced learners

John Osborne

When language learners produce "simple" errors (e.g. omission of 3rd person -*s*) on forms where their performance is predominantly target-like, are these errors random instances of backsliding, or is there some pattern to the contexts in which they appear? This chapter looks at four such errors – omission of 3rd person -*s*, inappropriate adverb placement, pluralized adjectives, and plural use of mass nouns – taken from two corpora of written productions by university level learners of English. The occurrence of these errors, even in careful written production, is facilitated by certain phraseological effects. Three types of effect are described – "blending", where items used together share or transfer their features, "bonding" when collocational links override the requirements of syntax, and "burying", where elements which are embedded inside larger units become less salient, and so lose grammatical features that they would normally be expected to carry. It is argued that persistent errors do not surface at random, but are triggered by the context.

1.   Formulaic effects and fossilization

It is easy to gather evidence that formulaic effects are a possible source of errors in the earlier stages of language learning. Inappropriate segmentation of chunks results in morphological errors such as *I'm like swimming, She's work in a bank*, or *His name's is Xavier* (these and following examples are from data collected for analysis of written productions in a French *lycée*, reported in Michael 1995). Before sequences such as *How old are you?, What's his job?* etc. have been appropriately unpacked and can be used productively, they may be directly recycled to form questions such as *How old are you Sonia?*, for *How old is Sonia?* (Chini 1999; see Myles et al. 1999 for comparable examples in L2 French). Somewhat later, at pre-intermediate level, they may continue to appear as incompletely analysed blocks, in utterances such as *I live in a flat with Sarah and I want to know what's his job.* At more advanced stages of learning, error-inducing phraseology effects are less immediately obvious, since non target-like usage appears in more subtle and diffuse ways, not in the form of unanalysed chunks, but as collocational or other associational patterns that favour the appearance of grammatical errors. Typically, these residual errors in post-intermediate learners' productions involve choices where the learners are aware of the constraints imposed by the L2 grammar, as evidenced by their capacity to formulate explicit pedagogical rules concerning the choice in question. Since such errors run counter to learners' metalinguistic knowledge, and persist until relatively advanced stages of learning, surviving even in endstate grammars, they are sometimes perceived as cases of fossilization (Long 2002; Han 2003, 2004).

Alongside exemplars of divergent usage, however, learner productions display a majority of alternative, target-like uses involving the same grammatical phenomena. It appears, then, as if learners are operating with rules which are not categorical but probabilistic in nature, resulting in productions where "correct" choices dominate, but non target-like choices reappear in certain contexts (cf. Sorace 2000, 2003). Sporadic use of non-target forms is potentially frustrating for language learners, and doubtless for their teachers too, particularly when the forms in question do not appear to be inherently complex. However, as Han (2004: 139) remarks, "[T]here are times when linguistic features that are not complex nevertheless appear to be difficult for learners to acquire." Below are four examples of apparently straightforward statements about English grammar, with which post-intermediate learners are generally familiar, but which are nevertheless occasionally ignored in their productions, as the sample L2 sentences given here in (1) to (4) illustrate.

Adjectives are invariable for number:

> (1) *English as a second language is nowadays something needed and studied by* <u>*vasts*</u> *amounts of people who are either self taught learners or enrolled in languages courses.* (ICLE-SP)

Nouns such as "information", "advice", etc. do not pluralize or take an indefinite article:

> (2) *Why shouldn't gardeners watch their favourite programme full of clever* <u>*advices*</u> *and innovations?* (ICLE-CZ)

Present-tense verbs take -*s* in the 3rd person singular:

(3)   *I believe that technology <u>prevent</u> humans' ability to use their imagination.*
      (ICLE-SW)

Adverbs are not placed between a verb and its direct object:

(4)   *Such people don't know the world around them but <u>they know perfectly the TV</u>*
      <u>programmes</u>. (ICLE-CZ)

All of these examples are taken from samples of university-level L2 English (see below for details of the corpora). What causes non-target forms such as these to surface in the careful production of relatively advanced learners, despite long-standing metalinguistic knowledge that they are not allowed by the grammar? Are they simply cases of random backsliding, or is it possible to identify specific contexts in which they appear? To investigate this question, occurrences of the four error types illustrated above, two noun-phrase errors (pluralized adjectives and pluralized mass nouns) and two verb-phrase errors (missing 3rd person -*s* and Verb-Adverb-Object order) were examined in a number of written corpora consisting of argumentative or descriptive essays. The two principal corpora used were a 1m word corpus of essays by French-speaking students in the 2nd and 3rd year of an English degree course at the University of Savoy (the *Chambéry Corpus*) and the *International Corpus of Learner English* (Granger et al. 2002), containing 11 sub-corpora of 200–270,000 words each, from learners of different L1s. Examples given here from the *Chambéry Corpus* are identified with the abbreviation CHY, followed by the year of study and the year of collection (thus CHY-2.04 indicates a 2nd year essay collected in 2004); examples from the *International Corpus of Learner English* are identified according to the national sub-corpus (ICLE-SP, ICLE-RU, etc.) from which they are taken. Two comparable native-speaker corpora were also included, to check whether the forms under investigation were indeed significantly more frequent in L2 production and were not, for example, the result of random typing errors that might crop up in any fairly large corpus. These two corpora were a 165,000 word collection of essays from undergraduates at a British university, and the *LOCNESS* corpus,[1] containing 95,000 words of essays from British universities and 168,000 from the United States. At the other end of the proficiency scale, a small corpus of lower-level learners in the 11th

---

1.   The Louvain Corpus of Native English Essays (LOCNESS) is made up of 90 literary/expository and argumentative essays from British university students (95,000 words) and 232 mostly argumentative essays from American university students (168,000 words). The LOCNESS corpus also contains 60,000 words of British A-Level essays, but these were not included in the comparison.

Table 1 Pluralized qualifiers (after disambiguation)

	Occurrences	/100,000 words
ESCALE	27	102
Chambéry Corpus	72	6.8
ICLE	131	5.1
NS students	1	0.2

grade (*Première*) in French secondary schools was also included – the *ESCALE* corpus – to give an indication of the evolution in the use of these forms between earlier and later stages of learning.

2.   Pluralized adjectives: *What happened to the good olds times?*

Pluralized adjectives were extracted from the corpora by exploiting a shortcoming in the tagging system. The corpora were tagged using a Brill tagger intended for standard English. Since the tagset obviously does not include a tag for pluralized adjectives, forms such as "goods", "olds", "remarkables" etc. were systematically tagged, by default, as plural nouns, <NNS>. A search for sequences of two adjacent <NNS> tags therefore yielded examples of plural nouns preceded by a qualifier marked for number. A small number of unwanted occurrences were removed by hand: possessives without an apostrophe (*childrens stories*) or genuine sequences of plural nouns, for example in unpunctuated enumerations. Table 1 shows the results of this search.

Only one example of a pluralized adjective was found in the native-speaker corpora, in (5) taken from *LOCNESS*.

(5)   *...great revelations in all areas come from breaks in tradition, new insights, and differents perspectives.* (LOCNESS-US)

In the small *ESCALE* corpus, pluralization of adjectives is relatively frequent. As would be expected, it is considerably less common in the productions of more advanced learners, but continues to appear, with comparable frequency, in both the *Chambéry Corpus* and in *ICLE*. It should be noted, however, that the overall frequency given for *ICLE* masks considerable variation between the different language groups, with few occurrences in the Bulgarian, Dutch, German and Swedish components, and the greatest number of occurrences appearing in the Italian and Spanish components. It is not clear to what extent these variations should be ascribed to differing L1 influence or to different levels of general proficiency in English (an issue also discussed in Wray and Fitzpatrick, this volume). All learn-

Table 2. Types of pluralized qualifiers

	Chambéry	ICLE
loose compounds	51.5% (37 occurrences)	53.4% (70 occurrences)
formulaic units	29% (21 occurrences)	29% (38 occurrences)

ers in the various components of *ICLE* are at comparable levels in their respective educational systems, but the productions in some of the sub-corpora are noticeably more target-like than in others.

Closer examination of the occurrences of pluralized qualifiers allows them to be roughly grouped into two main types (see Table 2). The first type, loose compounds, are words whose function gives them an indeterminate grammatical status in between adjective and noun: adjectivized nouns such as *adults smokers*, noun+noun combinations (*bathrooms fittings, diets ads*) and nominalisable adjectives (*heterosexuals couples*). These two-word units present a double ambiguity: in the grammatical status of the first element, and in their collective identity, as neither free associations nor fully lexicalized compounds.

A similarly ambiguous identity can be seen in the other main error context, formulaic units, which make up the same proportion of pluralized qualifiers in both the *Chambéry Corpus* and in *ICLE*. The adjectives included in this grouping do not have any obvious formal or semantic features in common, but all share the characteristic of appearing in collocational or other phraseological units. Examples are: *in others words, in theses cases, the good olds times, basics rights, youngs men, natives speakers, negatives consequences, publics opinions, humans beings, materials goods, historics monuments, feminists movements, extremes positions, mains features, others factors, gays couples, vasts amounts, violents films, primitives cultures, essentials rights, blacks leaders, extremists groups, remarkables aspects, financials problems.*

These collocations represent 60% of all the "true" pluralized adjectives found in the learner corpora (i.e. excluding adjectivized nouns and other non-adjectival qualifiers). Their collocational status is intuitive, but is confirmed by frequent co-occurrence in native-speaker usage, with for example 49 occurrences of *historic monument(s)* in the BNC and more than 3000 for *in other words*. Some of them are near-miss phraseological units: *old times* and *good old days* are both frequent collocations in the BNC, but *good old times* is not.

Why should frequent association favour pluralization of adjectives in learner English? It may be that the associations between strongly collocated words cause the characteristics of one member of the pair to transfer to the other. To adapt Bybee's observation (2006:721), "items that are used together frequently come to be processed together as a unit" – or at least they get pluralized together. This

Table 3. Count-like usage of mass nouns

	Number of occurrences as a "count" noun / total occurrences, followed by percentage of occurrences as a count noun (in brackets)						
	ESCALE		Chambéry		ICLE		NS students
freedom	2/11	(18%)	15/247	(6.1%)	28/825	(3.4%)	5/226 (2.2%)
information	4/11	(36%)	51/408	(12.5%)	33/1081	(3.1%)	0/103
advice	n/a		8/40	(20%)	10/91	(11%)	0/18
understanding	n/a		22/58	(37.9%)	45/280	(16.1%)	11/61 (18%)
behaviour	0/2		66/264	(25%)	86/827	(10.4%)	6/91 (6.6%)
training	n/a		10/61	(16.4%)	31/234	(13.2%)	0/32
research	1/9	(11%)	32/214	(15%)	45/275	(16.4%)	0/79

kind of morphological mimesis between co-occurring words is also apparent in the second error-type to be discussed here.

3.   **Pluralized mass nouns: *A huge amount of informations in our goggle-box***

Rules for the pluralization or singularization of mass nouns are less categorical than for pluralization of adjectives. Some mass nouns almost never pluralize or singularize; no examples were found in the NS corpora for use of indefinite *a(n)* or plural *-s* with *information, advice, training* or *research*. Others are more open to use of *a(n)* or *-s*, particularly if some differentiating quality is introduced through the use of an adjective, as in *a better social understanding, irrational human behaviors* (from *LOCNESS*). Non-native users of English tend to over-generalize this characteristic; count-like use of mass nouns is more frequent, both for those nouns that NSs do sometimes make count-like and for those, notably *information* and *advice*, which they generally do not. Table 3 shows the percentage of count-like uses, in relation to the total number of occurrences, for selected mass nouns. The percentages are generally higher for the all-French *Chambéry Corpus* than for *ICLE*, where there is once again variation between the sub-corpora, with the proportions being higher in the French, Spanish and Italian components, for example, and lower in the Swedish, Dutch and German. The main point at discussion here, though, is the contexts in which these count-like usages appear.

The first contextual factor is the presence of an adjective (as in *...taking out the most essential advices*), which appears to have a strongly facilitating effect on the count-like use of mass nouns. Between 46% and 76% of the count-like uses of a given noun in the *ICLE* are preceded by an adjective, whereas the overall

Table 4. Adjectives and mass nouns in ICLE

	percentage of adjectives in count-like occurrences	percentage of adjectives in non-count occurrences
freedom	50%	15%
information	46%	17%
advice	50%	21%
understanding	73%	6%
behaviour	60%	39%
training	76%	35%
research	51%	36%

frequency of adjective use with other, non-count uses of the same nouns is much lower (see Table 4).

A similar effect is produced by the presence of a quantifier, as in (6), responsible for 12% of count-like uses.

(6)   *Many <u>researches</u> have been conducted in this field.* (ICLE-PO)

The other main factor, and the second most frequent, accounting for 23% of count-like uses, is the mimetic pluralization of coordinate nouns. This occurs when a mass noun appears in a coordinate phrase with another (count) noun, and both nouns carry the mark of the plural, as in the following examples:

(7)   *...rejection of the values or <u>advices</u> of the elder generation.* (ICLE-FR)

(8)   *I don't mean concealing and changing facts or <u>informations</u>.* (ICLE-CZ)

(9)   *It is a subject of innumerable debates and <u>researches</u>.* (ICLE-FI)

These coordinate structures have clear phraseological characteristics, in that they form sequences whose features (in this case sub-categorization) are generalized to the whole unit instead of being applied separately to its components. The other two triggers for count-like use, involving qualifiers or quantifiers, may be more cognitively motivated, in that quantification and qualification emphasize discreteness and heterogeneity, normally seen as attributes of count nouns, and thus override metalinguistic awareness that, in English at least, the nouns in question do not normally function in this way. What all three contexts have in common, though, is that they facilitate the appearance of an error which consists not so much in pluralizing mass nouns in isolation as in pluralizing units, adjective+noun, quantifier+noun or noun+conj+noun, in which one of the components happens to be a mass noun.

Table 5. Singular nouns followed by verb without -*s*

	Occurrences	/100,000 words
ESCALE	50	189
Chambéry	71	6.7
ICLE	207	8
NS students	0	0

4.   Third person -*s*: *Modern life seem to be very chaotic*

At first sight, this is one of the more surprising errors to persist in post-intermediate L2 English. The rule in question is simple, categorical and purely morphological, requiring no knowledge of semantic properties. Third person -*s* is typically encountered in the very first stages of learning English as a foreign language, is highly frequent in the input, and its omission is not an obvious candidate for L1 transfer, since all of the languages considered here have more richly inflected verb systems than English. So what causes this error to continue to appear, not just in spoken L2 English, but in carefully monitored written production? Examples were extracted from the corpus by looking for occurrences of singular nouns, proper nouns or pronouns, followed by a non-inflected verb. Several search patterns were required in order to capture not only continuous sequences of singular noun + verb, but also, notably, verbs embedded within a relative clause. Extraneous examples of noun + non-inflected verb (complex NPs where the final element happened to be a singular noun, interrogatives containing a modal, etc.) were edited out by hand. In the lower-proficiency *ESCALE* corpus, examples where the non-inflected verb appeared to have past reference were also removed. Table 5 shows the overall results of these searches.

There is a sharp decline in the non-suppliance of -*s* from the *ESCALE* corpus to the more advanced corpora. However, even though its omission has become infrequent, particularly in relation to the high number of contexts requiring it, it is still not consistently supplied. The main contexts in which omission occurs are the following:

Complementizers:

(10)   *…due to the fact the player stay very static…* (CHY-2.04)

Relatives and cleft constructions:

(11)   *…children whose illness prevent them from going to school.* (CHY-2.03)

Table 6. Main contexts for omitted -*s*

	ESCALE	Chambéry	ICLE
complementizers	8%	8.5%	12%
relatives / clefts	32%	41%	36%
complex subject NPs	8%	8.5%	7%
collective subject Ns	16%	8.5%	7%

Compound/complex subject NPs (N's N / N of N / NN):

(12) *The progression of the white-collar sector __permit__ a growing number...*
       (CHY-3.04)

Collective subject nouns:

(13) *The mankind __consider__ itself rational...* (ICLE-IT)

These four contexts together account for two-thirds of the omitted subject-verb agreements (see Table 6 for details). Other, less frequent contexts include quantified mass nouns (*Many evidence have proved...*), indefinite subjects: (*...nobody oblige us to behave like this*) and what seem to be pseudo-subjunctives, such as *when a person try to image a feminist...* The principal contexts, though, involve syntactic complexity, and in particular various kinds of embedding.

In examples (14)–(17) below, syntactic units seem to merge into one other, blurring the distinction between the true grammatical subject (in bold) and other items (underlined) which are conceptually linked to the embedded verb and serve, in a sense, as grammatical distractors.

(14) __*Drugs*__ *are **an issue** which *arouse strong feelings and *provoke controversy.*
       (ICLE-PO)

(15) *We have to consider that **the invasion** of __images and films__ charged with violence *encourage agressiveness.* (ICLE-SP)

(16) __*Things*__ *that were previously regarded with __fear and superstition__ are put in **a context** which *make them understandable and natural.* (ICLE-SW)

(17) *Not to mention the __long hours__, the __highly stressful environment__, and **a workload** that *get heavier the better and more comitted you are to your job.*
       (ICLE-SW)

Even when there are no competing candidates for the role of grammatical or logical subject, embedding may result in diminished finiteness for verbs which get "buried" inside successive units, thus weakening their dependency on their subject:

(18)   *..loves when a tender and careful woman waits for him at home and after a busy day *meet him with a kind smile and moral support.* (ICLE-RU)

(19)   *...and one suggestion is that the fact that we are living at the end of the 20th century *make people insecure about the future.* (ICLE-SW)

(20)   *It is terribly sad that a criminal after killing somebody and doing harm to a family *enjoy the liberty or was punished with a ridicoulous penalty.* (ICLE-SP)

In these examples of omitted 3rd person *-s*, as with the noun phrase errors discussed above, the error is not a strictly localized phenomenon, affecting a single subject-verb relation, but a phenomenon operating across bigger units of text, which in many cases are not just multi-word units, but multi-phrasal units, inside which hierarchical relations have been flattened.

5.   Adverb placement: *People accept passively this brainwashing*

The last error-type to be discussed here is one which is potentially more closely linked to specific L1 influences, and which has been the subject of considerable attention in SLA research (notably: White 1991; Trahey & White 1993; Schwartz & Sprouse 1996; Vainikka & Young-Scholten 1996; Eubank 1996; Eubank et al. 1997; Beck 1998). Most existing studies, however, are based on elicited examples or on grammaticality judgements. Given the infrequent nature of unsolicited adverb use, access to corpus data is the only feasible way of collecting enough occurrences to reveal possible patterns in the spontaneous placement of adverbs. Examples (21)–(24) below, all from the *Chambéry Corpus*, illustrate the optionality apparent in L2 adverb placement, with the same adverb appearing in different positions, with the same or similar verbs:

(21)   *Sampson <u>clearly</u> explains that the Britons are aware of this difference...* (CHY-2.04)

(22)   *The fact that the characters are animals allows Orwell to underline the issue <u>more clearly</u>.* (CHY-2.99)

(23)   *Smith et al explain <u>clearly</u> the effects of too much time spent watching television.* (CHY-2.04)

(24)   *It is quite hard to define very <u>clearly</u> this word.* (CHY-2.04)

The first two of these examples are undoubtedly target-like; (23) might be perceived as unusual, but is not impossible in NS writing, given the complex nature of the direct object (see below for a discussion of this point). The remaining example (24) is improbable in mature NS production. However, given that variable

Table 7. Adverb placement (occurrences /100,000 words)

	all positions	V-Adv-O
Chambéry	2134	25.4
Fr ICLE	2401	22.5
All ICLE	2400	13.5
NS students	2279	6.10

placement of adverbs is also a feature of NS grammars, the question is in what way the optionality observed in learner grammars is different. To extract examples of V-Adv-O order from the corpora, possible variants of the basic Verb-Adverb-Noun sequence were identified, to take account of additional elements such as adjectives, determiners, intensifying or other adverbs, and of the fact that the direct object could be a noun, proper noun or pronoun. The search strings were thus variants of the pattern [V (adv) ADV (det) (adv) (adj) N/Pro], and were searched for using the batch search facility in *MonoConc*. The results are shown in Table 7, along with the overall frequency of all adverbs, irrespective of their position in the sentence.

It will be seen that the number of V-Adv-O sequences is similar in the all-French *Chambéry Corpus* and in the French component of *ICLE*, but lower in *ICLE* as a whole, and lower still in the native corpora, while the overall frequency of adverb use remains fairly constant. Generally, the results obtained from the learner corpora indicate that V-Adv-O order is most frequent in the productions of learners whose L1 has verb-raising (French, Italian and Spanish), and least frequent with speakers of V2 languages (Dutch, German and Swedish), with speakers of non-raising languages (Russian, Polish, Czech and Bulgarian) in between. Once again, these results may also be affected by the overall proficiency of the learners in question. Apart from L1 influence, choice of adverb placement may depend on a number of factors, such as heavy noun-phrase shift, but the emphasis here will be on phraseological factors, and specifically on verb-adverb collocations.

Many of the V-Adv-O sequences found in the learner corpora contain conventional combinations of verb and adverb. Some examples of these collocations are the following (given here in order of their frequency in the *BNC*): *reduce drastically, choose freely, enforce strictly, eliminate completely, accept passively, follow blindly, denounce publicly, change permanently, influence positively, refuse categorically, analyse objectively, grasp desperately, scrutinize thoroughly, describe meticulously, solve jointly, enrich culturally, accomplish brilliantly, choose unbiasedly, applaud frenetically, elect freely, facilitate enormously, differentiate distinctively.*

Like the adjective-noun combinations discussed earlier, many of these are frequent co-occurrences in native-speaker usage, with the *BNC* yielding for example 95 occurrences of *reduce drastically* and its variants. A number of these collocations also appear in the native-speaker student essays, as illustrated in examples (25) to (28) below:

completely + eliminate

    (25)   *...nearly impossible to completely eliminate all of the different drug uses.* (LOCNESS-US)

strictly + enforce

    (26)   *...to more strictly enforce marijuana laws.* (LOCNESS-US)

blindly + follow

    (27)   *...the majority of the population blindly follows what they say.* (LOCNESS-US)

categorically + refuse

    (28)   *...and refused categorically to discuss salaries.* (LOCNESS-GB)

It will be noticed, however, that although these are undoubtedly genuine collocations, used and recognized by native speakers, their collocational status does not normally cause them to occur in V-Adv-O sequences, but more typically in Adv-V-Complement, Adv+PP or in to-Adv-V (split infinitive) combinations. For example, the most frequently used of these collocations in the BNC, *reduce + drastically*, occurs overwhelmingly with the adverb preceding the verb. Out of the 95 co-occurrences of *reduce* and *drastically*, only 8 have the order V-Adv-O, all with a non-finite verb.

When V-Adv-O sequences do appear in NS usage, the collocational tie is often so strong that the adverb is effectively indissociable from the verb, and its removal would destroy the meaning of the predicate, as in (29), or at best seriously undermine it, as in (30):

    (29)   *the University takes very seriously its responsibility to justify these contributions through continued excellence in research and teaching.* (Alec Broers, former Vice-Chancellor of Cambridge University, quoted in CHY-3.03)

    (30)   *By giving this quote the author is not stating directly the relationship between freedom of speech and church and state.* (LOCNESS-US)

Learner collocations, on the other hand, tend to be weaker, as in (31) and (32), or even frankly tautological, as in (33):

    (31)   *This illustrates well that stereotypes are not ...* (CHY-2.04)

    (32)   *The reader, himself, understands very quickly the subterfuge.* (CHY-2.00)

(33) *In the kingdom of television, radio and press a man is not able to differenciate distinctively the border between the truth and the imagined reality.* (ICLE-PO)

Another possible cause for the persistence of V-Adv-O combinations is their use as semi-lexicalized units to compensate for lexical deficiencies. These uses, illustrated in (34)–(37) below, effectively split the semantic content of a verb into two parts, expressed separately by a more general verb and an adverb. Reuniting the semantic content into a single verb would avoid the necessity of using an adverb, but it is conceivable that, if the verb is not available to the user, the strong interdependence between substitute verb and adverb and their joint function as carriers of a single meaning will cause them to appear as an uninterrupted unit, even at the expense of a syntactic violation.

(34) *Undeniably, the language affects badly (hinders?) the learning process.* (CHY-2.03)

(35) *People who dream lead happy lives and their inner happiness affects positively (benefits?) those who suffer.* (ICLE-PO)

(36) *Consequently I classified again (reorganized?) my ideas and I imagined a new outline.* (CHY-2.03)

(37) *At the end of my arguments I would like to write again (restate?) my main thought.* (ICLE-CZ)

Another possible factor in the use of V-Adv-O order is heavy NP shift. This is certainly a factor in NS writing, where heavy object NPs get shifted to the right in order to avoid distending the link between a verb and a sentence-final adverb. This results in V-Adv-O sequences like that in (38), taken from the *LOCNESS* corpus.

(38) *... the articles that oppose prayer in public schools refute and weaken considerably the arguments for the reintroduction of prayer in public schools as a way to cure modern social ills.* (LOCNESS-US)

If NP shift is taking place in the learner productions, it is being applied, on average, to much lighter NPs. In the native-speaker essays, half of the NPs appearing in V-Adv-O sequences have 7 words or more, and typically contain relatives or complementizers. Another third contain between 4 and 6 words (typically N *of* N constructions), with the remaining 20% being light NPs of 1 to 3 words. In the learner corpora the proportions are variable, according to L1, but in the three sub-corpora that account for the greatest number of V-Adv-O sequences, roughly half of the

NPs concerned are light (40%, 55% and 60% respectively in the French, Italian and Spanish sub-corpora), and only 16–22% are heavy NPs of 7 words or more.

Unlike the first three error types discussed in this chapter, which mostly violate categorical rules of standard English, the constraints governing adverb placement are probabilistic in native-speaker usage. End position and pre-verbal position for adverbs are strongly preferred, but V-Adv-O order appears in certain conditions, and is probably subject to a degree of individual variation. The two main factors that favour V-Adv-O order in NS usage are collocational ties between verb and adverb, and heavy NP shift. In post-intermediate learner usage, end position and pre-verbal position are also preferred, but less strongly so, and the two factors favouring V-Adv-O order appear to have a lower threshold: NPs can be lighter and collocational ties less exclusive. The number of more or less strongly collocated verb-adverb pairings appearing in adjacent position may in fact be evidence of developing proficiency; if language learners are starting to form associations in their lexicon between collocates – appropriate or otherwise – then this could facilitate joint placement of the pairings inside syntactic structures. It is perhaps a case where the developing phraseological competence that leads to fluent and idiomatic use of the target language sometimes produces slightly inauthentic surface patterns.

6.   Phraseological effects: *Blending, bonding and burying*

The focus of this chapter has been on certain phraseological effects in a small number of L2 errors. Clearly they are not the only factors responsible for the emergence and persistence of these errors. Third person -*s* is anomalous in a language that otherwise has weak agreement; it is inconsistent that English should preserve plural marks on nouns but not on adjectives; (non)countability is not a stable either/or feature of nouns; contemporary patterns of adverb placement are a consequence of *do*-support and the loss of verb-raising in Early Modern English, and are still subject to a degree of optionality in present-day usage. But although these points may help to understand why the language features in question are not so straightforward to acquire, and why learners therefore continue to produce errors from time to time, they do not necessarily help to discern any pattern in the appearance of residual errors, nor to identify what distinguishes the occasions where learners produce these errors from all those where they do not.

Probably there is some randomness in learner errors, but the L2 samples analysed here were produced in conditions likely to maximise attention to form. All are written productions, mostly untimed, and written in non-examination conditions, with access to dictionaries and other reference tools. These task conditions, which apply to all of the samples in the *Chambéry Corpus* and to two-thirds of the *ICLE* samples (Granger et al. 2002: 18–19), reduce the probability of errors due to memory lapses, distraction or processing pressures. The errors that remain, therefore, have succeeded in passing through various monitoring, checking and re-reading filters, and if they have survived, it is probably because something in the context has a facilitating effect which counteracts metalinguistic knowledge and its attendant monitoring processes. Close examination of the contexts in which the errors appear shows up a number of recurrent features which, although they cannot provide a plausible account for all error occurrences, do seem to be a contributing factor in many cases. This chapter has attempted to identify some of these effects, which can be summarized into three main types, *blending, bonding* and *burying*:

Blending: This occurs when elements which are combined to form a larger unit share or transfer grammatical features amongst themselves, resulting in one or more of the components taking on features that are not allowed by the grammar. For example, in the multi-word units *natives speakers* and *the values or advices,* plurality is marked throughout the unit rather than on just one component. In the multi-phrasal unit *Drugs are an issue which arouse strong feelings,* the head word is plural, and causes the whole unit to function as plural. These multi-word or multi-phrasal units are *ad hoc* units; some, like *natives speakers,* are identifiable with units found in native usage, but others are not.

Bonding: lexical or grammatical elements that have formed associations in the learner's lexicon or grammar may become bonded to each other in such a way that they not only co-occur, appropriately or not, but also appear in adjacent position. This seems to be the case, for example, with adverb + verb collocations such as *follow blindly everything...* Another example, not discussed here, is the (pedagogically induced) association between *since* and the perfect *have -en,* resulting in appearance of the perfect even when *since* is being used not in its temporal sense but as a logical connector: *It is obvious that the sinking of the Titanic remains one of the most significant tragedies of the century since 1,518 out of 2,223 persons have died that terrible night.* (CHY-2.00).

Burying: Elements which are embedded inside larger units may become less salient, and so lose grammatical features that they would normally be expected to carry. An example of this is the diminished finiteness of verbs as they get further and further removed from their subject, as in (19) *...loves when a tender and careful woman waits for him at home and after a busy day meet him with a kind smile and moral support,* where the first verb governed by *woman* carries the mark of the 3rd person, but the second verb does not. Partly this may be a consequence of the processing effort involved in producing syntactically complex structures, which distracts attention from morphological details inside the structures. But phraseological frames can have the effect of neutralizing grammatical features even where the syntax is not complex. For example, the additive frame *not only ... but also*, perhaps because it is associated with plurality, can neutralize subject-verb agreement in its second part:

(39)   *...imagination is not only a factor which serves the individual needs, but also a factor which help to obviate the needs of others.* (ICLE-PO)

(40)   *... an essential role, not only as the person who teaches, but also as the person who learn a new reality.* (ICLE-SP)

These errors are not necessarily evidence of fossilization. If, as a growing body of research suggests, chunking, formulaic sequences and other phraseological phenomena play an important role in language learning, then it is not surprising that, in the development of L2 proficiency, they should also be responsible for the appearance of certain errors. Some kinds of phraseological mishap are immediately apparent. I once had a student who had assiduously worked his way through a slightly out-of-date book of English idioms and who made a point of using them at every opportunity, frequently with entertaining results. But others are less obvious, particularly as there is no reason, in principle, why interlanguage phraseology should have exactly the same characteristics as L1 phraseology. Since the errors themselves are relatively infrequent at this level, and since there are various context-types in which they appear, it is only by compiling examples from a sizeable corpus that patterns are likely to emerge. Looked at in isolation, possible phraseological error-inducing effects will probably not be noticeable, making individual errors seem random. Taken collectively, they may not be as random as they seem.

References

Beck, M.-L. (1998). L2 Acquisition and obligatory head movement: English-speaking learners of German and the Local Impairment Hypothesis. *Studies in Second Language Acquisition 20* (4), 311–348.

Bybee, J. (2006). From usage to grammar: The mind's response to repetition. *Language 82* (4), 711–733.

Chini, D. (1999). Un exemple de médiation problématique: La technique des blocs lexicalisés. In Bailly, D. (ed.) *Actes des journées d'étude du GEPED*, 79–94. Paris: Université Paris 7.

Eubank, L. (1996). Negation in early German-English interlanguage: More valueless features in the L2 initial state. *Second Language Research 12* (1), 73–106.

Eubank, L., J. Bischof, A. Huffstutler, P. Leek & C. West (1997). "Tom eats slowly cooked eggs": Thematic-verb raising in L2 knowledge. *Language Acquisition 6* (3), 171–199.

Granger, S., E. Dagneaux & F. Meunier (2002). *The international corpus of learner English. Handbook and CD-ROM*. Louvain-la-Neuve: Presses Universitaires de Louvain.

Han, Z. (2004). *Fossilization in adult second language acquisition*. Clevedon: Multilingual Matters.

Han, Z. (2003). Fossilization: From simplicity to complexity. *International Journal of Bilingual Education and Bilingualism 6* (2), 95–128.

Long, M. (2002). Stabilization and fossilization in interlanguage development. In Doughty, C. & M. Long (eds.) *The handbook of second language acquisition*, 487–535. Oxford: Blackwell.

Michael, A. (1995). Teaching English in a French high school: A look at errors in the written production of English. MA dissertation, Department of English, University of Savoie.

Myles, F., R. Mitchell & J. Hooper (1999). Interrogative chunks in French L2: A basis for creative construction? *Studies in Second Language Acquisition* 21/1, 49–80.

Schwartz, B. & R. Sprouse (1996). L2 cognitive states and the Full Transfer/Full Access model. *Second Language Research 12* (1), 40–72.

Sorace, A. (2000). Syntactic optionality in non-native grammars. *Second Language Research 16*, 93–102.

Sorace, A. (2003). Near-nativeness. In Doughty, C. & M. Long (eds.) *The handbook of second language acquisition*, 130–151. Oxford: Blackwell.

Trahey, M. & L. White (1993). Positive evidence and preemption in the second language classroom. *Studies in Second Language Acquisition* 15, 181–204.

Vainikka, A. & M. Young-Scholten (1996). Gradual development of L2 phrase structure. *Second Language Research 12* (1), 7–39.

White, L (1991). Adverb placement in second language acquisition: Some effects of positive and negative evidence in the classroom. *Second Language Research 7*, 133–161.

Contrasting English-Spanish interpersonal discourse phrases

A corpus study

JoAnne Neff van Aertselaer

This chapter presents the results of a contrastive study of interactional phrases (discourse strategies intended to actively engage the reader in the argumentation process) as used by novice and expert writers of argumentative texts of both English and Spanish. The novice writer texts, those produced by Spanish EFL and American university writers, were compared to expert Anglo writers' texts, opinion editorial articles. The Spanish editorials were used to trace the transfer of interactional patterns in the Spanish EFL texts. The phrases searched for in the various corpora consisted of the following types of interpersonal expressions: certainty markers, attitudinal markers and those constructions which are used for the presentation of evaluations in argumentation (adverbial phrases, such as *clearly, certainly*, etc.; *it* + adjective phrases: *it is possible, un/likely + that/to; it is necessary, clear, certain, obvious, true,* etc., *+ to/that*; and, the transfer of the *se* passive impersonal construction from Spanish to the EFL texts). The results show that the interactional phrases used by Spanish EFL students in comparison with those used by the other three groups are influenced by incomplete mastery of the modal system, choice of adjectival lexical phrases and transfer of the reflexive passive impersonal construction from Spanish.

1. Introduction

This study[1] contrasts discourse-level phrases used by expert writers of argumentative texts in English and Spanish with those used by novice writers, Spanish EFL and American university writers, in an attempt to distinguish novice writer features from preferred or non-preferred rhetorical features, as shown in the experts' texts. Discourse phrases (Thompson 2001) may be subcategorized into interactive

---

1. I am grateful for the suggestions offered by the two anonymous reviewers.

phrases – those involved in managing the flow of information (i.e., *first, in the following paragraph, on the one/ other hand, as can be seen in Table 1*, etc.) – and interactional phrases – those discourse strategies intended to actively engage the reader in the argumentation process (reader-in-the text strategies, evaluative statements, etc.). These comprise impersonal phrases and hedges, such as *it is generally thought; as is well-known; one could say that; it is probable that*, but also less impersonal, evaluative phrases or certainty markers, such as *it is clear, clearly, surely, it is obvious, obviously*, etc. This functional division coincides, in general terms, with Stainton's (1996) reworking of previous frameworks for metadiscourse by Vande Kopple (1985) and Crismore et al. (1993). Stainton (1996) presents a subdivision of metadiscourse into attitudinal and informational, which broadly correspond to Hallidays' (1973) interpersonal and textual metafunctions.

Due to space constraints, this chapter examines only the interactional phrases, although as Thompson (2001:61) points out, the interactive and interactional aspects are "two sides of the same coin". That is, interactional phrases which involve the reader also frequently signal future discourse moves, an interactive function. This study is part of a larger project, the aim of which is to describe the phraseological competency of Spanish EFL university students, particularly those features which affect the expression of certainty and the attitude markers. For this, it is first necessary to provide base-line information on native-speaker phraseological preferences (Howarth 1998), in this case, those of English and Spanish.

2.   English-Spanish contrastive metadiscourse studies

Previous English-Spanish contrastive studies of metadiscourse (Dafouz 2000; Neff et al. 2003; Neff et al. 2004) have shown that there are significant differences in the use of both interpersonal and textual metadiscourse in signed editorial texts and in student argumentative texts written in English. This is true for the different types of novice writers, that is, for both native and non-native speakers, including non-native speakers of various mother tongues.

2.1   English-Spanish studies on interactional phrases in EFL
student writing

In a study of the use of interactional elements such as modal verbs in the construction of impersonal authorial voice, Neff et al. (2003) found that Spanish EFL writers, in comparison with American college writers, have only partial competency in the use of the modal verbs *can, could, may, might* and *must*. The limited

Table 1. Constructions used by graduate and undergraduate students in expressing authorial voice

1. *The unaccusative (AVS) pattern* (Mendikoetxea 1999; Biber, et al. 1999), which involves the end-weight construction
    – *Then appears the shadow of war...*

2. *The hedging, attitudinal, emphatic or attribution pattern* (Hewings and Hewings, 2002), an extraposed *it* in an impersonalization construction in English
    – It would be better for all the creation of ...

3. *The reflexive 'se' passive pattern* (Contreras, 1976), an impersonalization strategy in Spanish.
    – It will be observed the image...

    Cf.: Undergraduate students' strategy: *WE as metadiscourse marker*
    – At the beginning of the play we can identify that there is a sort of introduction.

use of *may* and *might* hinders these students' ability to hedge statements and often *must* and *can* are used as unnecessary lexical phrases that introduce topics (i.e., *To finish, we must indicate that in the 19th century, people* ...).[2] The presence of these features is related to at least three factors: incomplete acquisition of EFL, a typological mismatch between the L1 and the L2 (in Spanish, there are few modal verbs, but the subjunctive is frequently put to use in subordinate clauses) and a transfer of discourse conventions from the L1 to the L2.

In a more recent study of the use of impersonal lexical phrases, Neff & Bunce (2006) examined three different underlying structures in Spanish which seem to trigger many word order errors in Spanish EFL writers' academic texts, as shown in Table 1.

In a comparison of Spanish EFL graduate students' texts with those written by undergraduates, we found that, although the graduate students produced a surprising number of sentences with rather serious errors (clauses with two subjects), their texts actually did reflect developmental trends. Most of the graduate student errors reflected either pattern 2 or pattern 3 structures, as shown in Table 1. That is, in sentences with hedging, certainty or attitudinal markers, many Spanish students constructed English clauses with double subjects (a preposed *it* and the logical subject placed after the verb: *It is possible the beginning of another*

---

2. Both of these EFL characteristics (limited use of modals and the utilization of modals and reporting verbs to introduce new topics) are shared by the French-speaking (Belgian) and Italian novice writers, although these two groups make greater use of *may* and *might* than Spanish EFL students.

world war).[3] Another source of error in the texts of more advanced EFL writers (graduate students) was the transfer of a very sophisticated discourse strategy for impersonalization in Spanish, the reflexive '_se_' passive, as in pattern 3. The main discourse strategy transferred from Spanish into English by the less advanced undergraduate students was, however, comparatively much simpler: the use of _we_ + modal verb (usually _can_) + verb of mental process (_we can see, we can think, we can wonder_). They made fewer attempts to transfer into their English texts the more sophisticated _se_ passive strategy, which would involve the use of passive modal constructions not yet mastered. As observed in the texts of the more advanced graduate students, the transfer of this '_se_' strategy often causes students to construct English clauses with double subjects, and with the same result as sentences including hedging or attitudinal markers: an extraposed _it_ and the logical subject placed after the verb. Consequently, the graduate students appear to be making more fundamental mistakes than the undergraduates, but these are a result of the attempts by more advanced students to use more sophisticated strategies.

3.   The present study

This study carries the analysis of Spanish EFL academic writing a step further in that it focuses specifically, as outlined below, on the following interpersonal expressions: certainty and attitudinal markers and those constructions which are used for impersonal presentation of arguments.

1. Anticipatory _it_ + adjective phrase: _it is possible, un/likely_ + _that/to_ and their counterparts in Spanish [hedging expressions]
2. Anticipatory _it_ + adjective phrase: _necessary, clear, certain, plain, obvious, sure, true_ + _to/that_ and their counterparts in Spanish [certainty expressions], and adverbials which could be used instead of the anticipatory _it_ + adjective phrase: _certainly, clearly, obviously, plainly, surely_ and their counterparts in Spanish [certainty adverbs]
3. Passive constructions as an impersonalization strategy and the corresponding reflexive passive in Spanish (the _se_ passive)

The four corpora used are listed in Table 2: two novice writer groups (Spanish EFL and American university writers) contrasted with one expert Anglo-American group and one expert Spanish group. The Spanish EFL corpus is part of the

---

3.   Even quite advanced users of English with Spanish as a mother tongue frequently construct such clauses, as do advanced users with Italian as a mother tongue (Amanda Murphy, Università Cattolica, Milan, personal communication).

Table 2. Corpora used in this study

Name of corpus	No. of words
SPICLE (Spanish EFL ADVANCED LEARNERS) – NOVICE	194,845
LOCNESS (American university writers) – NOVICE	149,790
Spanish editorialists (Peninsular Spanish texts)	115,186
English editorialists (British and American texts)	113,475

International Corpus of Learner English and the American university writer corpus is part of the LOCNESS corpus, both held at the Centre for English Corpus Linguistics, Louvain. The two corpora comprising the texts of the expert writers are part of the English-Spanish Contrastive Corpus, held at the Universidad Complutense, Madrid.

Wordsmith Tools 3.1 (Scott, 1999) was used to find the most frequent clusters and collocates in all of the texts. The figures for each pattern were normalized for 10,000 words. Then the results of the Spanish EFL writers were compared to those of the reference group, the signed editorial texts, by using a simple T-test to calculate significance. In an attempt to distinguish negative transfer factors from novice writer factors, statistical tests were also carried out for the comparison of the American novice writers' and the Spanish expert writers' texts with those of the expert writers in English. That is, the Spanish editorial texts were used to confirm possible transfer of discourse patterns into the Spanish EFL texts. The LOCNESS corpus (American college students) was used to corroborate the existence of novice-writer features, since previous research (Neff et al. 2004) has suggested that all novice writer texts, including those written by native speakers, contain various types of problems in establishing an authorial voice.

4.   Results and discussion

The results for the use of interactional patterns by the Spanish EFL students are set out in Table 3 (including the original errors) and those of the expert English writers, in Table 4.

The first significant difference (P<.005) revealed by the data is low occurrence of hedging phrases (pattern 1) in the student texts in comparison with the occurrence of this pattern in the English editorials. One might assume that such results reflect novice writer overstatement of propositions, i.e., little hedging being a feature present in the texts of inexperienced writers, even in those written by native speakers (Shaughnessy 1977: 240–241). However, the American college writers (as seen in Table 5) used even more pattern 1 hedges than the English-

Table 3. Interactional patterns used by Spanish EFL student writers

Patterns used by Spanish EFL writers	Examples (with errors included)
1. *It* + be + *possible/likely/unlikely* + *that* (hedging), or adverbs *possibly, probably* N = 14/ 0.74 per 10,000 words	– If we destroy Nature, we destroy our source of life, *it is possible that it does not be inmediately*, but we have to think in our descendents.
2. *It* + be + Adjective + *that* (Expressing degree of truth, or evaluation of what is said), or modal adverbs . *certain* = 2/ *certainly* = 0 . *clear* = 7/ *clearly* = 11 . *evident* = 0/ *evidently* = 1 . *obvious* = 31/ *obviously* = 15 . *sure* = 5/ *surely* = 7 . *true* = 20 N = 100 total/ 2.315 per 10,000 words	– It is <u>certain</u> that the prision system is outdated. The prisoners get out frequently when they are not rehabilitated... – Where has censorship to be imposed? I think it is <u>clear</u> that it must be imposed mainly in the mass media. – It is <u>obvious</u> the lack of cultural formation in the major part of the society. [*double subject: "it" and "the lack of cultural formation..."*] – It is <u>sure</u> that many criminals are going to kill and rob again.
3. *It* + passive verb + *that* (impersonalization strategy) N = 30/ 1.6 per 10,000 words (including 10 structures that seem impossible)	– It is believed that we live together ... – *?It is said that many young people... – *It is known that "the more you know, the less sure you are"... – *It is demonstrated that the TV channels not only ... – *It is proved that it beats the theatre... – *It is considered that there is no difference between... – It <u>could be thought</u> that the current human's only worry is working besides the way of how to earn more money <u>but</u>, the reality is quite another. The increasing fact of joining to any voluntary activity is, from my modest point of view, a proof for that.

speaking experts, although the difference between the latter group and the novice American writers (P<.06) is not as great as that between the English experts and the EFL students. This finding seems to point to a possible transfer from L1 rhetorical strategies.

In order to verify this possibility of transfer of an L1 pattern, the texts of the Spanish expert writers were examined for the same hedges. These searches revealed a significant difference (P<.007) between the very few hedges used by the Spanish expert writers and the more frequent use found in the English-speaking expert texts. Thus, one may hypothesize a transfer from L1 writing conventions, although caution must be exercised here, as some of the hedging of Spanish ex-

Table 4. Interpersonal patterns used by expert writers in English

Patterns used by expert writers in English (signed editorials)	Examples
1. It + be + possible/likely/ unlikely + that (hedging), or adverbs *possibly, probably* N = 95/ 8,6 per 10,000 words	– Permanent self-exclusion would almost certainly lead to a wholly disastrous withdrawal from the EU. When the case for monetary union and for the EU is eventually put to the British people, it is <u>likely</u> that, as in 1975, the result will be resoundingly positive.
2. It + be + Adjective + that (Expressing degree of certainty, or evaluation of what is said), or modal adverbs . *certain* = 7/*certainly* = 18 . *clear* = 2/ *clearly* = 11 . *evident* = 2/ *evidently* = 1 . *obvious* = 3/ *obviously* = 4 . *sure* = 0/ *surely* = 15 . *true* = 6 N = 68/ 6.2 per 10,000 words	– Pro- and anti-agreement unionists have equal numbers inside the devolved assembly. The agreement provided careful checks and balances to protect the narrow pro-agreement unionist block from being undone by the anti-agreement DUP. It is <u>clear</u> to all that Mr Trimble is still dogged by unionist critics inside and outside his party and will have difficulty each step of the way ahead. <u>But</u> he must be cheered by the realisation that his own waverers stood firm … – It is <u>true</u> that France and Germany could benefit from reforming their pensions and labour markets, from streamlining bureaucracies and privatising state-run industries. <u>But</u> all this needs to be explained and justified in the German or French national context – and not as the "price" of keeping some ill-starred "rendezvous with Europe" which most of the voters would far rather avoid. – It is <u>apt</u> that left-wing Peruvian rebels should recognise the political importance of Guatemala's model. <u>Yet</u> Guatemala's path into the future will not be easy. – To such a mentality, it is <u>inconceivable</u> that a consensus *should* be discovered, or a former killer like Martin McGuinness *might* have a useful part to play in government.
3. It + passive verb + that (impersonalization strategy) N = 2 tokens total	– It has given Britain the best leaders in the world, so <u>it is said</u>. In the 1980s the trade unions pleaded just this case when the Tory government …

pert writers may be found in dependent subjunctive clauses. This finding does seem to coincide, however, with a feature which other English-Spanish researchers (Williams 2005) have found for expert writing in Spanish: the "forcefulness"

Table 5. Interpersonal patterns used by novice writers (native speakers) in English

Patterns used in LOCNESS (American university writers)	Examples
1. *It* + be + *possible/likely/unlikely* + *that* (hedging), or adverbs *possibly*, *probably* N = 49/ 9.47 per 10,000 words	– The bottom line is that crime does not pay and that it destroys your life. The idea that seems at first to be in harmony with our perceived values of equality in American society. Although <u>it is likely</u> that most Americans, if asked, <u>would</u> profess to the belief that equal work deserves equal pay, equality of work as defined by specific task, physical difficulty, or cognitive difficulty, is not the real issue. The real issue, in a discussion of relative contribution to society, involves our deeper cultural assumptions about ….
2. *It* + be + Adjective + *that* (Expressing degree of truth, or evaluation of what is said) . *certain* = 1/ *certainly* = 19 . *clear* = 6/ *clearly* = 28 . *evident* = 1/ *evidently* = 1 . *obvious* = 9/ *obviously* = 16 . *sure* = 0/ *surely* 0 0 . *true* = 5 N = 86/ 5,7 per 10,000 words	– It has already been seen that when there was prayer in schools, there existed social ills as serious as the ones that exist today. It is <u>obvious</u> that required prayer <u>would</u> not eliminate the problems. On the other hand, with youngsters willingly and enthusiastically participating in religious activities… – The white person in many cases, feels uneasy towards those of another color because of stereotypes carried amidst white culture. It is <u>true</u> that this scenario is not always the case with a person of color, as obviously not all of the white population holds racist views, <u>but</u> it is quite obvious that it is a very significant problem.
3. *It* + passive verb + *that* (impersonalization strategy) N = 5 (none with modal verbs)	– One particularly painful test is the Draize eye Irritancy Test, where chemicals are squirted into a rabbits' eye to see if it causes blindness. How can this be ethical if <u>it is known</u> that there is pain being implemented on the animals? –*? <u>*It is proven*</u> that whites and black alike, who live in poverty, must deal with a higher crime rate unaffected by the color of one's skin.

of stating opinions as compared with the negative politeness strategies used in the texts of expert Anglo-American writers.

Regarding the use of pattern 2 (*It is* + Adjective of certainty + *that/to* to express the degree of truth or the evaluation of the following proposition), there was no significant difference between any of the groups. Per 10,000 words, the Spanish EFL texts contained 5.3 tokens; the expert English texts, 6.2; the American uni-

Table 6. Interpersonal patterns used by expert writers in Spanish

Patterns used by expert writers in Spanish	Examples
1. Es im/possible/probable; Lo que probable es [*It* + be + *possible/ likely/unlikely* + *that*], or adverbs *posiblemente, probablemente* [*possibly, probably*] [hedging] N = 28/ 2.4 per 10,000 words	– El problema es que su detección es enormemente difícil. Aunque *consiguiéramos* acercarnos a esos planetas, cosa hoy por hoy *impensable*, y en ellos hubiera vida, *lo más seguro* es que no podríamos observar desde el espacio alteraciones locales debidas inequívocamente a su presencia. Como no es <u>posible</u> para un hipotético observador extraterrestre que *pasara* por las cercanías del Sistema Solar observar dichas alteraciones locales…
2. *It* + be + Adjective + that (Expressing degree of truth, or evaluation of what is said), or modal adverbs . Es *in/cierto(Lo cierto es que)* = 16/ *ciertamente* = 0 . Es/está claro = 5/ *claramente* = 9 . Es evidente = 3/ *evidentemente* = 4 . Es obvio = 3/ *obviamente* = 3 . Es seguro = 3/ *seguramente* = 11 . Es verdad (*La verdad es que*) = 5 N = 67/ 5.9 per 10,000 words	– El origen de tales conflictos no ha provenido, por lo tanto, del poder judicial, sino de una inadecuada actuación de los otros dos poderes, particularmente el ejecutivo. Por otra parte, también es <u>cierto</u> que el poder judicial puede, en un determinado momento, limitar notablemente la capacidad de actuación de los otros poderes. <u>Pero no es menos cierto</u> que esa capacidad controladora se halla sometida a límites muy importantes. Habría que recordar aquí que, por mandato …
3. *It* + passive verb + *that* (impersonalization strategy) N = 30 (all in the present passive, except 2)	– <u>Se dice</u> que corrupción la ha habido siempre y la hay en todos los ámbitos de la sociedad. Y que la clase política no es sino un reflejo de los modos y conductas de la ciudadanía. <u>Se dice</u> y es verdad.

versity texts, 5.7; and the Spanish expert texts, 5.9. However, when one examines the individual adjectives and adverbs used by each of the groups, one finds that both the novice writer groups use many more phrases that make a strong appeal to general perception (Quirk 1985: 620), in particular: *it is obvious + that* (Spanish EFL, 31 tokens; American students, 9; expert English, 3; expert Spanish, 4) and *obviously* (Spanish EFL, 15 tokens; American students, 16 tokens, expert English, 4; expert Spanish, 3). As other researchers have argued (Hewings & Hewings 2002), such features tend to give novice writer texts less of a hypothetical tone than is usually required for carefully reasoned argumentation. In addition, the Spanish EFL students, unlike their American counterparts, also used other forceful evaluative adjectives and adverbs, notably, *it is true + that* (20 tokens) and *surely* (7 tokens).

True (5 tokens) and *clear* (2 tokens) were also used, although sparingly, by the professional Anglo-American writers, but in their texts these emphatic adjectives are always tempered by adversative particles, often accompanied by modal hedges (as in the two examples of pattern 2, Table 4, with the posterior use of *but*). These lexical phrases usually signal a subsequent reversal of opinion, posed as a suggestion. In general, the EFL students do not modulate propositions introduced by a forceful adjectival phrase or adverb, nor do they include subsequent epistemic verbs (or other hedges) which might allow the reader to distinguish between propositions put forth as claims, not facts. Consequently, the EFL writers' sentences containing *true, obvious* and *clear* give the impression of wanting to force the reader to accept their opinions.

Since the American university writers also overuse this second pattern (or the corresponding adverbial forms), in comparison with the expert writers in English, at least part of the EFL students' lack of constructing balanced argumentation can be attributed to novice writer characteristics. Although the American university writers frequently use a hedging modal in subsequent clauses, which somewhat mitigates the force of the evaluation, the use of a strong evaluative adjective on the part of the novice writers (both American and Spanish) allows the readers fewer options of reaching an opinion on their own.

In spite of the novice writer characteristics corroborated in this second pattern, the use of strong evaluative adjectives and adverbials is also very common in the Spanish expert writers' texts, as can be seen in Table 6. This would suggest that the results of the Spanish EFL writers may reflect a combination of factors: a transfer of Spanish rhetorical conventions, but also novice writer features.

Some English-Spanish contrastive work has suggested that Spanish expert writers prefer the adjectival pattern to the use of modal adverbials (*obviously, clearly, surely*), which, in turn, are preferred by the expert writers in English. Hoye (1997:257) reports that Spanish-speaking students (Chilean) make more use of periphrastic constructions; that is, he noted that a VP-adverb, such as *surely*, was frequently translated as *(Es) seguro que* ("it is sure that..."). He cites the Butt & Benjamin grammar (1989:215) of (peninsular) Spanish, which states that modal adverbs ending in *-ly* (*-mente* in Spanish) are specifically proscribed by Spanish writing manuals. However, the data from the present study do not suggest that the grammarians' proscription regarding adverbs ending in *–mente* necessarily affects expert writing in Spanish. While it seems that the Anglo-American writer and American university student groups both prefer the adverbial forms (*certain*, 7 tokens, *certainly*, 18; *clear*, 2 tokens, *clearly*, 11, etc.), the Spanish expert writers appear not to favour one form over another. That is, they seem to prefer some adverbials over the periphrastic adjectival constructions: *está claro*, 7 tokens, *claramente*, 9 ("it is clear"/ "clearly", respectively); *es seguro*, 5 tokens, *seguramente*, 11 ("it is certain"/ "certainly", respectively). But there are also some very common periphrastic adjectival phrases in the Spanish expert texts, such as *es in/cierto* ("it is un/certain"), 16 tokens versus the adverbial *ciertamente* ("certainly"), 0 tokens. Arguably, therefore, one cannot consistently predict that Spanish EFL writers might prefer to use periphrastic structures in their second language writing. More thorough research will have to be carried out to find out if the preference for periphrastic forms in Spanish really does exist, or if the preference involves only certain adverbials.

The third interactional strategy, the use of the passive, is much favored by the Spanish expert (25 tokens of the reflexive *se* passive[4]) and Spanish novice writers (30 tokens), and somewhat surprisingly, not at all by the expert English-speaking writers (2 tokens). Once again there was a significant difference between the Spanish EFL writers' use of this strategy and its use by expert English writers as well as between the Spanish expert writers and the English expert writers (P<.04 in both cases). Of the 28 passive constructions used by the Spanish EFL writers, all were in the present tense. This finding most probably reflects a translation of L1 *se* impersonal passive phrases, which, in the Spanish experts' texts, are all in the present tense, for example *se dice* ("it is said"). In the texts of both groups of novice writers, there were also non-existent passive English forms, for example: *It is proved that* (Spanish novice writers) or *It is proven that* (American novice writers). This again shows that novice writers, even native speakers, have difficulties in selecting the proper lexical phrases for academic writing.

The lack of the passive pattern in the English experts' texts may be due to the authors' reluctance to assume that readers and writers share many common assumptions, but may also be due to a difference in English and Spanish argumentation styles. Argumentation patterns in English require writers to set out their opinions very early on, but then to weigh up the "pros and cons". This is known as "retrogressive style" (Mauranen 1993). This style differs from Spanish argumentation, which could be said to follow the "progressive style" (Mauranen 1993). That is, in Spanish texts arguments are built up throughout the essay, towards a point at which the major decision is made in favour of one view or another. This type of argumentation pattern is reflected in Spanish metadiscourse, which differs significantly from that used in English argumentative texts. Spanish argumentative texts show more listing lexical phrases – *first, on the one/other hand*, etc. – and

---

4. · The reflexive *se* passive is used in some Romance languages, such as Italian, Romanian and Spanish as a means of focusing on the activity or event itself (Manoliu-Manea 1994: 93).

Table 7. A comparison of the use of each pattern per 10,000 words

Corpus	Use of pattern 1	Use of pattern 2	Use of pattern 3
Spanish EFL (Table 3)	0.74 per 10,000w	2.32 per 10,000w	1.6 per 10,000w Total: 14 tokens
Am. Univ (Table 5)	9.5 per 10,000w	5.7 per 10,000w	Total: 5 tokens
Anglo Experts (Table 4)	8.6 per 10,000w	6.2 per 10,000w	Total: 2 tokens
Spanish Experts (Table 6)	2.4 per 10,000w	5.9 per 10,000w	Total: 30 tokens

additive lexical phrases – *also, further, in addition*, etc., while English texts have more interactional lexical phrases, especially those which contain hedges.

Finally, Table 7 presents a global view of the strategies used by each of the four groups, in order to attempt to distinguish the effect of the various factors which may influence Spanish EFL writers: incomplete mastery of the English modal system; novice writer factors; and transfer factors.

As can be seen in Table 7, which focuses on the three types of structures discussed in this paper, the Spanish EFL students differ from both the American University writers and the Anglo expert writers, especially in terms of a less frequent use of pattern 1, a hedging strategy (*It is possible/likely/unlikely*), something the Spanish expert wirters also do. This result suggests, as previously noted, that Spanish EFL writers are affected by inadequate knowledge of the lexical phrases used in Academic Writing in English. However, there may also be an additional transfer effect from L1 writing styles. Regarding pattern 2, the Spanish EFL students seem to differ clearly from the other groups. Thus, in this case, the Spanish EFL writers seem to be less competent than their American counterparts in expressing less forcefully the degree of truth or evaluation of what has been stated as a claim. The American university writers appear to be much more similar to the expert Anglo writers. As for the passive impersonal strategy, pattern 3, Spanish writers, both novice and expert, prefer this strategy in comparison to Anglo writers, a finding which does not coincide with what is usually stated in textbooks about academic writing in English.

5.   Conclusion

This study of interactional lexical phrases used by Spanish EFL students in comparison with those used by expert writers of English and Spanish, and those written by American university students, has shown that Spanish EFL writers are influenced by a range of factors:

1. Incomplete mastery of the English modal system, including modal adverbs: EFL developmental stages
2. Novice writer factors: the use of forceful adjectival lexical phrases and adverbs and also of doubtful passive constructions
3. Transfer from L1: the Spanish use of fewer lexical phrases for hedging; the Spanish preference for the reflexive passive impersonal constructions in the present tense

Spanish EFL argumentative texts show that these students lack mastery in the use of modal verbs to modulate authorial voice in stating propositions and this fault is compounded by their overuse of very forceful evaluative adjectives in lexical phrases such as *it is* + adjective + *that*. The combination of these two factors often results in statements which come across as too forceful for English argumentative texts. In addition, the EFL texts also contain novice writer characteristics, similar to those of the American university writers, in that they use impersonal passive constructions that do not appear to be possible in English. Spanish EFL writers may also be influenced by a transfer of pragmatic preferences from Spanish. English-speaking professional writers prefer the modal adverbs (*certainly*, *clearly*, *obviously*, etc.) to the adjectival *it is* + Adj + *that* construction, which Spanish expert writers seem to prefer. However, more corpus work needs to be carried out in order to ascertain whether this preference really does correspond to rhetorical preferences in Spanish.

Overall, these results seem to support the conclusions set out by Mauranen (1993) in her study of Finnish and English-speaking research writers. Rhetorical practices may vary according to cultural preferences. In the case of the EFL students, their limited competency in academic English may hinder them from choosing more appropriate interpersonal strategies.

The implications of this research for the teaching of Academic English in tertiary institutions are fairly clear. ESL and EFL students need to have at hand a stock of lexical phrases for evaluating the claims that they wish to make. With this objective in mind, the EFL research group at the Universidad Complutense has used some of these findings in order to create exercises for the students of Academic Writing (a second year course for students in English Language and Linguistics). It is hoped that future research will provide some answers on how to improve our teaching of Academic Writing.

References

Biber, D., S. Johansson, G. Leech, S. Conrad & E. Finegan (1999). *Longman grammar of spoken and written English*. London: Longman.

Butt, J. & C. Benjamín (1989). *A new reference grammar of modern Spanish*. London: Edward Arnold.

Crismore A., R. Markannen & M. Steffensen (1993). Metadiscourse in persuasive writing. A study of texts written by American and Finnish university students. *Written Communication 10* (1), 39–71.

Contreras, H. (1976). *A theory of word order with special reference to Spanish*. Amsterdam: North Holland.

Dafouz, E. (2000). El metadiscurso como estrategia retórica en un corpus de textos periodístico. Estudio contrastivo de lengua inglesa y lengua española. PhD dissertation, Universidad Complutense de Madrid.

Halliday, M. A. K. (1973). *Explorations in the functions of language*. London: Edward Arnold.

Hewings, M. & A. Hewings (2002). "It is interesting to note that...": A comparative study of anticipatory 'it' in student and published writing". *English for Specific Purposes, 21* (4), 367–383.

Hoye, L. (1997). *Adverbs and modality in English*. London: Longman.

Howarth, P. (1998). The phraseology of learners' academic writing. In Cowie, A.P. (ed.) *Phraseology. Theory, analysis and applications*, 161–184. Oxford: Clarendon Press.

Manoliu-Manea, M. (1994). *Discourse and pragmatic constraint on grammatical choices*. Amsterdam: Elsevier.

Mauranen, A. (1993). *Cultural differences in academic rhetoric*. Frankfurt: Peter Lang.

Mendikoetxea, A. (1999). Construciones inacusativas y pasivas. In Bosque, I. & V. Demonte (eds.) *Gramática descriptiva de la lengua española*, 1575–1778. Madrid: Espasa Calpe, S.A.

Neff, J., E. Dafouz, M. Díez, F. Martínez, J.P. Rico, R. Prieto & C. Sancho (2003). Contrasting learner corpora: The use of modal and reporting verbs in the expression of writer stance. In Granger, S. & S. Petch-Tyson (eds.) *Extending the scope of corpus-based research*, 211–230. Amsterdam: Rodopi.

Neff, J., F. Ballesteros, E. Dafouz, M. Díez, F. Martínez, R. Prieto, R. & J. P. Rica (2004). Stance in native and non-native argumentative texts. In Facchinetti, R. & F. Palmer (eds.) *English modality in perspective. Genre analysis and contrastive studies*, 141–161. Frankfurt: Peter Lang.

Neff, J. & C. Bunce. (2006). Pragmatic word order errors and discourse-grammar interdependence. In Mourón C. & T. Moralejo (eds.) *Actas del IV Conferencia de Lingüística Contrastiva*, 697–705. Santiago de Compostela: Universidad de Santiago.

Quirk, R., S. Greenbaum, G. Leech, & J. Svartvik (1985) *A comprehensive grammar of the English language*. London: Longman.

Shaughnessy, M. (1977). *Errors and expectations: A guide for the teacher of basic writing*. New York: Oxford University Press.

Stainton, C. (1996). Metadiscourse: The rhetorical plane of text. *Nottingham Working Papers 2*.

Thompson, G. (2001). Interaction in academic writing: Learning to argue with the reader. *Applied Linguistics 22* (1), 58–78.

Vande Kopple, W. (1985). Some explanatory discourse on metadiscourse. *College Communication and Composition 36*, 82–93.

Williams, I. (2005). Thematic items referring to research and researchers in the discussion section of Spanish biomedical articles and English-Spanish translations. *Babel 51* (2), 124–160.

Exemplification in learner writing

A cross-linguistic perspective

Magali Paquot

The aim of the case study reported in this chapter is to examine the potential influence of the mother tongue on learners' production of both correct and incorrect multi-word units that are typically used to fulfil an important rhetorical function, namely exemplification, in academic writing. The phraseological patterns of five exemplifying lexical items are analyzed in five sub-corpora of the *International Corpus of Learner English*. These patterns are extracted from Paquot's (2007) productively-oriented academic word list and include the two fixed conjuncts *for example* and *for instance,* the noun *example* and the verbs *illustrate* and *exemplify.* The analysis aims to distinguish between aspects of phraseological use characteristic of learners from one mother tongue background (and therefore probably L1-dependent) from phraseological patterns shared by most learner populations (and hence more likely to be developmental or teaching-induced). Results suggest that there are two different types of transfer of L1 multi-word units: the first type applies to word-like units and the second to less salient multi-word units. The study also indicates that transfer of form often seems to go together with transfer of frequency and register.

1. Introduction

Recent corpus-based studies (e.g. Biber et al. 1999; Oakey 2002; Biber 2004; Biber et al. 2004) have pointed to the existence of a specific phraseology within English for Academic Purposes (EAP) characterized by word combinations that are essentially semantically and syntactically compositional, e.g. *as a **result** of, in the **presence** of, the **aim** of this **study**, the **extent** to which, for **example**, it has been **suggested**, it should be **noted** that, it is **likely** that, as **shown** in **figure/fig.**, in **addition**,* etc. These word combinations are built around typical EAP or sub-technical words (in bold), i.e. words that are common to a wide range of academic texts and disciplines (cf. Nation 2001), and fulfil organizational or rhetorical functions prominent in academic writing, e.g. introducing a topic, hypothesizing, summarizing, contrasting, exemplifying, explaining, evaluating, concluding, etc.

Comparisons of native and learner corpora of academic writing have highlighted a number of features of non-nativeness or 'unconventionality' in the phraseology of learners of English as a Foreign Language (EFL). EFL learners have been shown to overuse a limited number of frequent English collocations and prefabs but to underuse a whole set of native-like phraseological units, especially typical EAP multi-word units, e.g. *claim that, the issue of, a strong argument* (De Cock 2003: 364). Nesselhauf (2004: 141) suggests that the unavailability of pragmatic chunks for the learners is most probably responsible for a number of deviant multi-word units which are used to structure the body of the essay, e.g. *Only have a look at; If you have a look at; Let us have a look at; A first argument I want to name for this.* Nesselhauf also shows that among the nouns most often used with deviant verbs are typical EAP nouns like *action, aim, attitude, problem, question, statement, step* and *conclusion.*

Most of these studies have also pointed to the potential influence of the mother tongue on learners' multi-word units. For example, Granger (1998) finds that the few English collocations involving intensifiers that are used by French learners typically have a direct translation equivalent in French (e.g. *closely linked* 'étroitement lié'). Similarly, De Cock (2003) shows that French learners underuse a number of multi-word units which have no cognate forms in French (e.g. *sort of*), misuse some English sequences that have French partially deceptive cognates (e.g. *on the contrary* ≈ 'au contraire', *in fact* ≈ 'en fait') and use atypical combinations that are literal translations of French multi-word units (e.g. *according to me* 'selon moi').

Many studies mention the potential influence of the mother tongue on learners' production of multi-word units but very few, whether corpus-based or not, have tackled the issue systematically and examined the conditions under which multi-word units are most potentially transferable. In a number of studies based on acceptability tests and translation tasks, Kellerman (1977, 1978, 1979, 2000) suggests that L2 learners seem to work on the hypothesis that there are constraints on how similar the L2 can be to the L1, and these constraints seem to hold, even when the two languages are closely related and the structures congruent. Kellerman (1978) investigates the 'transferability' of the different meanings of the Dutch verb *breken* into its English cognate *break*. He shows that while Dutch learners of English accept the structures that are the least 'marked' in their mother tongue (*he broke his leg, the cup broke*), they tend to reject what they perceive as language-specific items (*his voice broke when he was thirteen, some workers broke the strike*). Marked in this context means "semantically odd, or syntactically less producible or less frequent when compared with 'normal' forms" (Kellerman 1979:46). In the 2000 study, Kellerman expands on these findings and argues that the dimension of prototypicality largely determines Dutch learners' judgements about the transferability of the different usages of *breken* into *break*.

Although Kellerman acknowledges that learners' intuitions about what can be transferred in an L2 may not accurately reflect what they actually do when using the target language, his findings suggest that the further word combinations are situated from the central core of phraseology, i.e. semantically opaque, syntactically and collocationally inflexible multi-word units, the more potentially transferable they may be. This conclusion is challenged by Nesselhauf in a study of learners' multi-word combinations with the two verbs *take* and *make* in which she claims that "it does not seem to be the case that transfer decreases with the degree of idiomaticity of a combination [...] but rather that locutional combinations [restricted collocations] – at least in the case of the verb-noun combinations with the two verbs investigated – are the type of combination that is most susceptible to transfer" (Nesselhauf 2003:278), e.g. **make part of* (Fr. 'faire partie de') for *be part of*, **make profit* (Fr. 'faire profit'), for *make a profit*, **make dreams* (Fr. 'faire des rêves') for *have dreams*. However, the author makes this claim on the basis of erroneous collocations only and does not examine potential L1 influence on native-like multi-word units produced by learners.

The aim of this case study is to examine the potential influence of the mother tongue (L1) on learners' production of both correct and incorrect multi-word units that are typically used to fulfil an important rhetorical function, namely exemplification, in academic writing. In second language writing research, L1 influence has been shown to manifest itself in idea-generating and idea-organizing activities (Wang & Wen 2002). It may be suggested that EAP multi-word units are most potentially transferable not only because they are essentially semantically and syntactically compositional, i.e. typically unmarked word combinations, but also because they are directly anchored to an organizational or rhetorical function. The phraseological patterns of five exemplifying lexical items extracted from Paquot's (2007) productively-oriented academic word list – the two fixed conjuncts *for example* and *for instance*, the noun *example* and the verbs *illustrate* and *exemplify* – are analyzed in five sub-corpora of the *International Corpus of Learner English* (Granger et al. 2002) with a view to distinguishing between aspects of learner phraseological use characteristic of learners from one mother tongue background and therefore probably L1-dependent and phraseological patterns shared by most learner populations and hence more likely to be developmental or teaching-induced.

2. Data and methodology

This case study makes use of both native and learner corpora. The learner data consist of five sub-corpora of the *International Corpus of Learner English* (henceforth ICLE) of approximately 150,000 words each. Texts in each sub-corpus were carefully selected in an attempt to control external variables which may affect the written production of learners: they are all untimed argumentative essays written by higher-intermediate to advanced EFL university students of five different mother tongue backgrounds: Dutch, French, German, Polish and Spanish. An extended version of the *Louvain Corpus of Native Speaker Essays* (Granger 1996) (henceforth LOCNESS), a 326,746-word corpus of argumentative essays written by American university students (309 essays; average number of words per essay: 1057), is used as the comparable corpus. Argumentative essay titles in both corpora include topics such as *death penalty, euthanasia, crime does not pay* and *money is the root of evil*. Although numerous scholars have questioned the native speaker's status as the most relevant model for teaching English (e.g. Seidlhofer 2001; Jenkins 2005),[1] demonstrating a command of standard written English remains a high-priority requirement in academic settings (Flowerdew 2000; Hinkel 2004).

Jarvis's working definition of L1 influence refers to "any instance of learner data where a statistically significant correlation (or probability-based relation) is shown to exist between some feature of learners' IL [*interlanguage*] performance and their L1 background" (2000: 252). The author suggests that to establish convincingly that interlanguage behaviour exhibits L1-related effects, three potential effects of L1 influence should be systematically investigated, i.e. (1) intra-L1-group similarities, (2) inter-L1-group differences and (3) L1-interlanguage (IL) performance similarities. Intra-L1-group similarities are similarities in the use of a common second language (L2) by learners from the same L1 background; inter-L1-group differences refer to differences in the use of a common L2 by learners from different mother tongue backgrounds; and L1-IL performance similarities are similarities in L1 and IL behaviour by learners who share the same mother tongue.

The *Integrated Contrastive Model* (Granger 1996; Gilquin 2000/2001) provides a very useful framework within which to investigate these three potential effects of L1 influence on the basis of naturally occurring samples of learner language (Ellis & Barkhuizen 2005: 25–30). The model combines *Contrastive Analysis* (CA)

---

1. These authors call for the development of a model based on proficient users of English as a Lingua Franca (ELF) on the basis that English is now used by many more non-native speakers than native speakers (cf. Modiano's (1999) Modified Concentric Circles). However, I share Mukherjee's (2005) doubts about "the suitability of this kind of English as a target norm for the ELT classroom."

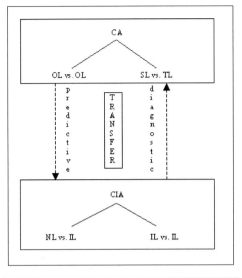

Figure 1. The Integrated Contrastive Model (Granger 1996)[2]

and *Contrastive Interlanguage Analysis* (CIA). CIA consists of two types of comparison. First, it involves a comparison of native and non-native production of the same language which aims to "highlight a range of features of non-nativeness in learner writing and speech, i.e. not only errors but also instances of under- and overrepresentation of words, phrases and structures" (Granger 2002: 12). Second, CIA includes a comparison of different interlanguages of the same language, e.g. the English of French learners, Spanish learners, Dutch learners, etc. This second type of comparison allows for the analysis of the first two types of L1-related effects: an investigation of a learner corpus made up of texts written by learners of the same mother tongue background may reveal intra-L1-group similarities, whereas a comparison of interlanguages by learners from at least two different L1 backgrounds may reveal inter-L1-group differences.

The combination of CA and CIA proposed by Granger (1996) helps analysts to link interlanguage behaviour to performance in the mother tongue and thus investigate the third type of potential effect of L1 influence, i.e. L1-interlanguage performance similarities. Similarities in L1 and IL behaviour by learners from the

---

2. CA: Contrastive Analysis; OL: Original Language; SL: Source Language; TL: Target Language; CIA: Contrastive Interlanguage Analysis; NL: Native Language; IL: Interlanguage

same mother tongue background are probably the strongest type of evidence as this "elucidates the relationship between the source and effects of L1 influence" (Jarvis 2000: 255). Corpora of texts written in the learners' mother tongues are therefore used to investigate L1-IL performance similarities.

As illustrated in Figure 1, the *Integrated Contrastive Model* proposes two types of approaches to CA and CIA data. From CA to CIA, the approach is predictive and consists in formulating CA-based predictions about L2 production which are then checked against CIA data. From CIA to CA, the approach is diagnostic:[3] it aims to explain CIA findings, i.e. errors but also overuse and underuse, in the light of CA descriptions. The latter approach is adopted in this study but the more neutral term "explanatory" is preferred. Figure 2 shows that after a comparison of the learner corpora, i.e. different interlanguages, with the English native corpus (EN_{L1}) and subsequent comparisons between the learner corpora, results per L1 are paralleled with contrastive findings from L1 corpora when available.

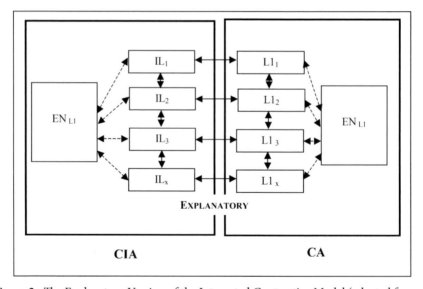

Figure 2. The Explanatory Version of the Integrated Contrastive Model (adapted from Granger 1996)

---

3. It should be noted that, in the *Integrated Contrastive Model*, the terms 'predictive' and 'diagnostic' refer to working hypotheses which will either be confirmed or refuted by corpus data (cf. Granger 1996: 46).

3.   Exemplification in native writing

There are two types of lexical items most frequently used to fulfil an exemplifying function and that appear in Paquot's (2007) productively-oriented academic word list: (1) word sequences that intuitively appear to be single units and that will be called "word-like" units in this study, i.e. *for example* and *for instance* and (2) collocations and frames which do not intuitively appear to be single units as they are characterized by a high degree of variability but which are nevertheless repeatedly used to introduce examples, i.e. collocations and frames with the noun *example* and the verbs *illustrate* and *exemplify* (cf. Table 1).

For example is the most frequently used lexical item to introduce an example in LOCNESS (104 occurrences). It is typically used at the beginning of a sentence or after the subject:

(1)   *The arguments in favour of capital punishment revolve around the ancient biblical concept of "an eye for an eye".* **For example,** *a criminal who murders should himself be murdered to fulfil what is considered by many to be justice.* (LOCNESS)

(2)   *Many of the fuels being developed today have little or no impact on the environment. Hydrogen,* **for example,** *burns completely clean.* (LOCNESS)

For example differs significantly from *for instance* both in terms of frequency and register. Table 2 shows the distribution of *for example* and *for instance* in the four sub-corpora of the BNC-Baby, i.e. a four million word sampling of the 100 million word British National Corpus which represents the four main genres of academic

Table 1. Exemplifying function

Word-like units	Collocations and frames with...
For example	example
For instance	illustrate
	exemplify

Table 2. Distribution of *for example* and *for instance* in the Baby BNC

	for example	*for instance*
Academic writing	707 [85%]	121 [65%]
Spontaneous conversation	23 [3%]	15 [8%]
Fiction	19 [2%]	31 [16%]
Newspaper texts	83 [10%]	20 [11%]
Total	**832 [100%]**	**187 [100%]**

writing, fiction, newspaper texts and spontaneous conversation.[4] A comparison of the four sub-corpora reveals that *for instance* is less typical of academic prose. Overall, *for instance* is also generally much less frequent than *for example* in English: it appears 187 times in the whole BNC-Baby whereas *for example* appears 832 times.

Productive frames with the noun *example* and the verb *to be*, i.e. X *is* DET (ADJ.) *example of* Y and DET (ADJ.) *example of* Y *is* X, are also commonly found in student and professional academic writing:

(3) *This is a prime example of thinking that does not follow in old footsteps but breaks away from convention and forges new routes.* (LOCNESS)

(4) *Some of these diseases are life threatening. AIDS is a perfectly good example of these diseases.* (LOCNESS)

(5) *An example of forest knowledge is that of the "hunter gatherers" on the Philippine island of Mindanao, who recognize 1600 categories of plants.* (BNC-Baby – academic)

In LOCNESS, almost 50% of the occurrences of the noun *example* outside the conjunct *for example* appear in productive frames.

Finally, the verbs *illustrate* and *exemplify* are also used to introduce an example but *illustrate* is much more frequent. They are typically found in the passive (cf. sentence 6) or in the active with non-human subjects such as *example, figure, table, case* and *approach* (cf. sentence 7).

(6) *The problem is well illustrated by the debate that preceded the Medical Research Council's study on the prevention of neural tube defects.* (BNC-Baby – academic)

(7) *As the above cases illustrate, the prayer that is proposed to be said in schools may have the opposite effect than what is intended.* (LOCNESS)

4. Exemplification in learner writing

An analysis of *for example, for instance, example, illustrate* and *exemplify* in learner writing shows that there are striking differences in use between native and learner writers of English. In Section 4.1, patterns shared by the five learner populations

---

4. For more information on the British National Corpus and the BNC Baby, cf. http://www.natcorp.ox.ac.uk/

are described while Section 4.2 gives a description of features that are specific to the French learner population.

4.1   Shared multi-word units

Learners' use of word-like units displays similar patterns of overuse among the five mother tongue backgrounds: *For example* is overused by the five learner populations under investigation (cf. Figure 3) and *for instance* is massively overused by all learner populations, with the exception of German learners (cf. Figure 4).[5]

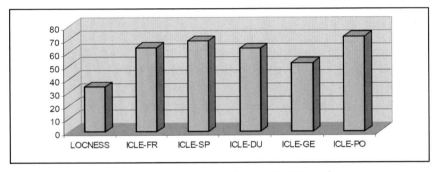

Figure 3. Number of occurrences of for example per 100,000 words

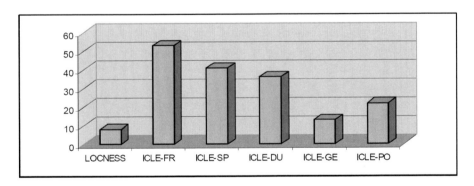

Figure 4. Number of occurrences of for instance per 100,000 words

---

5.   Siepmann (2005) found that both *'for example'* and *'for instance'* were slightly less frequent in his non-native corpus of German student essays than they were in his native corpus. This difference in results is most probably due to a difference in text type as the author compares EFL student writing to professional writing.

Unlike in native writing, the two conjuncts are repeatedly found at the end of a sentence in learner writing:

(8) *I find the pronunciation of English much more difficult than the pronunciation of Italian, **for instance**.* (ICLE-POLISH)

(9) *Furthermore the psyche surpassed the nature of cosmic allegorism, which involved the representation of thunderstorm as a performance of the god Zeus **for example**.* (ICLE-DUTCH)

The non-native writers' tendency to overuse the fixed formulae *for example* and *for instance* is clearly in line with Granger's (1998: 156) conclusion that "learners' repertoires for introducing arguments and points of view are very restricted and they therefore 'cling on' to certain fixed phrases and expressions which they feel confident in using."

It is most probable that learners cling on to these word-like units for two main reasons. First, each first language has a direct equivalent to *for example*, i.e. *par exemple* in French, *por ejemplo* in Spanish, *bijvoorbeeld* in Dutch, *zum Beispiel* in German and *na przyktad* in Polish, which provides a clear anchor in learners' minds. Second, word-like units are typically emphasised in instruction and teaching materials. Grammars and writing textbooks often only provide lists of adverbial connectors in sections on discursive functions (e.g. Oshima & Hogue 2006: 291–299). Similarly, instruction is most likely responsible for the massive overuse of *for instance* in EFL students. *For example* and *for instance* are often taught as two synonyms and as a result, learners use them interchangeably. Learners presumably write *for instance* instead of *for example* when they have already used *for example* in their essay and want to change for the sake of variety. However, it was shown in Section 3 that *for instance* is much less frequent than *for example* in L1 academic writing.

Another explanation for the general overuse of *for example* and *for instance* may also be that these word-like units are repeatedly used when they are unnecessary, redundant or even when other rhetorical functions should be made explicit. Sentence 10 is an example of redundant exemplification:

(10) *The mob **for instance** is a very good **example**.* (ICLE-SPANISH)

The mirror image of this tendency is the underuse of the less salient multi-word units, i.e. productive frames with the noun *example* and the verb *to be*, of which learners appear to be unaware. This underuse is also most probably reinforced by teaching as teaching materials rarely put emphasis on these unmarked multi-word units (cf. Laws 1999: 48–49). It is therefore not surprising that they are underused by almost all learner populations. The Dutch learners are the only ones who do not underuse these frames. This may be due to a difference in proficiency level as the Dutch sub-corpus seems to include a larger proportion of highly rated essays than other ICLE sub-corpora[6] Another possible explanation may be in terms of L1-related effects. In a comparable corpus of Dutch formal writing, productive frames with the verb *zijn* were found to be quite frequent:

(11) **Een goed voorbeeld is** *het akkoord dat eurocommissaris Bolkestein met de VS sloot over de verstrekking van passagiersgegevens van vluchten naar Amerika.*
[*A good example is the agreement that the Euro-commissioner Bolkestein reached with the US on passenger data disclosure on flights to America.*]

(12) **Een bekend voorbeeld is** *Linux, het alternatief voor het bestruringssysteem van Microsoft.*
[*A well-known example is Linux, the alternative to Microsoft operating system.*]

Finally, learners turn out to underuse the verb *exemplify*. As for the verb *illustrate*, they underuse it only in the passive but overuse active structures with a human subject (13)–(14) and the phrase *To illustrate this, ...* used at the beginning of a sentence (15)–(16):

(13) **I would like to illustrate that by means of some examples** *which, as you will see, are very diverse.* (ICLE-DUTCH)

(14) **What I wanted to illustrate is that** *an obviously simple and clear solution turns out to be not the best one at a closer look – at least for one part of the people.* (ICLE-GERMAN)

(15) **To illustrate the truth of this,** *one has only to mention people's disappointment when realizing how little value has the time spent at university.* (ICLE-SPANISH)

(16) **To illustrate this,** *we can mention the notion of culture and language in the north of Belgium.* (ICLE-FRENCH)

---

6. A number of texts written by learners from the 11 mother tongue backgrounds found in the first edition of *International Corpus of Learner English* have recently been rated externally by a professional ESOL rater according to the descriptors for writing found in the Common European Framework of Reference for Languages. Results show that learner essays rate from B2 to C2 and that the proportion of B2, C1 and C2 texts differs between the 11 mother tongue backgrounds (cf. Thewissen et al. 2006).

4.2   Multi-word units specific to French learner writing

French learners repeatedly use the sequence *let us/let's take the example of,* a frame that is not incorrect but certainly very infrequent in native academic writing. The sequence does not appear in LOCNESS and occurs once in a slightly different form in the academic subpart of the BNC-Baby:[7]

(17)   **Let us take as an example** *an infinitely long, infinitely thin distribution of charges as shown in Fig. 2.8.* (BNC-Baby – academic)

Academic writing is a genre characterized by high degrees of formality and detachment and the speech-like nature of this sequence leads to an overall impression of stylistic inappropriateness:

(18)   *One form of this is nationalism. To show what I mean,* **let's take the example of** *an Englishman in Belgium.* (ICLE-FRENCH)

(19)   *One of them is the loss of contacts in families. (..)* **Let us take an example**: *many people eat while watching TV. I personally think that this is a pity.* (ICLE-FRENCH)

Whereas the conjunct *for example* is significantly overused in most ICLE subcorpora, the frame *let's take the example of* is quite rare in other interlanguages and seems to be specific to French learners. This over-representation is most probably an L1-related effect as the sequence has a congruent counterpart in French, i.e. *Prenons l'exemple de …,* which is commonly found in student and professional formal writing. The following sentences come from the *Corpus de Dissertations Françaises* (CODIF), a 200,000-word corpus of essays written by French-speaking students collected at the University of Louvain:

(20)   **Prenons l'exemple des** *sorciers ou des magiciens au Moyen Age.*

(21)   **Prenons l'exemple d'un** *individu qui postule pour un emploi.*

(22)   **Prenons l'exemple du** *port du voile qui a créé une polémique il y a tout juste 10 mois.*

The overuse of *let's take the example of* is part of a more generalised and massive overuse of *let us / let's* in ICLE-FRENCH. Figure 5 shows that although *let us* (or *let's*) is generally more frequent in learner writing than in LOCNESS, the sequence is massively overused only in the French learner corpus.

---

7.   The sequence *let's take the example of* does not appear in the British Academic Written English corpus described in Nesi et al. (2004).

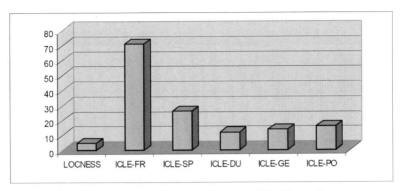

Figure 5. Number of occurrences of *let* us and *let's* per 100,000 words

A few examples of sentences introduced with *let us* or *let's* in ICLE-FRENCH are:

(23) ***Let's consider*** *the situation in Belgium.*

(24) ***Let's first have a look at*** *what is Europe actually.*

(25) *Now* ***let's move on*** *to our third category of criminals.*

(26) ***Let's try*** *to find the most important principles which are urging people to react as they do.*

(27) *So* ***let us analyse*** *the potential assets of this country…*

(28) ***Let us comment on*** *the second statement: …*

(29) ***Let us now examine*** *the second solution.*

(30) ***Let us explain*** *these two points.*

This overuse can be compared to the very frequent use of the first person plural imperative to organise discourse in French formal writing:

(31) ***Citons*** *comme exemple le jugement difficile des autorités françaises sur les activités du régime de Vichy dans le cadre du procès de Touvier.* (CODIF)

(32) ***Envisageons*** *tout d'abord la question économique.* (CODIF)

(33) ***Examinons*** *quelques exemples pour tenter d'y voir plus clair.* (CODIF)

(34) *Et* ***notons*** *que ces réalisations nous inspirent des rêves insoupçonnés jusque là,*(CODIF)

(35) ***Considérons*** *un instant le cinéma actuel.* (CODIF)

(36) ***Pensons****, par exemple, à l'Espagne, qui, pendant quatre à huit siècles, a appris à côtoyer les peuples arabes.* (CODIF)

Table 3. First person plural imperative forms in ICLE-FRENCH and CODIF

Corpora	Relative frequencies per 100,000 words
ICLE-FRENCH	71
CODIF	85

Table 3 shows that frequencies of first person plural imperative forms in ICLE-FRENCH and CODIF are quite similar and suggests that frequency in the learners' L1 may be reflected in their interlanguage.

This hypothesis is further supported by the similarity in frequency of first person plural imperative forms in ICLE-Spanish and in the written part of the *Corpus de Referencia del Español Actual* (CREA).[8] The two sequences *let's* and *let us* appear in the Spanish learner corpus though not as frequently as in French learner writing. Similarly, Spanish first person plural imperative forms are quite frequent in formal writing though less frequent than their French equivalents. The following sentences are examples of Spanish first person plural imperative forms used as metadiscourse markers:

(37) **Consideremos** *ahora la distribución de la producción mundial de energía y de las emisiones de CO2 ... (CREA)*

(38) *Pero* **veamos** *lo que se nos dice. (CREA)*

(39) *Como ilustración,* **tomemos** *el caso de las alas de los pájaros. (CREA)*

Finally, the infrequent use of *laten we* in Dutch formal writing (1.4 occurrence per 100,000 words in the written part of the PAROLE corpus[9]) is also reflected in Dutch learner writing as ICLE-DUTCH is the only learner corpus in which the overuse of *let us* is not statistically significant.

5.   Transfer of L1 multi-word units

From this case study, there appear to be two types of transfer of L1 exemplifying multi-word units. The first type applies to word-like units and the second to less salient multi-word units. L2 word-like units tend to be overused by learners

---

8. We make use of this corpus for lack of any comparable corpus of essays written by Spanish-speaking students. For more information on the *Corpus de Referencia del Español Actual*, see http://www.rae.es.

9. For more information on the PAROLE corpus, see http://parole.inl.nl/html/index.html

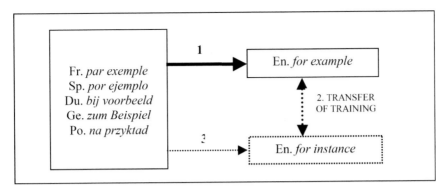

Figure 6. Transfer of L1 word-like units

especially if there are similar units performing similar functions in their L1s. The overuse is often reinforced by instruction as teaching materials tend to focus exclusively on these units. This case study suggests that learners not only establish equivalence between *for example* and the functionally equivalent word-like unit in their L1 (cf. Figure 6) but they also extend the equivalence to *for instance*. One possible explanation for this rough equivalence is again the influence of instruction or 'transfer of training' (cf. Selinker 1972): although they differ in terms of frequency and register, *for example* and *for instance* are taught as functionally equivalent forms.

The second type of transfer concerns more variable or less salient multi-word units that are essentially semantically and syntactically compositional, i.e. typically unmarked word combinations. French learners' use of the multi-word unit *let's take the example of* is a direct translation of the French *Prenons l'exemple de* but can be regarded as a case of positive transfer as the sequence is found in English. However, this multi-word unit in learner writing does not have the same stylistic profile as in native English writing. Figure 7 shows that transfer of form may not only go together with transfer of function but also with transfer of register and frequency. Thus, the L1 multi-word unit *Let's take the example of* .. mirrors the stylistic profile of the French sequence *Prenons l'exemple de* .. and is repeatedly used in EFL French learner formal writing. An even more convincing example is the generalised overuse of the first person plural imperative in EFL French learner writing, a rhetorical strategy that does not conform to English academic writing conventions but rather to French academic style.

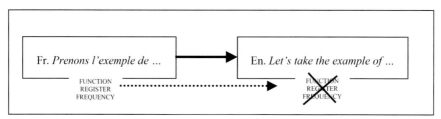

Figure 7. Transfer of L1 less salient multi-word units

6.   Pedagogical implications

Descriptions of EAP vocabulary and its phraseology in native corpora are becoming available (cf. Verdaguer & González 2004) but information derived from learner corpus analysis, and more crucially, L1-specific information, is currently sorely lacking (Granger 2004). Patterns shared by all learner populations can be used to increase the pedagogical value of teaching materials which would incorporate information on aspects of overuse, underuse, misuse and learners' idiosyncratic use of lexico-grammatical means to fulfil rhetorical functions (cf. Flowerdew 1998). Learner-corpus analyses will enable the lexical means typically underused by all learner populations to be presented as useful alternatives to learners' preferred patterns. Thus, EAP textbooks should draw learners' attention to the fact that EFL students generally tend to overuse *for example* and *for instance* and advise them to also use productive frames such as X *is a* (adj.) *example of* Y and *a* (adj.) *example of* Y *is* X as well as the verbs *exemplify* and *illustrate*. These verbs should be taught in context, in their precise rhetorical use, and their preferred environments (i.e. passive structures such as *BE exemplified in/by*, *BE illustrated in/by*, *as illustrated in/by* and *as exemplified in/by*) should be introduced to EFL learners.

The findings presented in this study also support the view of contrastive rhetoric that "the linguistic patterns and rhetorical conventions of the L1 often transfer to writing in ESL and thus cause interference" (Connor 2002: 494). They have important implications for EAP teaching as they suggest that the mother tongue deserves a place in the academic writing class. Although L1-specific findings may be more difficult to incorporate into generic EAP textbooks, these findings may prove particularly useful to EFL learners to help them conform to "the native stylistic norms for a particular register", which "entails not only making appropriate grammatical and lexical choices but also selecting conventional [multi-word units] to an appropriate extent" (Howarth 1998: 186). It is highly desirable that they be incorporated into EAP textbooks specifically targeting EFL learners sharing the same mother tongue background or into electronic dictionaries and newly developed teaching materials such as writing aid software tools, where space is no longer so much of an issue (cf. Granger 2004).

7.   Conclusion

The study shows that L1-related effects contribute significantly to learners' use of multi-word units in L2 together with other factors like transfer of training and level of proficiency. Results suggest that transfer of form often goes together with transfer of function and supports the hypothesis that multi-word units with a pragmatic anchor are more easily transferred. Transfer of form also seems to go together with transfer of frequency and register. These two types of transfer are less documented and well worth exploring in more detail. For learners, things can go wrong at each level: the function of a formally equivalent multi-word unit in the L2 is not always the same as in the L1; the frequency of a multi-word unit in L2 is often different from the frequency of its counterpart in L1 and in addition, there may be mismatches in register as shown by the example of the first person plural imperative in French vs. English academic writing.

Finally, this study has demonstrated the usefulness of the *Integrated Contrastive Model* to identify L1 influence. If we want to learn more about EAP multi-word units in learner writing and the conditions under which L1 sequences are most potentially transferable, we need three types of comparison: (1) comparisons of EAP vocabulary and its phraseology in learner vs. native writing, (2) comparisons of EAP vocabulary and its phraseology in different L1 learner corpora and (3) detailed descriptions of EAP vocabulary and its phraseology in other languages (see the work of Siepmann (2005, and this volume). It is only through a "constant toing and fro-ing between CA and CIA" (Granger 1996: 46) that we can hope to gain a better understanding of the interaction between the L1 and L2 phrasicons.

Acknowledgements

I gratefully acknowledge the support of the Communauté française de Belgique, which funded this research within the framework of the 'Action de recherche concertée' project entitled 'Foreign Language Learning: Phraseology and Discourse' (No. 03/08–301). I would also like to express my deep gratitude to Professor Sylviane Granger for her guidance and support.

References

Biber, D. (2004). Lexical bundles in academic speech and writing. In Lewandowska-Tomaszc-zyk, B. (ed.) *Practical applications in language and computers* (PALC 2003), 165–178. Frankfurt: Peter Lang.

Biber, D., S. Johansson, G. Leech, S. Conrad & E. Finegan (1999). *Longman grammar of spoken and written English*. Harlow: Longman.

Biber, D., S. Conrad & V. Cortes (2004). *If you look at* …: Lexical bundles in university teaching and textbooks. *Applied Linguistics 25* (3), 371–405.

Connor, U. (2002). New directions in contrastive rhetoric. *TESOL Quarterly 36* (4), 493–510.

De Cock, S. (2003). Recurrent sequences of words in native speaker and advanced learner spoken and written English: A corpus-driven approach. PhD dissertation, Louvain-la-Neuve: Université catholique de Louvain.

Ellis, R. & G. Barkhuizen (2005). *Analysing learner language*. Oxford: Oxford University Press.

Flowerdew, L. (1998). Integrating 'Expert' and 'Interlanguage' computer corpora findings on causality: Discoveries for teachers and students. *English for Specific Purposes 17* (4), 329–345.

Flowerdew, J. (2000). Discourse community, legitimate peripheral participation, and the non-native-English-speaking scholar. *TESOL Quarterly 34* (1),127–149.

Gilquin, G. (2000/2001). The integrated contrastive model: Spicing up your data. *Languages in Contrast 3* (1), 95–123.

Granger, S. (1996). From CA to CIA and back: An integrated approach to computerized bilingual and learner corpora. In Aijmer, K., Altenberg B. & Johansson M. (eds.) *Languages in contrast. Text-based cross-linguistic studies* [Lund Studies in English 88], 37–51. Lund: Lund University Press.

Granger, S. (1998). Prefabricated patterns in advanced EFL writing: Collocations and formulae. In Cowie, A. (ed.) *Phraseology: Theory, analysis and applications*, 145–160. Oxford: Oxford University Press.

Granger, S. (2002). A Bird's-eye view of learner corpus research. In Granger, S., J. Hung & S. Petch-Tyson (eds.) *Computer learner corpora, second language acquisition and foreign language teaching*. 3–33. Amsterdam: John Benjamins.

Granger, S. (2004). Computer learner corpus research: Current status and future prospects. In Connor, U. & T. Upton (eds.) *Applied corpus linguistics: A multidimensional perspective*, 123–145. Amsterdam: Rodopi.

Granger, S., E. Dagneaux & F. Meunier (eds.) (2002). *The international corpus of learner English. CD-ROM and Handbook*. Louvain-la-Neuve: Presses universitaires de Louvain. (Available from http://www.i6doc.com).

Hinkel, E. (2004). *Teaching academic ESL writing*. Mahwah, NJ: Lawrence Erlbaum Associates.

Howarth, P. (1998). The phraseology of learners' academic writing. In Cowie, A.P. (ed.) *Phraseology: Theory, analysis, and applications*, 161–186. Oxford: Oxford University Press.

Jarvis, S. (2000). Methodological rigor in the study of transfer: Identifying L1 influence in the interlanguage lexicon. *Language Learning 50* (2), 245–309.

Jenkins, J. (2005). ELF at the gate: The position of English as a Lingua Franca. *Humanising Language Teaching 7* (2). (Retrieved from www.hltmag.co.uk/mar05/idea.htm).

Kellerman, E. (1977). Towards a characterization of the strategy of transfer in second language learning. *Interlanguage Studies Bulletin 2* (1), 58–145.

Kellerman, E. (1978). Giving learners a break: Native language intuitions as a source of predictions about transferability. *Working Papers on Bilingualism 15*, 59–92.

Kellerman, E. (1979). Transfer and non-transfer: Where are we now? *Studies in Second Language Acquisition 2*, 37–57.

Kellerman, E. (2000). Lo que la fruta puede decirnos acerca de la transferencia léxico-semántica: Una dimensión no estructural de las percepciones que tiene el aprendiz sobre las relaciones lingüísticas. In Muñoz, C. (ed.) *Segundas lenguas: Adquisición en el aula*, 21–37. Barcelona: Ariel.

Laws, A. (1999). *Writing skills*. Oxford: Summertown.

Modiano, M. (1999). International English in the global village. *English Today 15*, 22–28.

Mukherjee, J. (2005). The native speaker is alive and kicking – Linguistic and language pedagogical perspectives. *Anglistik 16* (2), 7–23.

Nation, P. (2001). *Learning vocabulary in another language*. Cambridge: Cambridge University Press.

Nesi, H., G. Sharpling & L. Ganobcsik-Williams (2004). Student papers across the curriculum: Designing and developing a corpus of British student writing. *Computers and Composition 21*, 439–450.

Nesselhauf, N. (2003). Transfer at the locutional level: An investigation of German-speaking and French-speaking learners of English. In Tschichold, C. (ed.) *English core linguistics. Essays in honour of D.J. Allerton*, 269–286. Bern: Peter Lang.

Nesselhauf, N. (2004). *Collocations in a Learner Corpus*. Amsterdam: John Benjamins.

Oakey, D. (2002). Formulaic language in English academic writing: A corpus-based study of the formal and functional variation of a lexical phrase in different academic disciplines. In Reppen, R., S.M. Fitzmaurice & D. Biber (eds.) *Using corpora to explore linguistic variation*, 111–129. Amsterdam: John Benjamins.

Oshima, A. & A. Hogue (2006). *Writing academic English* (4th edn). White Plains NY: Pearson.

Paquot, M. (2007). Towards a productively-oriented academic word list. In Walinski, J., K. Kredens & S. Gozdz-Roszkowski (eds.) *PALC 2005 Proceedings*, 127–140. Frankfurt: Peter Lang.

Seidlhofer, B. (2001). Closing a conceptual gap: The case for a description of English as a lingua franca. *International Journal of Applied Linguistics 11* (2): 133–58.

Selinker, L. (1972). Interlanguage. *International Review of Applied Linguistics 10* (3): 209–231.

Siepmann, D. (2005). *Discourse markers across languages: A contrastive study of second-level discourse markers in native and non-native text with implications for general and pedagogic lexicography*. London: Routledge.

Thewissen, J., Y. Bestgen & S. Granger (2006). *Using error-tagged learner corpora to create English-specific CEF descriptors*. Paper presented at the Third Annual Conference of EALTA, 19–21 May 2006, Krakow, Poland.

Verdaguer, I. & E. González (2004). A lexical database of collocations in scientific English: Preliminary considerations. In Williams, G. & S. Vessier (eds.) *Proceedings of the Eleventh EURALEX International Congress*, 929–934. Lorient: Université de Bretagne-Sud.

Wang, W. & Q. Wen (2002). L1 use in the L2 composing process: an exploratory study of 16 Chinese EFL writers. *Journal of Second Language Writing 11*, 225–246.

Learning phraseological units

Why can't you just leave it alone?

Deviations from memorized language as a gauge of nativelike competence

Alison Wray and Tess Fitzpatrick

This chapter reports an investigation into the capacity of language learners to improve their performance through the memorization of specifically targeted linguistic material. Six intermediate/advanced learners of English memorized nativelike versions of conversational turns that they anticipated needing in future conversations. After rehearsal, they attempted to use the memorized material in real interaction. Recordings of all stages of the process were transcribed and analyzed, to identify the nature of the deviations made from the targets. Nativelike deviations are interpreted as a legitimate approximation of nativelike behaviour, since fully faithful reproduction of a memorized original is usually neither necessary nor desirable for those with the linguistic skill to make appropriate changes. Non-nativelike deviations are viewed as indicative of shortfalls in knowledge, poor attention focus, and over-optimistic risk-taking during memorization. Individual profiles of the learners are presented, and it is proposed that memorization could be used as a means of establishing the strengths and weaknesses of learners in relation to morphological, lexical and phraseological knowledge.[1]

1. Introduction

Formulaic language has proved difficult to characterize and challenging to harness for effective teaching and learning in the L2 context. As Wray (2002:ix) points out, it is often targeted in the early stages of classroom learning, so must presum-

1. This research was funded by an Innovation Award from the Arts and Humanities Research Board, UK. We are grateful for many helpful comments from colleagues at the various conferences and seminars where we have presented this work. In addition, we would like to thank the two anonymous reviewers of the present chapter for their feedback.

ably be relatively easy to master in one sense, yet it is also the final difficult hurdle for the proficient learner who wants to sound truly nativelike. Experiments with teaching multiword strings abound (see Wray 2002, Chap. 10 for an overview, and Wray 2000 for a comparative analysis of three approaches), but there is only limited research on the psycholinguistic processing that underpins it (see Schmitt 2004 for one collection of studies).

In order to ascertain the parameters of normal learning and processing, it can be useful to explore the extremes, and studies that focus on the role of rote memorization are one way of doing that. Wray (2004) conducted an in depth observation of a beginner learner of Welsh, who memorized a lengthy text in order to meet the challenge of presenting a cookery demonstration on television after only four days of language tuition. By investigating a beginner Wray was able to gauge with some accuracy the sum total of the subject's learning. In contrast, with more advanced learners, it will inevitably be harder to establish what they already knew before the intervention. Nevertheless, there are good reasons for believing that memorization, if effectively applied, can be highly beneficial to those who already have knowledge of a language (Ding 2007).

This chapter reports aspects of a detailed study of six intermediate/advanced learners who were given the opportunity to memorize and then use in real interaction complete nativelike sentences specifically created for them on the basis of their needs and wishes. The learning programme was intensive and thus not directly transferable to the classroom, but the purpose was not to develop a new teaching tool. Rather it was to establish what happens if learners are given every possible opportunity and encouragement to use pre-memorized nativelike material. The focus of the present account is an analysis of the deviations that were made from the memorized material, and how those deviations offer a profile of the learner's knowledge and approach to communication in the L2.

2.   Memorization and language learning

The role of multiword memorization in language learning is far from understood. Although it provides the learner with access to the specific targeted material, the extent to which it is an effective door to more general learning remains unclear. Jeremias (1982) advocates memorization for its communicative benefits, as a means of accessing expressive potential beyond the learner's current proficiency, and Hakuta (1976) suggests that it is important for a learner's motivation to supplement the communicative repertoire of words and rules with some useful longer strings. For Granger (1998), such benefits are all there is, for "there does not seem to be a direct line from prefabs to creative language" (p. 157). On the other hand, Ellis & Sinclair (1996) are amongst those who view memorized material as a legitimate and important means of learning its component units.

While 'parrot learning' is generally disparaged in the west, some learners ascribe to memorization their extremely high level of linguistic competence. Stevick's (1989) detailed account of seven successful language learners reveals such techniques as the deliberate mimicking of the teacher, structured rehearsal of fixed and variable material, text memorization and sentence 'stockpiling'. Chinese students, in particular, have been the focus of several explorations of memorization for successful learning (e.g. Au & Entwistle 1999; Cooper 2004; Dahlin & Watkins 2000; Ding 2007; Kennedy 2002; Ting & Qi 2001; Zhanrong 2002). A recurrent theme is the observation that, contrary to popular perceptions in the west, memorization does not need to be a superficial and therefore rather pointless activity; rather, its effective deployment lies "at the heart of the commonly found superior performance of Asian compared to Western students" (Dahlin & Watkins 2000:66). Memorization is effective when it is directly used to consolidate and/or facilitate understanding (ibid: 67; Cooper 2004:294).

In a study by Marton et al. (1993), Chinese teacher educators had very positive attitudes towards memorization, provided it linked with understanding in one of two ways. Either the student could memorize what had already been understood, or else memorization could be a process through which understanding occurred (p. 10). In the former case, the purpose would be to enhance the student's capacity to access useful material on demand – after all, you cannot use something you cannot remember, even if you do understand it. In the latter case, the mind would work unconsciously on material, identifying and consolidating patterns that were not, at the start, fully known, and leading to "the discovery of new meaning" (Dahlin & Watkins 2000:80). Marton et al's findings suggest that, in either case, the effectiveness of memorization comes down to the attention that the learner pays to the detail of the material, so that learning outcomes are contingent on accuracy – an issue central to this chapter.

However, since not every possible sentence can be rehearsed, effectiveness in using a language effectively must balance the flexibility to draw on large units where possible, with the facility to edit them to their precise context as required. Research into the nature of formulaic language more generally suggests that both native and non-native speakers can benefit from the economies of prefabricated material, but that adult L2 learners struggle to match the native speaker in balancing processing economy, expressive flexibility and accuracy (Wray 2002).

3.   What happens when we memorize text

If you ask a native speaker to memorize something and then recall it, any of the following might happen:

a.   Total success in recall, e.g. *I'd like to draw your attention particularly to the spandrel created by the arches beneath the dome.*
b.   Effective success, but with inconsequential differences in detail, e.g. *I'd* particularly *like to draw your attention to the spandrel* that is *created by the arches* under *the dome.*
c.   Partial failure in the recall of target forms, e.g. *I'd like to draw your attention particularly to the …those shapes there, created by the arches beneath the, er, high ceilinged area.*
d.   Failure to recall form, but because the meaning is recalled, production of a fluent and complete equivalent expression of the message (paraphrase), e.g. *I want to show you how the arches below the dome join to create that tapered shape, called a spandrel.*
e.   Failure to recall both meaning and form.

The list does not, of course, anticipate that a native speaker will introduce any non-nativelike deviations in relation to morphology, lexical choice, phraseology or word order (other than, perhaps, as a slip of the tongue). Yet the absence of such non-native deviations is not because native speakers are better memorizers of the detail of the target form. Rather, it is because their knowledge of the language is sufficient for the correct forms reliably to appear once the semantic prompt is given. Indeed, the details of form barely need be attended to (compare Sachs 1967). Unless the native speaker desires to ensure an exact memorization (as with the lines of a play for example) it will be sufficient to focus on the message content, perhaps along with a few key lexical items as mnemonics. Thus, a native speaker preparing for a job interview, for instance, need not memorize pre-constructed answers to anticipated questions. Unless s/he fears becoming incoherently tongue-tied with nerves, it will be enough to remember the ideas, and to rely on being able to construct the answer off-the-cuff.

The extent to which non-native speakers can afford not to attend to the detail of a memorized word string is a function of proficiency. At low proficiency, the failure to internalize lexical and morphological detail during a memorization task could, at worst, lead to irretrievable breakdown in the message delivery. Where the message did survive, the repairs necessary to make good the forgotten detail would rely on the individual's command of the target language, and where that command was incomplete, non-native errors would be introduced.

However, with increasing proficiency, non-native speakers can gradually adopt the hallmark strategy of the native speaker – less attention to detail. That is, they can dare to focus less on form than before, in the expectation that morphological details can be added quite naturally, and that if a lexical item should be forgotten, another of equal appropriateness can probably be retrieved to replace it. However, it is in the nature of knowledge – and of language indeed – that the assessment of the risk entailed in reducing attention to the form of the target for memorization will not always be an accurate one. That is, learners may not always fully appreciate the limitations of their command of a feature such as the plural marker or the distribution of present and present perfect tenses. On the basis of their receptive knowledge of the language, which reliably furnishes them with recognition and comprehension of the form in the target, they may believe that they will be able to reinstate it on demand when in fact their productive command of the form is less secure.

When a learner reproduces a target faithfully, we discover little about his/her linguistic knowledge, for the feat may be a simple reflection of memorization effort. Linguistic material that learners just repeat or recall can easily be precocious relative to what they could generate from scratch – this is, indeed, a central feature of formulaic language (Wray 2002). However, we can learn a great deal from what happens when the recall is incomplete. When memorizers find that a morphological detail, or a lexical item, or even a whole phrase from the target will not come to mind, what are they able to offer by way of a repair? As noted above, the native speaker can reinstate the morphology, and supply the same, or an equivalent word or phrase, without sounding non-nativelike. The extent to which a non-native speaker can do the same would seem to be a useful gauge of proficiency.

Deviation profiling – the proficiency measure explored in this chapter – characterizes the learner's knowledge by examining the distribution of nativelike and non-nativelike repairs to memorized but incompletely recalled targets. It has some useful advantages over standard error analysis. Firstly, when error analysis is conducted on open texts (essays, spontaneous speech, and so on), one can never be entirely sure what the learner was intending to say. In deviation profiling, however, we not only know what the target was, but also know that the learner has in fact encountered the nativelike form before, so that failing to reproduce it is an indication that the form lies outside what has been so far integrated into the learner's knowledge system. Secondly, error analysis is deficit modelling – it does not measure nativelike achievement as a counter-balance to the measure of errors (Dagneaux, Denness & Granger 1998: 164). In contrast, a deviation profile is composed of both nativelike and non-nativelike elements.

Although it is centred on a memorization task, deviation profiling is not sensitive to the effort put in by the individual learner. A fully correctly recalled word

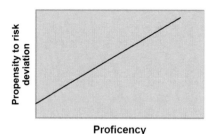

Figure 1. Relationship between proficiency and risk taking in relation to deviations from the memorized target

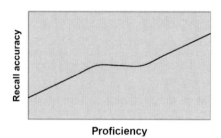

Figure 2. Predicted level of accuracy in reproduction of memorized material, according to proficiency

string tells you nothing about proficiency at all, since anyone, from native speaker to complete beginner, could achieve it with enough effort. It is the deviations that are indicative – these are the points at which incomplete recall relies on active linguistic knowledge to make a repair. With a more careful memorizer, the incidence of deviations will be lower, so that, simply, more material will be required to build the profile.

Of course, other factors play a part in the fidelity of recall. Concentration, confidence, the assessment of the risk of not recalling the target fully accurately, and the anticipated need for flexibility in using the material in the future, may all determine the level of attention paid to the target. The closer to a full command of a linguistic pattern or lexical set the individual perceives herself to be, the more likely she is to choose to bypass the effort of intense memorization of its form. Yet different individuals may perceive the same level of ability differently. Thus a deviation profile needs to include not only a gauge of nativelikeness but also a measurement of the level of risk taken as indicated by the overall closeness of the output to the target. This is important because while learners can safely take more risks in relation to deviating from the target as their proficiency increases – so that the propensity to deviate increases linearly with proficiency (Figure 1) – the accuracy of those deviations may temporarily plateau (Figure 2). This is because increasing the risk entails paying less attention to the detail of target form than before, so that a much greater strain will be placed upon the learner in repairing what are, now, much more likely to be incompletely recalled targets. Insofar as the learner accurately assesses what can be ignored, there will be no detriment in performance, but where the learner is over-optimistic about what can reliably be repaired in a nativelike way, levels of nativelikeness will fail to increase, until additional proficiency is achieved. In deviation profiling, therefore, measures must be taken both of the propensity to deviate and the nativelikeness of the outcome.

4. Profiling learner proficiency on the basis of memorization

4.1 The data set

The data set is the product of an in-depth study of six intermediate/advanced learners of English studying in the UK, engaging in cycles of memorization for the purposes of real conversations. In any given cycle, the subject worked one-to-one with a native speaker of English to identify a future conversation, and to predict utterances that would be useful and appropriate to that conversation. The native speaker provided a nativelike formulation of each utterance (the 'model', M) and recorded it onto CD. The subject then memorized the models at home, returning after a few days to rehearse them with the native speaker in a 'practice performance' (PP). Finally, the subject attempted to use the memorized utterances in the real situation that had been anticipated at the start of the cycle. This constituted the 'real performance' (RP). Some utterance sets were additionally subject to an unprepared recall test three or four weeks later, the 'delayed performance' (DP). All stages of the process were digitally recorded. Each cycle was a self-contained package that took place over 7 to 10 days. Subjects took part in between two and five such packages each. All subjects were female, aged 22 to 35 (mean age 28.8 yrs). Three (Ch, Hi and Sa) were L1 speakers of Japanese, and three (Jo, Lc and Lo) of Chinese. Further details of the study are reported in Fitzpatrick & Wray (2006).

The aim of the project was to observe the consequences for the subjects of memorizing their prepared utterances: the effect on their general accuracy and fluency, the impact on their self-perception, their projection of competence and confidence towards native speaker interlocutors, and the responses that their utterances prompted from those interlocutors. We also looked for correlations between the use and accuracy of memorized material in use and individual profiles of proficiency, aptitude, learning background and motivation.

The study was designed to avoid certain confounding variables that normally arise when looking at the efficacy of prepared conversation:

a. Material targeted for memorization is often deliberately generic (e.g. Gatbonton & Segalowitz 1988), and does not fit the learner's precise situation particularly closely. To counter this, the utterances were designed to meet the subject's own immediate needs in a specific situation identified by her.

b. Learners often lack confidence about whether or not they are making nativelike choices. To counter this, the utterances were known by the learner to be nativelike, having been generated by a native speaker in her presence.

c. A poor performance in real conversation can reflect the learner's lack of experience in producing the desired string fluently and accurately. To counter this, there was ample opportunity to learn the utterances and practise them with the native speaker.

d. Learners are often compromised by a lack of understanding about the material they are using. To counter this, we used subjects with a good independent knowledge of English, so they were not memorizing anything they could not understand.

Twenty-one conversation cycles formed the basis of our analysis, consisting of 227 model utterances, or an average of 10.8 model utterances per conversation. The mean number of words per model utterance was 10.05. The data were transcribed from digital recordings of the practice (PP) and real performance (RP) sessions and, as applicable, from the delayed performance (DP). Since we are not concerned here with the trajectory of retention over time (see Wray 2004 for a study that did examine this factor), the data from different stages have been amalgamated for the present purposes.

4.2 Data analysis

A total of 2416 memorized words contributed to the analysis: these constitute the words in the targets that were attempted. Targets that were never attempted were excluded, since it was unclear whether they had been memorized at all, and, if they had, whether they had ever been deemed relevant for use. Table 1 shows the distribution of target material across the six subjects.

Table 1. Profile of dataset

	Ch	Hi	Jo	Lc	Lo	Sa
Total words in attempted models	158	731	360	360	151	656

M	Oh I wonder if I could ask you something
PP	Oh I wonder if I can ask you something
RP	Oh if I want to I can ask you something
DP	Can I have some question

Figure 3. Model utterance and attempts for Jo 2:3

The subjects' outputs were analyzed and categorized according to deviations from the models. A deviation is not necessarily an error, other than in the very specific sense that it renders the output non-identical to the model. There are myriad reasons why deviations from a model might be legitimate and desirable. They include the need to embed the wordstring appropriately in the discourse (for instance, omitting an initial adjunct such as *then* or *so* because it is not necessary), and the need to alter the factual content (for instance, the time of a meeting, if the memorized time was not convenient). The capacity to effect such deviations is in itself a marker of proficiency: a beginner might be able to memorize a phrase successfully but not tailor it in order to extend its use (compare Myles et al. 1999, who found this lack of extension in learners of French as a foreign language).

Typically in our data set, a model utterance was recalled with two or more deviations over the various attempts, and each deviation was separately classified. For instance, Figure 3 represents the material associated with attempts at the model labelled 'Jo 2:3', that is, the third model utterance in Jo's second cycle, which was for a conversation in a shop about options for printing photographs. The model (M) is fairly accurately reproduced in the practice performance (PP), with one deviation, a substitution of *can* for *could*. This deviation was categorized as a nativelike morphological variant, that is, a change that a native speaker might make. In contrast, in the real performance (RP) the substitution of *if I want to I can X* for *I wonder if I could X* was judged to be non-nativelike. So too was the entire attempt in the delayed performance (DP).

In addition to being classified as nativelike or non-nativelike, deviations were classified as occurring at one of three levels: morphological, lexical or phrasal (multiword). Thus, in the RP attempt in Figure 3, *if I want to I can* was treated as a phrasal substitution, and hence a single deviation, rather than as a series of single word replacements, word order changes and so on. Although such judgements are not an exact science, decisions were applied consistently across the database, and checked at the end of the process, to ensure that similar linguistic behaviour had always been categorized in the same way.

The analysis identified a total of 922 deviations. However, two minor types of deviation were set aside in the subsequent analysis. One was the expansion of two-word contractions such as *I'd* and *wouldn't*. These constituted a total of 36 deviations, or 4% of the total. Although they occurred in all six subjects' output, it was considered inappropriate to include them in the further analysis since they did not constitute an instance of recall failure per se and, in fact, were indicative of knowing what the underlying form of the contraction was, rather than not knowing the contraction. There were no instances of incorrect expansions – that is, *I'd* was never mistakenly expanded to *I had* instead of *I would*, etc. – nor were there any introduced contractions of uncontracted target word pairs.

The second category excluded was slips of the tongue. There were, in fact, only two of these, both from the same subject and both entailing lexical replacement with a phonologically similar item: *problems* for *projects* (Sa 2:8) and *lecturers* for *lessons* (Sa 3:11), the latter possibly a semantic change (to *lectures*) followed by a phonological slip. These slips were omitted because they stood apart from all other deviations, as the only ones that might also be made by a native speaker yet result in a non-nativelike outcome. The distribution of the remaining 884 errors is shown in the Appendix. Deviations were nativelike in 57.7% of cases.

5.   Deviation profiling

5.1   Distributions of deviations

As Figure 4 shows, phrase-level deviations were most common (in fact, they constituted 42.6% of the total). Within that category almost two out of three (63.35%) were judged nativelike, that is, changes that a native speaker might make, e.g. *The dissertation title* → *The title of the dissertation* (Hi 3:5); *They usually learn* → *Usually they learn* (Lc 6:12).

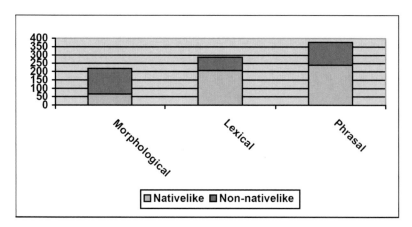

Figure 4. Distribution of nativelike and non-nativelike deviations by main type in the learners' production

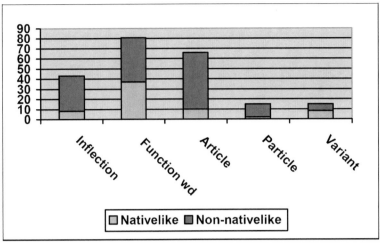

Figure 5. Distribution of nativelike and non-nativelike deviations in morphological type in the learners' production

Lexical deviations accounted for one third of the total (32.5%), and of these, 71.8% were nativelike, e.g. *Like this → Just like this* (Hi 4:10); *The trouble is → The problem is* (Sa 2:6). One quarter of the deviations (24.9%) were morphological, but here seven out of ten changes were non-nativelike (70.5%), e.g. *A question → A questions* (Jo 3:2); *I've got an idea → I've got idea* (Hi 1:3), and, indeed, 41.4% of the total non-nativelike changes were in the morphological domain. In order to explain these distributions, it is useful to break down each type, to establish which subtypes played the dominant roles.

The morphological deviation type was composed of eleven subtypes, which can be grouped by morpheme category (inflection, function word, article, particle or variant)[2], or by the nature of the deviation (substitution, omission or insertion). Grouped by morpheme category (Figure 5) the three main sources of deviation are function words (36.8%), articles (30%), and inflections (19.5%). Inflections and articles were the most likely to be changed in a non-native way. Only just over one in seven deviations in relation to the article were nativelike, and just over one in five in relation to inflections. Breaking down these two major contributors by change type (Figure 6) we can see that a change to the article was most likely to entail an omission and one instance of the 32 such deviations resulted in a native-

---

2.   Prepositions were viewed as part of the morphological system (subtype 'function word'), since they form a closed class; they are not subject to free lexical selection in the same way that content words are. For example, when Sa said *in the paper* when the model was *on the paper* (Sa 5:7) this deviation was viewed as a morphological error and not as a lexical substitution of the kind seen in *my project* for *my research* (Hi 3:6).

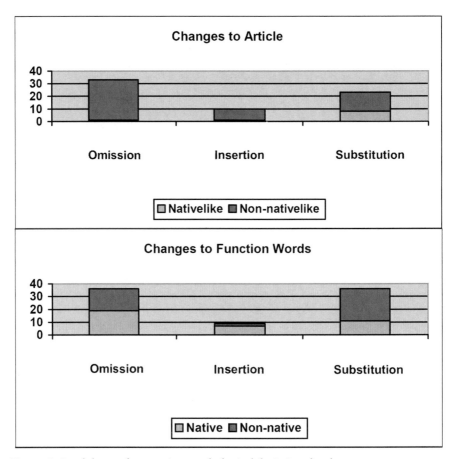

Figure 6. Breakdown of two main morphological deviations by change

like outcome. In contrast, for function words it was substitution that carried the most risk of a non-nativelike outcome.

Lexical deviations were identified on the basis of two sub-types, content words and adjuncts. Figure 7 shows that in both cases a deviation was more likely to be nativelike than not. However, the difference is particularly marked for adjuncts, where 83% of deviations were nativelike. The susceptible adjuncts were predominantly cotextual or temporal linkers such as sentence-initial *so, but, then* and *now*, and it might have been imagined that most deviations in relation to them would have been simple omissions. However, it was actually insertions that predominated (Figure 8). The most common insertion was initial *and* (48%), then *yeah* or *yes* (11%), *so* (8%) and *but* (7%). The remaining 26% of inserted adjuncts comprised 13 types, with between one and four tokens each.

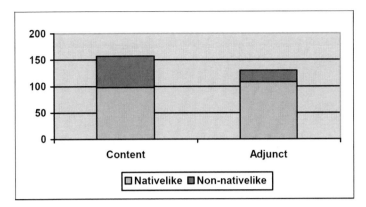

Figure 7. Lexical deviations by subtype

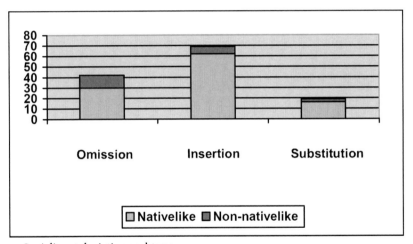

Figure 8. Adjunct deviations subtype

Inserted adjuncts constitute a special case in the sense that they could be viewed as standing outside the body of the memorized target, rather than being introduced into it. Similarly, it could be argued that even during memorization the subjects could have partitioned off certain adjuncts as intrinsically optional and only for use if the cotext required them. Nevertheless, adjuncts are a component of linguistic knowledge that the learner must command in order to communicate effectively and, with the subjects instructed to memorize the targets as provided, any changes made, for whatever reason, do still constitute deviations that could be – and indeed were – differently handled by different subjects.

At the phrasal level (Figure 9), substitutions (47.5%) were the most common form of deviation, with 59.8% of them being nativelike.

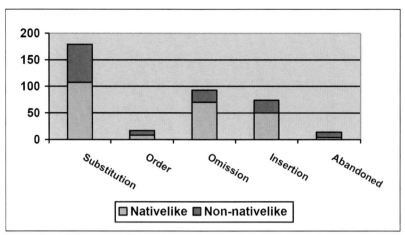

Figure 9. Phrasal deviations by subtype

5.2   Differences by L1

The deviation patterns across the morphological, lexical and phrasal levels probably reflect an interaction between the learners' knowledge and the nature of different languages. Proficiency differences notwithstanding,[3] it seemed highly likely
that learners with different language backgrounds would be found to struggle
with different things. In order to see if this was the case, the combined deviations
for the three Japanese and the three Chinese subjects were calculated as percentages of the total number of deviations for that subgroup. Figure 10 shows that the
Japanese subjects made more phrase-level deviations than the Chinese subjects,
and that morphological deviations were more likely to be non-nativelike for the
Chinese subjects than the Japanese ones. With only three subjects in each group,
we cannot draw strong conclusions, of course, but the contrast does at least indicate where future research might focus some attention.

Breaking down the morphological type (Figure 11) it is revealed that the
Japanese subjects made very few inflectional deviations (3.9%) compared with
the Chinese subjects (33.3%). For Japanese subjects, deviations in function words
and articles jointly contributed 82.5% of the morphological deviations, whereas
for the Chinese subjects it was only 53%. However, the Japanese subjects' deviations in function words were more likely to be nativelike than non-nativelike (e.g.
I know that I'll need to get... changed to *I know I need to get...* Sa 1:2), while the

---

3.   Naturally, increasing proficiency tends to make learners from different language backgrounds converge. However, certain errors associated with interference from an L1 often persist
to a late stage.

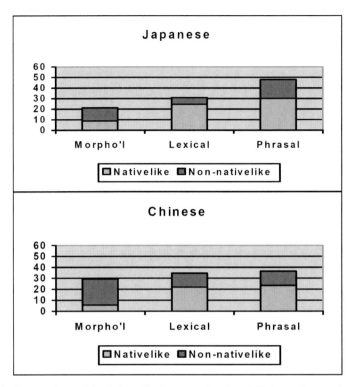

Figure 10. Proportions of deviations for Japanese (top) and Chinese (bottom) subjects

reverse was true for Chinese subjects, a contrast that was highly significant (χ^2 = 7.87, df =1, p < 0.01). This may suggest that Japanese and Chinese learners have different fundamental susceptibilities in relation to function word accuracy. An alternative explanation would be that it simply reflects the slightly higher overall proficiency of the Japanese learners in this study (see Figure 14, below). However, the absence of any significant difference in the distribution of native and non-native deviations for articles (χ^2 = 0.64) rather undermines that argument, unless the higher proficiency of the Japanese learners had enabled them to neutralize an underlying susceptibility to use articles less accurately than Chinese learners – a rather more convoluted explanation overall.

5.3   Individual profiles

Figure 12 presents profiles of the six subjects by deviation type, showing the nativelike, non-nativelike and combined distributions. Lo stands out as entirely unlike the others, in having few phrasal deviations and a high proportion of mor-

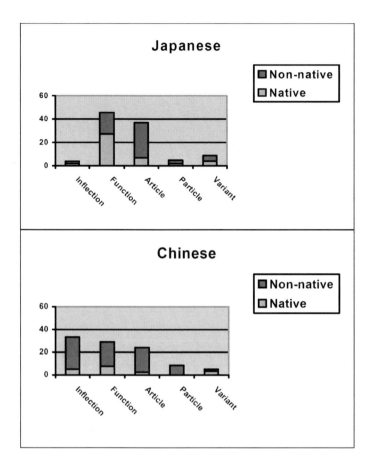

Figure 11. Proportions of morphological deviations for Japanese (top) and Chinese (bottom) subjects

phological deviations. Furthermore, almost all of her morphological deviations were non-nativelike, while all of her phrasal ones were nativelike. However, Lo contributed by far the smallest amount of data, with 49 deviations in total, from a target pool of 151 words. Whether the pattern is, therefore, a product of this small amount of data, or whether, conversely, the small quantity of data that Lo produced was the result of weaknesses in her morphological knowledge or focus, is impossible to say.

All six subjects were least successful with morphological deviations, being more likely (to a greater or lesser degree) to produce a non-nativelike change than a nativelike one. Conversely, at the lexical level, all were more likely (though again, by varying margins) to produce a nativelike change, and at the phrasal level all but Ch were more likely to be nativelike than not. Perhaps this general pattern

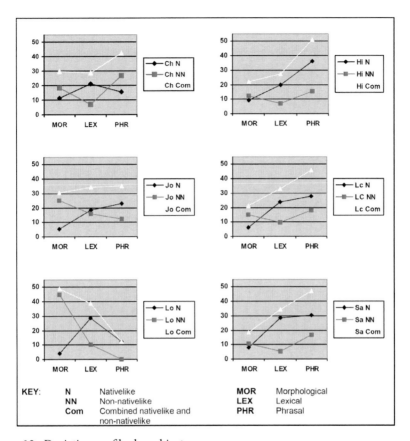

Figure 12. Deviation profiles by subject

is unsurprising. In any specific language context, the range of possible morphological substitutes is extremely limited, often to the extent that there is no possible nativelike substitute (in the case of a plural marker, for example). As a result, any morphological deviation from the model is likely to be a non-nativelike one. More flexibility is possible in the substitution of lexical items and phrasal items, which will appear nativelike so long as collocational and semantic/pragmatic constraints are observed.[4]

The similarities in the profiles in Figure 12 are consistent with the similarities between the subjects, who were all sufficiently proficient users of English to be enrolled on Masters programmes in the UK. There were, in other words, no beginners, though some subjects were quite clearly more effective users of English than others. A beginner's profile would be anticipated to feature mostly non-nativelike

---

4. We are grateful to one of the anonymous reviewers for drawing our attention to this.

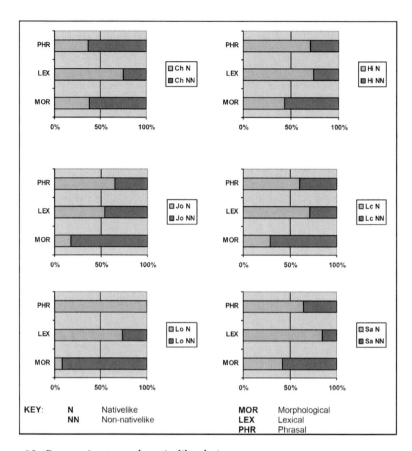

Figure 13. Progression towards nativelike choices

deviations and, indeed, a large proportion of them would be predicted to be features imported from the L1, or else phonological variants of the target rather than genuine 'repairs' that draw on other aspects of the L2 linguistic system.

Figure 13 presents the profiles in a way that makes it easy to see how far along the pathway from non-nativelike to nativelike each subject has progressed, in relation to morphology, lexis and phraseology. These profiles show that Hi, Lc and Sa were strongest overall, being able to make nativelike deviations fairly reliably at the phrasal and lexical levels, though none had reached the 50% threshold for morphological deviations. Jo was slightly weaker on all three fronts, and Ch's profile reveals that she had further to go than the others in making nativelike changes at phrasal level. Again, Lo's profile is unusual. It shows that she did not make any non-nativelike phrasal changes, but that she was particularly weak in relation to morphological detail.

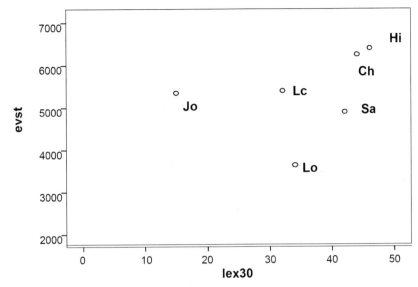

Figure 14. Scores on two language proficiency measures

Two independent measures of proficiency had been taken during the study. EVST[5] (Meara & Jones 1988) is a measure of receptive vocabulary knowledge. Lex 30 (Meara & Fitzpatrick 2000) is a measure of productive vocabulary knowledge. Both tests work by estimating the subject's total vocabulary on the basis of distributions of words known across generic frequency bands, and both have been found reliable predictors of general linguistic ability. Figure 14 plots the scores on the two tests, and shows that Lo, our outlier in the deviation profiles, scored particularly poorly on EVST. However, the relationship between deviations and EVST is not clear. There was no correlation between the nativelike or non-nativelike lexical derivations per word values and the EVST scores, nor between the nativelike lexical deviations per word and Lex 30. On the other hand, there was a significant negative correlation between non-nativelike lexical deviations per word and Lex 30 ($r = -.902$, $p = .014$), suggesting that having a good productive vocabulary makes it easier to avoid making non-nativelike changes to memorized material.

On the Lognostics Language Learning Aptitude Test (LLAT) (Meara et al. 2001), which we also administered in the study, Lo's profile was again striking. She attained the highest score in the group on aural memory, joint highest (100%) on a task linking unfamiliar sounds and symbols, but lowest on the recognition of unfamiliar words by sound (see Fitzpatrick & Wray 2006 for the full report).

---

5. Eurocentres Vocabulary Size Test, see http://www.swan.ac.uk/cals/calsres/lognostics.htm

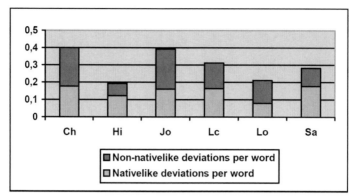

Figure 15. Deviations per word by subject

Overall, it must be said that the relationship between Lo's deviation profile and her performance on the other tests is not all that clear, and the same goes for the other subjects. Jo's low Lex 30 performance could be linked to her being the least likely of the six to make a nativelike change at lexical level, but here, too, there is a distinct danger of post hoc rationalization. While the absence of any clearly emerging correspondence between the deviation profiles and the other test results could mean that the deviation profiles are not an accurate measure of proficiency, it could equally be a case of fragmentation in relation to what 'proficiency' constitutes under these different profiling approaches. We are confident that the deviation profiles in Figure 12 and Figure 13 are a direct index of the subjects' access to the morphological, lexical and phrasal knowledge that most challenges them.

There is one more factor that needs to be introduced for a complete profile. We have proposed that a variable in the fidelity of reproduction is the level of risk taken, specifically in not attending to the fine detail during memorization. In Figure 15 we see each subject's propensity to deviate in nativelike and non-native-like ways, expressed as mean deviations per word. This shows that Ch and Jo took most risks, and Hi least.

As a rule of thumb it might be proposed that individuals like Ch, Jo and Lo, whose non-nativelike repairs exceed their nativelike ones, would benefit from paying additional attention to those aspects of their performance that are most troublesome – as revealed by the progression profile (Figure 13) and the data breakdown (Appendix). Conversely, a learner with a profile like Hi's, whose repairs were more likely to be nativelike than not, but who took few risks in relation to memorization, might be encouraged to experiment more with memorization focussed on message meaning rather than phrasal and lexical form, in the interests of greater expressive flexibility. An advantage of recommendations based on deviation profiling is that the learner has a robust basis for genuine learning, because the memorization task always provides a nativelike model.

6.   Conclusion

Deviation profiling appears to offer insights into the pattern of strengths and weaknesses in an individual's command of the L2. Because it refers back to a known target, it is able accurately to identify deviations in relation to a specific original, something that is not possible with open texts. In addition, the individual is known to have had some exposure to the nativelike target, so that deviations can reasonably be construed as representative of weaknesses in systematic knowledge.

Deviations are a necessary consequence of incomplete recall – to which native speakers are just as vulnerable as non-native speakers – and also are a positively desirable strategy in pursuit of flexibility of expression. For this reason, and also because nativelike changes are credited as a balance to non-nativelike ones, deviation profiling avoids appearing judgmental. A profile is a representation of knowledge, attention and perception of risk, and it is for the individual, ultimately, to decide whether the balance between them is optimal for her own goals. Nor should we assume that everyone's goals are the same. Lo, the outlier in the profiles, appeared to value freedom of expression over accuracy – a legitimate position, albeit considerably different from Hi's. Lo commented: *I just changed some different words but it is the same meaning.*

For others, cultural and national identity might also play a role in determining the extent to which nativelike models are faithfully reproduced. Da, a subject in our pilot study, observed: *Sometimes I change (the phrases) maybe I think there is a difference between British thinking and Chinese thinking... We have to do something in my thinking...actually we ...haven't really changed Chinese thinking to English thinking so sometimes I have to change some words just for me to easy to...find a good way to express my emotions....* While Da changed the sentences to match his patterns of thinking, Lc reported that the use of memorized nativelike sentences helped her think in a more British way, with the result that she was able to communicate more effectively with British people.

The subjects reported finding the use of memorized sentences in anticipated conversations a liberating experience, because it gave them exposure to an opportunity to sound nativelike, promoted their fluency, reduced the panic of on-line production in stressful encounters, gave them a sense of confidence about being understood, and provided material that could be used in other contexts too. Hi also noted that the rehearsal of the models had greatly improved her listening skills. It seems, then, that memorization has a number of potential advantages in relation to learning and confidence-building as well as proficiency evaluation.

More work still needs to be done, on developing deviation profiling as a tool. Should it prove reliable, it could be of benefit in at least two regards. Firstly, it could assist assessors in grading written or oral work that contains (or is suspected to contain) extensive memorized material (Wray & Pegg, forthcoming). Often, the use of memorized material is considered to be disguising the 'true' level of knowledge. Our approach somewhat endorses this view, but shows how to avoid adversely judging the learner who has sufficient proficiency to dare variations in what has been memorized, even though doing so could introduce more errors than there would be in a faithful reproduction of the memorized material.

Secondly, deviation profiling could be used for placement testing in language schools, where grading must be done quickly and effectively. Memorization tasks can be administered in any medium, including as a pen and paper test (though subjects would certainly benefit from the scope to rehearse aloud). Deviation profiling by test does not discriminate between the imaginative and less imaginative individual, nor the faster and slower writer. It does not confer benefit on those who have prepared for the test, since there is no obvious way to prepare for it – even memorization practice does not increase scores, only reduces the quantity of profiled material. Furthermore, because deviation profiling does not measure the fidelity of memorization, it does not matter if some subjects expend more effort on the task than others. The only constraint is that the task must be challenging enough to produce sufficient data from incomplete recall for profiling to be possible and to be reliable. This can be controlled either by requiring more memorization than can be achieved in the allotted time, or by introducing a new context topic in recall, so that the precise details of the memorized material are no longer applicable and must be modified. Our future research will explore the parameters of effective deviation profiling, with particular attention to the minimum dataset size required for reliability.

References

Au, C. & N. Entwistle (1999). Memorization with understanding in approaches to studying: cultural variant or response to assessment demands. Paper presented at the European Association on Learning and Instruction Conference, Gothenburg, August.

Cooper, B.J. (2004). The enigma of the Chinese learner. *Accounting Education 13*, 289–310.

Dagneaux, E., S. Denness & S. Granger (1998). Computer-aided error analysis. *System 26* (2), 163–174.

Dahlin, B. & D. Watkins (2000). The role of repetition in the processes of memorizing and understanding: A comparison of the views of German and Chinese secondary school students in Hong Kong. *British Journal of Educational Psychology 70*, 65–84.

Ding, Y. (2007). Text memorization and imitation: The practices of successful Chinese learners of English. *System 35*, 271–280.

Ellis, N. C. & S. G. Sinclair (1996). Working memory in the acquisition of vocabulary and syntax: putting language in good order. *Quarterly Journal of Experimental Psychology 49*A (1), 234–250.

Fitzpatrick, T. & A. Wray (2006). Breaking up is not so hard to do: individual differences in L2 memorization. *Canadian Modern Language Review 63* (1), 35–57

Gatbonton, E. & N. Segalowitz (1988). Creative automatization: principles for promoting fluency within a communicative framework. *TESOL Quarterly 22* (3), 473–492.

Granger, S. (1998). Prefabricated patterns in advanced EFL writing: collocations and formulae. In Cowie, A. P. (ed.) *Phraseology: Theory, analysis and applications*, 145–160. Oxford: Clarendon Press.

Hakuta, K. (1976). A case study of a Japanese child learning English as a second language. *Language Learning 26* (2), 321–351.

Jeremias, J.M.V. (1982). The 'social' component in the English classroom: semantic and pragmatic considerations. *Anglo-American Studies 2* (1), 63–73.

Kennedy, P. (2002). Learning cultures and learning styles: Myth-understanding about adult (Hong Kong) Chinese learners. *International Journal of Lifelong Education 21* (5), 430–445.

Marton, F., G. Dall'Alba & L.K. Tse (1993). *The paradox of the Chinese learner* [Occasional Paper no 93.1], Melbourne: RMIT, Educational Research and Development Unit.

Meara, P. & T. Fitzpatrick (2000). Lex30: An improved method of assessing productive vocabulary in an L2. *System, 28* (1), 19–30.

Meara, P. & G. Jones (1988). Vocabulary Size as a Placement Indicator. In Grunwell, P. (ed.) *Applied Linguistics in Society*, 80–87. London: CILT.

Meara, P., J. Milton & N. Lorenzo-Dus (2001). *Language aptitude tests: Lognostics.* Swansea: Express Publishing.

Myles, F., R. Mitchell & J. Hooper (1999). Interrogative chunks in French L2: A basis for creative construction? *Studies in Second Language Acquisition 21* (1), 49–80.

Sachs, J.S. (1967). Recognition memory for syntactic and semantic aspects of connected discourse. *Perception and psychophysics 2*, 437–42.

Schmitt, N. (ed.) (2004). *Formulaic sequences: Acquisition, processing and use.* Amsterdam: John Benjamins.

Stevick, E. W. (1989). *Success with foreign languages.* Hemel Hempstead: Prentice Hall.

Ting, Y. & Qi, Y. (2001). Learning English texts by heard in a Chinese university: A traditional literacy practice in a modern setting, *Foreign Language Circles 5*, 58–65

Wray, A. (2000). Formulaic sequences in second language teaching: principles and practice. *Applied Linguistics 21* (4), 463–489.

Wray, A. (2002). *Formulaic language and the lexicon.* Cambridge: Cambridge University Press.

Wray, A. (2004). 'Here's one I prepared earlier': Formulaic language learning on television. In Schmitt, N. (ed), *Formulaic sequences: Acquisition, processing and use*, 249–268. Amsterdam: John Benjamins.

Wray, A. & C. Pegg (forthcoming). The effect of memorized learning on the writing scores of Chinese IELTS test takers. *IELTS Research Reports.*

Zhanrong, L. (2002). Learning strategies of Chinese EFL learners: Review of studies in China. *RTVU ELT Express*, http://www1.openedu.com.cn/elt/2/4.htm [last accessed 11th July 2007].

Appendix

Distributions of deviations by type

Deviation type	NATIVELIKE RESULT Frequency							NON-NATIVELIKE RESULT Frequency						
	Ch	Hi	Jo	Lc	Lo	Sa	Total	Ch	Hi	Jo	Lc	Lo	Sa	Total
MORPHOLOGICAL														
Inflection change	0	0	0	6	0	2	8	1	1	20	5	8	0	35
Function wd omission	4	2	5	2	0	6	19	1	2	2	1	5	6	17
Function wd insertion	0	4	2	0	0	1	7	0	0	0	0	0	2	2
Function wd substitution	2	3	0	0	0	6	11	0	6	10	7	0	2	25
Article omission	0	0	0	1	0	0	1	6	4	8	1	7	6	32
Article insertion	0	1	0	0	0	0	1	1	0	1	1	0	6	9
Article substitution	1	4	2	0	0	1	8	0	6	6	1	0	2	15
Particle omission	0	0	0	0	0	0	0	2	0	4	4	2	0	12
Particle insertion	1	1	0	0	0	0	2	0	0	0	0	0	1	1
Particle substitution	0	0	0	0	0	0	0	0	0	0	0	0	0	0
Morphological variant substitution	0	1	2	0	2	3	8	2	2	0	2	0	1	7
Total	**8**	**16**	**11**	**9**	**2**	**19**	**65**	**13**	**21**	**51**	**22**	**22**	**26**	**155**
LEXICAL														
Content wd omission	2	9	7	2	1	10	31	1	2	9	2	0	4	18
Content wd insertion	3	5	7	4	4	5	28	1	2	4	3	2	0	12
Content wd substitution	8	7	1	6	0	17	39	2	4	8	7	3	5	29

	1	2	3	4	5	6	Total	7	8	9	10	11	12	Total
Adjunct omission	0	2	5	8	2	13	**30**	1	2	7	1	0	1	**12**
Adjunct insertion	2	4	15	10	7	24	**62**	0	2	2	1	0	2	**7**
Adjunct substitution	0	7	3	5	0	1	**16**	0	0	2	0	0	1	**3**
Total	**15**	**34**	**38**	**35**	**14**	**70**	**206**	**5**	**12**	**32**	**14**	**5**	**13**	**81**
PHRASAL														
Phrase substitution	5	35	18	17	1	31	**107**	7	17	11	13	0	24	**72**
Word/phrase order	0	1	3	1	0	3	**8**	0	0	6	0	0	3	**9**
Phrase omission	6	17	13	10	2	22	**70**	5	3	4	7	0	4	**23**
Phrase insertion	0	8	12	13	3	14	**50**	7	4	2	5	0	6	**24**
Entire model abandoned	0	0	0	0	0	4	**4**	0	2	2	2	0	4	**10**
Total	**11**	**61**	**46**	**41**	**6**	**74**	**239**	**19**	**26**	**25**	**27**	**0**	**41**	**138**
Grand totals	**34**	**111**	**95**	**85**	**22**	**163**	**510**	**37**	**59**	**108**	**63**	**27**	**80**	**374**

Phraseology and English for academic purposes
Challenges and opportunities

Averil Coxhead

No word is an island. Each word we teach and expect students to learn in English for Academic Purposes (EAP) carries with it many aspects of knowledge including meaning and or meanings, associations, referents, and contexts of use. In recognising that words of a feather seem to flock together, teachers and researchers are exploring new technologies to find out more about words in contexts and in use so as to meet the language needs of an unprecedented number of EAP students worldwide. Whilst this area of study is dynamic and interesting, it is somewhat fraught with doubts and frustrations. This chapter outlines some of the challenges of phraseology in EAP for teachers, researchers, and students. It also discusses some exciting opportunities for the future of phraseology in the teaching and learning of EAP.

1.   Introduction

"I like to learn verbs because you only have to learn one word." A Chinese first language speaker made this statement in an interview in a study on the use of words and phrases in an academic writing task (Coxhead in preparation). This student, and five others in my small pilot case study, had recently completed a credit-bearing undergraduate academic writing paper at Massey University in Aotearoa/New Zealand. Part of their paper focused on the students' learning of vocabulary from the Academic Word List (Coxhead 2000), training in noticing, and direct instruction on common phrases in their academic reading to support their academic writing development. The student's comment about learning verbs so that she could focus on one word at a time begs a methodological question operating outside the influence of teachers, researchers, texts and classrooms: why learn two words together when learning one seems hard enough? The other side of the coin for teachers is that to justify spending valuable class time on teaching and learning phrases or lexical bundles, we need to know which ones will give good return for learning and how to teach them successfully.

In this chapter I focus on two of the many faces of phraseology – those of English for Academic Purposes (EAP) teachers and learners. I will discuss the tension between current lexical teaching methodology and the principles underpinning this methodology, through asking the following questions: Why are phrases important in EAP? What phrases should we teach in EAP? What pedagogical approach should we use? And finally, what barriers do our students encounter in using formulaic sequences in their writing? Perhaps these questions might form the basis for a future research agenda to support teachers and learners in facing the challenges and taking the opportunities phraseology offers EAP.

2.   Phraseology and pedagogy in EAP

Michael Stubbs (personal communication) made the point that one of the major problems with corpus-based research is figuring out what questions would be useful to ask. In this section, I will address the importance of phrases in EAP, what phrases should be taught in EAP, and how.

2.1   Why are phrases important in EAP?

An overwhelming amount of dense language surrounds learners not just in EAP classrooms, academic reading and content classes but everywhere in the tertiary setting (Biber et al. 2002:9). There is no doubt that the learners need many words to cope with everyday (Adolphs & Schmitt 2003:436) and higher (Biber et al. 2004:377) educational requirements in both spoken and written contexts: perhaps more than previously thought. Words are important, but why would the phrases words occur in be worth time and effort in classrooms? Biber et al. (2004:371) refer to these sequences as 'lexical bundles' and call them '... basic building blocks of discourse'. Wray (2002:203) writes that formulaic sequences are important for second language speakers because they allow for speakers to process and interact, and express their identity with a group – in the case of my EAP students, as part of the academic undergraduate community. Schmitt (2005) has found clear benefits for idiomatic formulaic sequences in processing information while reading for both native and non-native speakers, and Cortes (2004:400) states that, "Many lexical bundles are not idiomatic: rather, their meaning is transparent, fully retrievable from the meaning of the individual words that make up the bundle."

Academic discourse is marked by formal lexis not found frequently in fiction (Coxhead 2000) and there is an expectation that a learner writing within the same context will use this vocabulary (Jones & Haywood 2004: 273). Corson (1995) calls this predominantly Graeco-Latin vocabulary a 'lexical bar' that acts as a barrier to accessing the academic community, not just for second language writers but for first language writers who do not have ready access to this vocabulary. Over 80% of the 570 word families of the Academic Word List (AWL) (Coxhead 2000), for example, are Graeco-Latin in origin. The 'lexical bar' presents more difficulties for learners from non-Romance languages. Howarth (1998: 186), in his chapter on the phraseology of postgraduate second language writers, points out that 'Conforming to the native stylistic norms for a particular register entails not only making appropriate grammatical and lexical choices but also selecting conventional collocations to an appropriate extent'. Cortes (2004) reports that history and biology students do not use lexical bundles very often in writing, tend to rely on a small number, and do not use them the same way as professionals writing in those fields do.

2.2   What phrases should we teach in EAP?

Howarth (1998: 186) makes the point that one of the key issues surrounding learners' use of phrases in academic writing is that EFL teachers lack understanding of 'phraseological mechanisms of the language'. Granger (1998) points out that teachers do not know what to teach and there is a lack of training in language-in-use in current teacher training programmes in the area of writing (Coxhead & Byrd forthcoming). Vocabulary itself has recently gained more attention from researchers, teachers and materials designers, but we are at the beginning stages of understanding the nature of formulaic sequences. The diversity of the EAP field, with students from a wide variety of language backgrounds and educational systems, is a second source of difficulty. Some students require finesse in their use of expressions whilst others are building academic language foundations at a lower level and are working towards becoming part of the undergraduate community. EAP courses differ in duration, level, textbooks and purpose. Massey University's credit-bearing academic writing paper, for example, caters for undergraduates and sometimes postgraduates from a wide range of majors and uses materials from EAP textbooks, the students' own textbooks, internet sources, reference books and occasionally journal articles. How do we accommodate such diversity and know that we are teaching the phraseological units students need to know?

One way to attempt to answer this question is to look at recent research into EAP vocabulary at the word level. The AWL, for example, has provided some guidance on words with reasonable frequency and range in a corpus of written academic texts (Coxhead 2000) that provide around 10% coverage. One of the challenges of the AWL is that it was released solely as a list of individual words and their families, with no indication of the context and patterning in which these words occurred. As a result, learners and teachers often focus merely on the recognition of individual AWL words alone, without considering wider and vital aspects of knowing a word including learning and using common collocations and phrases containing these words. A further problem for teachers and learners is that even a short search of AWL Sublist One words such as *data, estimate, contract* and *require* (let alone their family members) in one academic text can yield a daunting number of concordance entries and combinations. For example, the word family *require* occurred 3632 times in a corpus of approximately 3,500,000 running words of written academic texts; that is 590 occurrences in arts, 993 in commerce, 1216 in law and 833 in science (Coxhead 1998: 119). Schmitt (2000: 81), in his book on language teaching and vocabulary, states "One of the main pedagogical hurdles is the sheer number of collocational possibilities to deal with." Stubbs (2004: 7) points out that with access to major databases and software for identifying phrases in corpora, the major problems have become how to generalise with so much data and working out which questions to ask. Coxhead et al. (forthcoming) are expanding on the AWL by identifying its common collocations and recurrent phrases initially in a corpus of academic writing, and later in academic speaking, as one way to assist teachers with selecting phrases which are common enough for EAP learners to get a good return for learning. Coxhead et al. are basing the selection of items on their frequency, range and uniformity, as Coxhead (2000) did in the development of the AWL.

Another approach to identifying common formulaic sequences in academic context has been operationalised by Biber et al. (2004) in their frequency-based analysis of lexical bundles in university textbooks and classrooms. This interesting study provides useful insights into lexical bundles and EAP. The researchers find that in both function and frequency, these bundles differ from each other as well as conversation and academic prose (2004: 382–384). Some of the common bundles identified in this study include *I don't know if, I don't know* and *the fact that the* (2004: 384). Such items highlight several difficulties with selecting phraseological items for teaching using frequency alone. Firstly, what is frequent in one academic text, subject area or realm of use in an academic setting may not be so in another. Secondly, high frequency items such as *I don't know if* would perhaps hold little face value for learners in an EAP course, despite their frequency in classroom teaching and conversation. The co-occurrence of such items in two areas of student life should be helpful for teachers and learners in that prior knowledge of high frequency items should support new learning. However, learners may well believe they already know all about a high frequency word or not recognise or value a pattern it occurs in.

An exploratory study by Jones & Haywood (2004) focussed on learning and teaching the formulaic phrases found in (and shared by) four EAP course books of academic writing, selected on frequency through a corpus search and sorted according to Biber et al.'s (1999) grammatical categorisations of lexical bundles. This approach highlights the relatively new development in EAP textbooks towards presenting and practising lexical bundles. However, it also makes clear that such books select items for teaching by relying mostly on teacher intuition (Jones & Haywood 2004: 274), as many academic vocabulary EFL textbooks have done in the past. Jones and Haywood focus on approximately 80 lexical bundles the students encountered during the course, including noun phrases such as *the relationship between, there were no significant differences,* and *studies have shown that* (2004: 295). Here we have high frequency words such as *differences* being used with *significant,* which occurs in the AWL.

Yet another approach to find out what phrases to teach comes from Simpson & Ellis (2005), who include statistical measures such as Mutual Information and Log Likelihood in their corpus-based analysis of academic speech and prose, as well as teacher intuition, to allow teachers to make distinctions that are relevant to the data, in a way that frequency alone cannot. The resulting Academic Formulas list is to be based on similar principles as the AWL, in that the high frequency lexical bundles found in both academic corpora and general English corpora will be separated from the academic list, much in the same way as the General Service List (West 1953) was in the AWL study (Coxhead 2000). This approach will ensure that the contexts of occurrence are taken into account and may help identify formulaic sequences that have high frequency and are of general use, as well as ones that are more academic in nature.

Soon we may have a wealth of information about academic language-in-use. Lists of formulae or common collocations and phrases or lexical bundles are certainly useful tools for moving the field of language teaching for academic purposes ahead on surer ground. The question of how to teach such items requires attention.

2.3   What pedagogical approach should we use?

Teachers are under pressure to ensure that learners gain training in noticing collocations and lexical bundles, exposure to pedagogically sound methods of learning vocabulary, and opportunities to practise and gain feedback, as well as further opportunities to develop and maintain fluency in using the target language. All of this is expected to take place often in part-time three month courses whilst students are studying other subjects concurrently. As Kennedy (2003:483) points out, there is a need "…to devise a curriculum that maximises the opportunities for learners to get enough experience of the units of language in use in order to internalise them." Exactly what those units of language, elements of the curriculum and approaches to learning and teaching should be when teaching and learning formulaic sequences still requires research and evaluation (Jones & Haywood 2004:290).

Wray (2000), in an article in which she examines the approaches to teaching formulaic sequences put forward by Willis (1990), Nattinger & DeCarrico (1992) and Lewis (1993), identifies a basic contradiction behind teaching such sequences in an analytical way in language classrooms. She argues that the main idea behind a speaker choosing to use a formulaic sequence is to avoid the need to analyse the string; but language classrooms encourage the analysis of strings (Wray 2000:480). If educators are to somehow balance the analytical with the formulaic, Wray warns we need to be careful because as '… the potential for the very idiomaticity of an expression to make it less open to generalization than it may seem at first glance' (Wray 2000:484). It appears that teachers may well be at an impasse.

Learning a word in order to use it in writing is more difficult than learning a word for receptive purposes (Nation 2001:182). Researchers have been attempting to find ways to measure the effectiveness of teaching activities. Hulstijn & Laufer (2001) have developed the Involvement Load Hypothesis, whereby task-induced involvement is measured through three components: need, search, and evaluation.[1] They found that a composition task led to the highest amount of target word retention when compared with a reading comprehension task and a gap-fill and comprehension task. Folse (2006) compared the involvement load in three fill-in-the-blank activities and a composition task, in regard to verbs. Contrary to the previous study, he concluded that the gap-fill task led to more retention because of the repetition of target words. Folse's study shows the value of repetition or retrieval in classroom tasks. Knowledge of a word for production in writing is not limited to spelling and meaning, but includes context of use, grammatical accuracy, word parts and more (Nation 2001:28). Read (2004)

---

1. The components of the Involvement Load Hypothesis are *need, search* and *evaluation*. The load is calculated by the presence or absence of each of these components. *Need*, the motivational component, can be moderate or strong, depending on whether the motivation is extrinsic (moderate) or intrinsic (strong). *Search* involves finding the L2 meaning of a word, while *evaluation*, either moderate or strong, involves comparison between a word and other words to establish which would be better in a particular context (moderate) or 'how additional words will combine with the new word in an original context (as opposed to given) sentence or text (strong) (Hulstijn & Laufer 2001:544).

identifies three constructs of vocabulary knowledge vital for accurate productive use of words and phrases: precision of meaning, comprehensive word knowledge, and network knowledge.[2] These constructs have implications for testing, as Read points out. Clearly developing, measuring, and demonstrating lexical knowledge is not an easy task.

There is a lack of theoretical underpinnings directly related to teaching and learning formulaic sequences (Granger 1998). In vocabulary studies, theories and principles have been drawn on from psychology and linguistics. For example, three psychological conditions of learning that are useful for remembering words are outlined by Nation (2001:75). These principles are 'noticing' (Schmidt 2001) whereby learners are encouraged to notice and fill gaps in their learning, 'retrieval' whereby the learner retrieves either the form or meaning of a word from memory thereby strengthening the memory of that word (see Baddeley 1990) and 'generation' which Nation (2001:68) says "... occurs when previously met words are subsequently met or used in ways that differ from the previous meeting with the word." If such principles support individual word learning, they could or should perhaps also be useful with lexical bundles as well.

It is still unclear however whether teachers (should) provide explicit instruction on lexical phrases in the classroom or rely on rich exposure to these items to increase the students' knowledge (Schmitt et al. 2004:69). In vocabulary literature, there are mounting arguments for direct teaching and learning (Nation 2001). Laufer (2005:321) advocates for 'word-focused classroom instruction', or Planned Lexical Instruction (PLI) – an approach similar to form-focussed instruction where teachers ensure that students notice vocabulary presented accurately and have opportunities to develop their lexical knowledge through direct practice. Simpson & Ellis (2005) recommend a variety of direct learning activities including access to sound files and written corpora as well as classroom tasks. Hoey (2005:8), in his work on lexical priming, states that 'As a word is acquired through encounters with it in speech and writing, it becomes cumulatively loaded with the contexts and co-texts in which it is encountered, and our knowledge of it includes the fact that it co-occurs with certain kinds of context.' If direct learning is needed, what kind is best? How many encounters and what kind of exposure exactly and when?

---

2. *Precision of meaning* relates to 'the difference between having a limited, vague idea of what a word means, and having a much more elaborated and specific knowledge of its meaning' (Read 2004:211). *Comprehensive word knowledge* involves knowing about a word's meaning, collocations, syntax, morphology, orthography, and pragmatic relationships. *Network knowledge* involves including the word in the mental lexicon, along with being able to either connect it to other related words or to distinguish it from them.

Jones & Haywood's (2004) study used a variety of teaching methods to focus on the target formulaic sequences in reading activities. They drew attention to the words through highlighting, encouraging students to memorise and use the sequences in their writing, and using tools such as concordances. The learners also took part in writing classes in which they reviewed the sequences, analysed them in context, and completed gap-fill exercises (Jones & Haywood 2004: 276–278). The study found that although student awareness of formulaic sequences had increased during the period of the study, students did not do so well at learning and using the phrases in their writing. The researchers attributed this finding to students seeming not to memorise the target chunks well, or appearing to just focus on the target word they knew well and that was more salient (Jones & Haywood 2004: 289).

Like Jones & Haywood (2004), in my EAP classroom teaching and materials preparation I have employed the three psychological conditions of noticing, retrieval, and generation. The students work on *noticing* common collocations and phrases by reading texts with highlighted target lexical phrases as well as finding and teaching each other common collocations in authentic academic reading materials. Web-based tools such as the AWL Highlighter and AWL Gapmaker (Haywood, no date) are also used. *Retrieval* is practised through students retelling key sections of source text with or without source texts, constructing individual word cards for self-study and recycling target items and collocations regularly in class. *Generation* is encouraged through isolating target collocations in sentences and creating new texts around them. We also manipulate target items in source texts by paraphrasing, summary writing and quotation practice. Further practice is gained by composing longer essays and reports for feedback and end assessment.

However, the question of how effective these techniques are still remains. We need to know whether other learners, like those in the Jones and Haywood study, report that faulty memorisation techniques and an overriding focus on a salient and sole target word are major factors inhibiting their learning and use of formulaic sequences in writing. Or do risk, lack of instruction on how to use lexical bundles, or use of other bundles in writing cause difficulty (Cortes 2004: 421)? It is important to ask students in order to find out whether they express value or difficulty in the teaching and learning of phraseological units in EAP.

3.   What barriers do our students encounter in using formulaic sequences in their writing?

All six students in my small pilot study had just completed their first year of university study and on average had spent two and a half years in New Zealand studying a variety of majors: Human Resource Management, English Literature, Media Studies, Communication, Education and Economics/Mathematics. The study focussed on vocabulary use in writing. Participants wrote a timed essay on the topic of global warming, using either one or two input texts, and were then interviewed on their vocabulary use in the task (Coxhead in preparation). In the interviews the students were asked to talk about: any words in the reading texts they would have liked to have used in their writing but decided not to; the words and phrases used in their writing that were not in the input text/s; and whether they tried to include specific vocabulary items or phrases in their writing. These writers had much to say about the barriers they encountered in their writing for university, particularly with trying to use particular words and phrases successfully.

All participants reported on specific phrases or collocations they had noticed in the text/s. Some had incorporated such items in their writing, in the form of quotations or as part of a paraphrase or used them in a generative way, in particular if they were closely related to the topic of global warming (for example, *carbon emissions*) or were either reasonably transparent or easily translated into their first language (as in *ride-share*). A lack of knowledge of the words or a lack of time was given as a reason for not using noticed items in the writing task. One participant put it succinctly: 'I had not enough time to learn how to use this word yesterday when I was writing'. Another also made the comment that 'Highlighting words and telling students to use words is more important. If (they) are just underlined, we see and check and understand but may not use it'. Although lexical bundles had been noticed and not used, the participants demonstrated that they had acquired some level of knowledge about them by giving the meaning of the items when asked.

Risk was a factor most students reported as a hindrance in using freshly encountered phrases in context. Avoidance was the main coping strategy in this case. An extreme example of risk aversion was one writer who refused to use *emit pollution* in his writing because '*Emission* is connected to *emit* but if I write *emission*, it will be plagiarism because it is a special word' even though to have used his own collocation with the verb would have been appropriate in this context. A lack of motivation to use words was reported if any risk taking might lead to a lower assessment mark in an academic assignment because of language errors.

All participants called on lexical bundles they had been taught within language classes in China or foundation classes in New Zealand. In some instances they had read about the topic in newspapers or magazines or as part of their studies at Massey in subject areas such as Finance. Not all retrieval of previously learned phrases was accurate, as Jones & Haywood (2004) and Cortes (2004) reported in their studies. One participant used the expression 'a danger phenomenon' and identified it as one she knows well because she learned it from a text in

Chinese and also in her academic study. Others tried hard to incorporate known phrases into their writing. Several tried but gave up because of inaccurate recall or being unable to locate the sequence in a dictionary (one participant checked the dictionary for 'the cat race' when he actually wanted to write about 'the rat race'). Another problem was connecting the target phrase with the topic at hand. Most students reported that they did not think about collocations at all during the reading and writing task.

There was a genuine concern amongst participants to use academic and professional phrases in their writing so their writing 'sounds academic'. The main reasons for this concern were that lecturers might think their essays were 'easy' if the students just used easy words, that there was an expectation from lecturing staff that specific words and phrases from subject areas would be used by students, and that in doing so, the texts would be improved. It seems that these students might almost have read Wray's (2002) work on formulaic sequences facilitating the expression of identity within a group.

A final barrier to learning and using phrases was a pragmatic learning approach outlined by one participant but touched upon by several others. This particular student had decided that learning one word was hard enough, so why learn two or more? Verbs were her target, supposedly because they occur on their own. She did not bother with adverbs or adjectives because they required extra learning. Another student writer reported that she would be more confident in using in her writing a noun that she had just encountered in her reading, than a verb or adverb, because their meanings are 'more difficult to guess'. Schmitt & Zimmerman (2002), in their study of derivative word forms, found that students' knowledge of adverbs and adjectives was not as strong as that of nouns and verbs. Pragmatic approaches to learning such as deciding to only learn verbs or to focus on learning one word at a time have a major impact on the lexical knowledge of students and on their ability to take advantage of what lexical bundles have to offer their language development. When more research on EAP lexical bundles becomes more readily available, we might have more students recognising their value as one student did when he reported finding the AWL words really useful because he constantly encountered them in his university studies.

4.   Conclusion

In this chapter I have briefly outlined a dilemma for language teachers and learners. We need to apply contemporary research and concepts in our teaching of phrases and collocations, but how can we support the so-called 'end-users' in their endeavours to make progress when the nature and extent of these items has yet to be described? One way we might be able to answer this question is described by Wible (this volume), in which he discusses the contribution digital environments might make to support the acquisition of multi-word expressions and the development of resources for teachers and learners. A number of researchers are working in a variety of exciting ways to identify lexical bundles that give good return for learning. Meanwhile, the lack of theoretical underpinnings directly related to teaching and learning collocations and phrases causes difficulties, as does the problem of the analytical nature of language classrooms encountering the unanalysed chunks of formulaic sequences (Wray 2000). Research into whether current teaching methodologies are successful in their approach to teaching and learning such sequences is beginning through the development of such measures as the Involvement Load Hypothesis (Hulstijn & Laufer 2001). It appears that stipulating the use of target structures in tasks helps learners focus on them. Listening to students' voices is also important, because they have much to contribute to the discussion. Taking up the challenge of further research into phraseology and EAP may lead to opportunities to convince teachers and learners that it is worth focussing on more than just one word at a time.

References

Adolphs, S. & N. Schmitt (2003). Lexical coverage of spoken discourse. *Applied Linguistics 24* (4), 425–438.

Baddeley, A. (1990). *Human memory*. Hillsdale, NJ: Lawrence Erlbaum Associates.

Biber, D., S. Johannson, G. Leech, S. Conrad & E. Finnegan (1999). *Longman grammar of spoken and written English*. Harlow: Pearson Education.

Biber, D., S. Conrad, R. Reppen, P. Byrd & M. Helt (2002). Speaking and writing in the university: A multidimensional comparison. *TESOL Quarterly 36* (1), 9–48.

Biber, D., S. Conrad & V. Cortes (2004). *If you look at…*: Lexical bundles in university teaching and textbooks. *Applied Linguistics 25* (3), 371–405.

Corson, D. (1995). *Using English words*. Dordrecht: Kluwer Academic.

Cortes, V. (2004). Lexical bundles in published and student disciplinary writing: Examples from history and biology. *English for Specific Purposes 23*, 397–423.

Coxhead, A. (1998). The development and evaluation of an academic word list. M.A. thesis. Wellington, New Zealand: Victoria University of Wellington.

Coxhead, A. (2000). A new academic word list. *TESOL Quarterly 34* (2), 213–238.

Coxhead, A. (in preparation). Exploring vocabulary use in an EAP writing task. Massey University, Palmerston North, New Zealand.

Coxhead, A. & P. Byrd (forthcoming). Preparing writing teachers to teach the vocabulary & grammar of academic prose. *Journal of Second Language Writing*.

Coxhead, A., J. Bunting, P. Byrd & K. Moran (forthcoming). *The Academic Word List: Collocations and recurrent phrases*. Boston: University of Michigan Press.

Folse, K. (2006). The effect of type of written exercise on L2 vocabulary retention. *TESOL Quarterly, 40* (2), 273–293.

Granger, S. (1998). Prefabricated patterns in advanced EFL writing: Collocations and formulae. In Cowie, A. P. (ed.) *Phraseology: Theory, analysis and applications*, 145–160. Oxford: Clarendon Press.

Haywood, S. (n.d). *The AWL highlighter.* Available at http://www.nottingham.ac.uk/~alzsh3/acvocab/awlhighlighter.htm on 8 March 2005.

Hoey, M. (2005). *Lexical priming.* London: Routledge.

Howarth, P. (1998). The phraseology of learners' academic writing. In Cowie, A. P. (ed.) *Phraseology: Theory, analysis and applications*, 162–186. Oxford: Clarendon Press.

Hulstijn, J. & B. Laufer (2001). Some empirical evidence for the Involvement Load Hypothesis in vocabulary acquisition. *Language Learning 51* (3), 539–558.

Jones, M. & S. Haywood (2004). Facilitating the acquisition of formulaic sequences: An exploratory study in an EAP context. In Schmitt, N. (ed.) *Formulaic sequences*, 269–291. Amsterdam: John Benjamins.

Kennedy, G. (2003). Amplifier collocations in the British National Corpus: Implications for English language teaching. *TESOL Quarterly 37* (3), 467–487.

Laufer, B. (2005). Instructed second language vocabulary learning: The fault in the 'default hypothesis'. In Housen, A. & M. Pierrard (eds.) *Investigations in instructed second language acquisition*, 311–329. Berlin: Mouton de Gruyter.

Lewis, M. (1993). *The lexical approach.* Hove: Teacher Training Publications.

Nation, I. S. P. (2001). *Learning vocabulary in another language.* Cambridge: Cambridge University Press.

Nattinger, J. & J. DeCarrico (1992). *Lexical phrases and language teaching.* Oxford: Oxford University Press.

Read, J. (2004). Plumbing the depths: How should the construct of vocabulary knowledge be defined? In Bogaards, P. & B. Laufer (eds.) *Vocabulary in second language teaching*, 209–228. Amsterdam: John Benjamins.

Schmidt, R. (2001). Attention. In Robinson, P. (ed.) *Cognition and second language instruction*, 3–32. Cambridge: Cambridge University Press.

Schmitt, N. (2000). *Vocabulary in language teaching.* Cambridge: Cambridge University Press.

Schmitt, N. (2005). Processing advantages of formulaic sequences vs non-formulaic sequences in text passages. In Cosme C., C. Gouverneur, F. Meunier & M. Paquot (eds.) (2005) Proceedings of the Phraseology 2005 conference. 381–382. Université catholique de Louvain: Louvain-la-Neuve, 13–15 October 2005.

Schmitt, N. & C. Zimmerman (2002). Derivative word forms: What do learners know? *TESOL Quarterly 36* (2), 145–171.

Schmitt, N., Z. Dörnyei, S. Adolphs & V. Durow (2004). Knowledge and acquisition of formulaic sequences: A longitudinal study. In Schmitt, N. (ed.) *Formulaic sequences*, 55–71. Amsterdam: John Benjamins.

Simpson, R. & N. Ellis (2005). 'An academic formulas list'. In Cosme C., C. Gouverneur, F. Meunier & M. Paquot (eds.) (2005) Proceedings of the Phraseology 2005 conference. 391–394. Université catholique de Louvain: Louvain-la-Neuve, 13–15 October 2005.

Stubbs, M. (2004). On very frequent phrases in English: Distributions, functions and structures. Paper presented at ICAME 25, Verona, Italy, 19–23 May, 2004. Available at http://www.uni-trier.de/uni/fb2/anglistik/Projekte/stubbs/icame-2004.htm.

West, M. (1953). *A general service list of English words*. London: Longman, Green and Co.

Willis, D. (1990). *The lexical syllabus*. London: Harper Collins.

Wray, A. (2000). Formulaic sequences in second language teaching. *Applied Linguistics 21* (4), 463–489.

Wray, A. (2002). *Formulaic sequences and the lexicon*. Cambridge: Cambridge University Press.

Multiword expressions and the digital turn

David Wible

> So when she seemed disturbed or absent-minded, it was in fact, I think,
> that she was aware of too many things, having no principle for selecting
> the more from the less important, and that her awareness could never be
> diminished, since it was among the things she had thought of as familiar
> that this disaster had taken place.   Marilynne Robinson, Housekeeping

Increasingly the target language input that second language learners are exposed
to is digital. This chapter traces some of the implications of this digital turn for
the learning of multiword expressions. The underlying question being addressed
in the chapter is what sorts of digital resources and tools can foster learners'
mastery of multiword expressions. First, it is shown how multiword expressions pose a fundamentally different acquisition challenge for learners who rely
primarily on textual input compared to those who depend mainly on spoken
input. Unlike most literature on the acquisition of multiword expressions, the
chapter then concentrates on the challenge to the text-oriented learner. The
limitations of traditional paper and ink lexical resources are described in terms
of three qualities: they are static, centralized, and passive. The significance of the
digitalization of these resources (for example, machine-readable dictionaries)
is analyzed then through the lenses of these three qualities. Finally, the nature
of the Web as a massive, noisy digital archive is taken as an environment for
embedding a radically different sort of lexical resource for learning multiword
expressions, one that is dynamic, distributed, and active. An existing tool that
exemplifies this alternative, called Collocator, is described in terms of these
qualities.

1. Introduction

One of the few widely accepted tenets in second language research is that successful language learning requires exposure to target language input. A central motivation of this chapter is the fact that, increasingly, the input that learners encoun-

ter is digital.[1] From one point of view, this digitalization, or digital turn, could be seen as irrelevant to language learning. What difference does it make whether the news story I read appears to me on newsprint or on a computer screen? Why should it matter whether I look up an unknown word by turning the pages of a paper dictionary or by typing a query into an electronic one? If the content of the dictionary entry or the news story is the same in both cases, what difference could it make to my language learning whether it is represented to me with ink or pixels? Described from a Saussurean perspective, digitalization even at its most potent would seem to be an 'etic' rather than an 'emic' feature of language. An even weaker view could construe the digital dimension of language input as mere noise, on a par with whether or not spoken input comes from a speaker with laryngitis. It is perhaps for this reason that the digital turn, while having generated plenty of literature concerning language learning and teaching, has yet to appear on the radar screen of language acquisition theory.

This oversimplifies, of course, the potential impact of digitalization on language learning and education. Its effects go far beyond simply the material form of representation of language instances to language users. One of my purposes in this chapter is to trace some of these broader effects and their implications for learning multiword expressions.[2] Since currently so much of our digitally mediated exposure to language occurs on the World Wide Web, I eventually relate my discussion to the Web as the prototypical digital environment.

Before turning to digital technology, however, I describe a set of assumptions about the challenges that multiword expressions pose both to learners and to those designing lexical resources for learners. These will serve then to frame my approach to the role that digital environments can play in the learning and teaching of multiword expressions.

---

1. This is true not only of the language input learners encounter but of the language output they produce. A consideration of learner output in digital environments is important, but would deserve its own chapter. My graduate students and I have been doing work on learner output of multiword expressions in digital environments (Liu 2002; Wang 2005; Chen 2007). Wible (2005) devotes some chapters to learners' digital output and the conceptual issues involved in aspects such as automatic error detection, though the focus there is not on multiword expressions. In this chapter, however, I deal exclusively with digital environments as sources of input.

2. While Wray (2002: 9) lists more than fifty terms used to refer to multiword expressions of various sorts, for simplicity's sake, in this chapter I generally use the term *multiword expression* and in places for variety I use the term *lexical chunk* or *chunk* as its synonyms. I use the term *collocation* for a specific sort of two-word expression that is a sub-type of these as described in the text.

2. The challenge to learners

A common assumption in discussions of multiword expressions and language acquisition is that these strings first appear in the repertoire of the L1 or L2 learner as wholes which are only later discovered by the learner to contain subparts. For example, in her extensive review of formulaic expressions in second language acquisition, Weinert points to "…L1 and L2 acquisitional data which show that learners may initially operate with unanalyzed units which later become analysed" (1995: 198). Similarly, according to Schmitt & Carter "(T)here is a consensus that some L1 acquirers do learn and use formulaic sequences before they have mastered the sequences' internal makeup" (2004: 11). Nattinger & Decarrico describe this "from whole to parts" view of acquisition in more detail:

> One common pattern in language acquisition is that learners pass through a stage in which they use a large number of unanalyzed chunks of language in certain predictable social contexts. They use, in other words, a great deal of 'prefabricated' language. Many early researchers thought these prefabricated chunks were distinct and somewhat peripheral to the main body of language, but more recent research puts this formulaic speech at the very center of language acquisition and sees it as basic to the creative rule-forming processes which follow. For example, first language learners begin with a few basic, unvarying phrases, which they later, on analogy with similar phrases, learn to analyze as smaller, increasingly variable patterns. They then learn to break apart these smaller patterns into individual words and, in so doing, find their own way to the regular rules of syntax.
> (Nattinger & DeCarrico 1992: x)

Notice that this perspective does not account for how learners acquire lexical chunks as chunks. Rather, it suggests what happens subsequently: the learner next discovers that the chunk consists of component words. Instead of explaining how multiword chunks enter the competence of the language user as such, this view often assumes their existence in the learner's repertoire already and exploits this assumption to ascribe to them a role in the acquisition of words and syntax. Bybee (1998) has argued for a version of this view as an account of how the lexicon develops in L1 learners and has dubbed it the "emergent lexicon." Bolinger urged this view on several occasions (1976; 1977; inter alia) in a compelling corrective to the oversimplified notions of lexical knowledge in modular linguistic theories. For example, he says: "My claim is that *the dog* contrasts with *dog* before *dog* contrasts with *the*" (1977: 157).[3] That is, words are recognized after (and because

---

3. Neither Bybee nor Bolinger focuses on multiword expressions or lexical chunks per se, but considers all sorts of multiword strings (whether conventionalized expressions or simply

of) the larger strings they occur in. For example, an encounter with *dog* used independently of *the dog* (or an encounter, say, with the verb *give* used independently of the phrase *gimme*) is the child's chance to detect that these longer strings (*gimme* and *the dog*) may have separable parts. (Child: <u>*Gimme*</u> *cookie!* Parent: '<u>*Give*</u> *you what?*').

This sort of process involving unanalyzed chunks yielding to analysis by way of contrasts plausibly holds true for the emergence of substantial portions of the child's lexical repertoire: from *gotcha* to *got* and *you*; from *whatsat* to *whats that* to *what is that*, and so on. I will refer to this view as a "whole to parts" view or, following Bybee, as an emergent view of lexical acquisition.

There are two points I would like to make concerning this view relevant to this chapter's theme. First, as I noted above, it does not touch upon how lexical chunks or multiword expressions are mastered. It is intended rather to make the point that they appear in the language user's repertoire as wholes before the learner detects their parts. This view, therefore, is not particularly helpful in addressing how second language learners can come to master multiword expressions.

The second and more important point I want to make concerning the "whole to parts" view of lexical chunks is that it rests on an assumption which, while convincing for child L1 acquisition, is unwarranted in the case of a substantial portion of the second language learners in the world. Specifically, it assumes that the primary target language input to the learner (L1 or L2) is spoken input. In the case of spoken input, word boundaries are not reliably flagged in the speech stream. It is for precisely this reason that learners who rely on spoken input must discover these boundaries and the identity of words between them through such delicate, indirect means, for example by contrasting them with related variations: *gimme* vs. *give you*; *thedog* vs. *mydog* vs. *dog*, and so on. Notice, however, that this view loses force for learners whose input comes as text rather than speech. Unlike speech, text does contain conspicuous word boundaries in a hefty portion of the input the learners encounter: white space separates strings of alphabetic characters from each other.[4] Moreover, a substantial proportion of the world's adult language learners are learning in a foreign language rather than second language

---

compositional sequences as in Bolinger's example of *the dog*) to be fodder for learners' discovery of words within these strings.

4. This holds true of course only for particular sorts of writing systems. In the cases of highly isolating languages such as Chinese where a written character corresponds more or less directly to a morpheme, word segmentation is far from a trivial task for the reader; there are no typographic clues such as white space that correspond to lexeme boundaries. It is a shortcoming of this chapter, then, that in focusing upon English I assume with others (e.g., Carter (1998:4) cited in Bishop 2004) that word boundaries correspond quite closely to white space in text.

setting and in traditional classrooms where the primary source of target language input is text not speech.

These text-oriented learners require from researchers a different construal of the challenge that multiword expressions pose for the learner. Basically, for them the task is not one of unbundling what they first considered to be unanalyzed wholes without parts and discovering the word boundaries and the words inside, but the reverse: discovering that some sequences of the discrete units occurring between white spaces in text are in some respects best considered as bundled wholes despite the lack of typographical evidence that this is so. As far as I know, this challenge to the text-dependent learner has rarely been noted in the literature on the pedagogy and acquisition of multiword expressions.[5] It is, nevertheless, a central challenge for this population of learners, and I will suggest that digital language input can play a unique facilitating role in addressing it.

3. The challenges to lexicography

In making available useful knowledge about words, lexicographers traditionally have faced two major tasks: discovering lexical knowledge and representing it in forms useful to those who need it. I will refer to these as the tasks of discovery and representation. The digital turn has seen a revolution in how lexicographers approach both. There is a burgeoning literature on this that includes results from the fields of corpus linguistics and computational lexicography (for example, Boguraev & Briscoe (1989), Hanks (2003), Zernik (1991), Walker et al. (1995), inter alia). I would be doing this body of work a disservice and straying from my topic if I were to try to summarize it here. Instead I intend to sketch some implications that a phraseological perspective can contribute in applying lexical knowledge resources to foreign language education. Still for this, I use the perspectives of lexical knowledge representation and lexical knowledge discovery in turn.

4. Knowledge representation

Here I consider some implications of the digital turn for lexical knowledge representation and in particular for representing multiword expressions. The central purpose of this section is to suggest eventually that multiword expressions highlight the limitations of current conventions for representing lexical knowledge,

---

5. Some exceptions are Wray (2002: 206) and Bishop (2004).

and as such, they provide an opportunity both to examine the assumptions that underlie these conventions and to motivate alternatives to them.

Traditionally, the prototypical lexicographic artifact – the paper and ink dictionary – is static, centralized, and passive. I consider each of these traits of representation and sketch the impact wrought on them when the lexical resources become digital.

First, such lexical representations are static. Publishers of paper dictionaries must make irreversible decisions on what organizing principles will govern the ordering of information throughout an entire reference work and within each entry of that work. Once such volumes are published, their form of representation is fixed in indelible ink. For example, a traditional dictionary that lists entries in alphabetical order of their headwords serves as an extremely poor rhyming dictionary for lyricists. Even though an alphabetically organized dictionary has the same crucial phonetic information for its headwords that a rhyming dictionary relies upon, it is not a rhyming dictionary because of how that pronunciation information is ordered and represented. Likewise, a rhyming dictionary will be an awkward reference source if I encounter an unknown word in my reading and want to find out what it means. Alternatively, when I have an idea but lack the words to express it, an alphabetically ordered dictionary would leave me without a suitable entry point for my query; a thesaurus or a lexicon would serve me better.[6]

Machine-readable dictionaries can overcome some of the static qualities constraining paper representations. The same lexical resources represented in machine-readable form offer the possibility that this information can be represented to the user in a variety of ways, organized according to different lexical properties depending on the need of the user. Moreover, each of these representations can be supported by the same lexical database simply searched according to different fields.

More profoundly perhaps, the computer has made possible the creation of certain lexical resources that simply would not have been feasible under the constraints of paper and ink. WordNet has been designed as a machine-readable thesaurus structured according to lexical semantic relations among senses (Fellbaum 1998). I can query a specific word and, if it is polysemous, find the different senses of that word listed, much like a paper dictionary or thesaurus. WordNet 2.0, for example, lists four senses for the noun *medicine*. For any one of these four, I can be

---

6. Of course, this can be overcome in paper dictionaries by indexes and cross-indexing. And the design of such indexing is often a central criterion in judging the quality of a dictionary. Still, even the most user-friendly cross-indexing design requires a good deal of page turning back and forth and an exceptionally committed user.

shown all the words that share that same sense (that is, the set of synonyms denot-ing that single sense, what George Miller has dubbed a synset (1998: 23–24)). Just as easily, however, I can search for words that stand in a specific semantic rela-tion to any of those senses. A search for the hypernyms of each sense of *medicine* shows that *medicine* in its four different senses can be a kind of medical practice, a kind of medical science, a kind of drug, or a kind of punishment (as in the metaphorical expression 'take your medicine', which is listed as a synonym of *mu-sic* used metaphorically in 'face the music'). I can search downward from any of these senses for subordinate terms or hyponyms, and find, for example, 46 kinds of medicine in the sense of medical science (from allergology to virology) and 83 immediate subordinate terms for medicine in the sense of drug. I can continue seamlessly downward finding that a sedative is a kind of medicine and benzodi-azepine is a kind of sedative.

Because of the flexibility of machine-readable content, Miller and his col-leagues have been able to create a thesaurus that can instantiate a radically differ-ent conception of a lexicon, a net rather than a list. Notice, however, that it can be queried much the same way a paper dictionary would be, that is, by the spelling of a headword. WordNet has been adding definitions to the synset entries, providing a dimension of similarity to traditional dictionaries, with no need to completely rework its organizing principles. Medicine as a drug is defined in WordNet 2.0 as "something that treats or prevents or alleviates the symptoms of disease." Thus a word can be queried for its definitions, for its synonyms and for a path through a complex network of the lexical semantic relations it holds to other words and senses. In addition, nothing would prevent the addition of pronunciation data and the capacity to query for rhymes. This is one example of how digitalization can infuse flexibility into the otherwise static representations of lexical knowledge found in traditional dictionaries. A relational perspective on lexical knowledge (modeled on a net or web rather than a list) had to wait for the flexibility of digital representations before it could be instantiated in a usable resource. I hope to show below that likewise a phraseological perspective resists representation in the static list format of traditional dictionaries and calls for yet another alternative model made possible by machine-readable resources, still different from the relational model of WordNet.

A second limitation of the traditional dictionary representations of lexical knowledge is that they are centralized. The content is contained on pages bound between the covers of a volume or set of volumes. This limits their usefulness. How many steps am I willing to take from a comfortable armchair to retrieve a dictionary and look up an unfamiliar word I come across in my reading? Ma-chine-readable dictionaries can begin to narrow this distance. By dramatically reducing the space that the content occupies, a pocket-sized electronic dictionary, for example, is more portable than a paper version that would contain the same amount of content. One electronic dictionary currently on the market advertises 274,000 full definitions in a pocket device weighing 2.33 ounces.[7]

But digitalization supports a more radical portability since it enables one machine-readable resource to be viewed simultaneously by multiple users at great distances from the dictionary itself: the online dictionary. Any device that connects to the Internet and can browse the Web provides complete access to an online dictionary (in fact, to many of them), so for the user, the total size and weight of this lexical resource is zero.

Finally, in what would seem to be the ultimate step in bridging the gap between user and resource, digitalization opens the possibility that every line of text I read is shadowed by a dictionary. This is the possibility that arises when not only the dictionary is digital, but also the texts I read as well. For a number of years now there have been machine-readable dictionaries which can be queried from the text that the user is reading on a computer screen. The user clicks on an unknown word in the text and the dictionary entry for that form appears in a pop-up window. The software in this case performs a sort of string-matching between a string of characters in the text that the reader selects on the one hand and the word form variations of headwords in the dictionary on the other. A match between the selected string of text and a dictionary headword triggers the pop-up of that dictionary entry. The reading text itself may be a local file stored on the reader's computer or it may be a webpage stored on a server elsewhere and viewed from the reader's Web browser. In any case, this integration of text and dictionary made possible by digitalization closes the gap that typically has separated a reader holding a text here and the closest dictionary sitting on a bookshelf over there.

It would be unfortunate, however, to see the bridging of this physical gap as an end in itself. In what follows, I want to suggest instead that it puts us in a position to describe an alternative role for lexical knowledge resources and to recognize the specific constraints which prevent even current digital dictionaries from fulfilling such an alternative role. Multiword expressions provide the central motivation for this alternative; they are also a main reason current digital dictionaries are inadequate to support it.

---

7.   Without the two AAA batteries.

5.   Toward an alternative view of lexical knowledge and digital resources

Seen from a certain perspective, dictionaries that can be accessed by clicking on unknown words in a digital text share a deep similarity with stand-alone paper and electronic versions.[8] Though they differ in how they afford access to lexical knowledge, they share a certain view of what that lexical knowledge is. I will refer to this shared view as an "entry view" or "list view." It is the view, elucidated and incisively critiqued by Adam Kilgarriff (1993, 1997), that word meanings are discrete and can be readily discriminated and listed as individuated senses in an entry-type format familiar from the traditional dictionary. As Kilgarriff points out, this approach to representing lexical knowledge, rather than a reflection of a lexicographer's beliefs about word knowledge, is largely an artifact of the physical limitations of the book format to which lexicographers have traditionally had to conform.

One of the clearest illustrations that the entry view of word knowledge is inadequate comes, in fact, from multiword expressions.[9] Taking the verb *run* for example, if we consider some collocations in which *run* participates, then the idea of discrete senses for this verb starts to lose force.

Run a race
Run a company
Run a risk
Run a fever
Run a red light
Run amok

Clearly *run* has a different meaning in each of those expressions, yet it seems beside the point to try to capture each of them as discrete and definable within a dictionary definition. While a compositional semantics would require some individuated sense for the lexeme *run* in each case in order to build a meaning for the phrase *run a risk*, phraseological expressions pose a non-trivial challenge for such an approach to meaning and to the architecture of linguistic knowledge (Jackendoff 1995, inter alia). WordNet 2.0 distinguishes 41 senses of the verb *run*. Such a fine-grained yet discrete representation certainly plays a crucial role in a

---

8.   I should clarify that here I am referring to machine-readable dictionaries intended for direct access by dictionary users and not WordNet nor machine-readable lexicons found under the hood of various natural language processing applications such as machine translation systems.

9.   This discussion rehearses and extends the one found in Chapter 8 of Wible (2005).

range of computational linguistic applications; it might even successfully feed a compositional semantics for expressions containing *run*. Yet there is little appeal to the idea that a language learner's task in this case involves discovering which of the 41 discrete senses of *run* is denoted by that verb in *run a risk*. And it is unlikely that a language user's grasp of the expression *run a risk* derives from a bottom-up contribution of a discrete definition of *run*.[10]

The point here is that multiword expressions seen from a learner's point of view bring the lexicographer to the limits of the entry view of representation and call for a different picture. What we want is a perspective that would be more directly relevant to the needs of a language learner and that could suggest a representation of lexical knowledge more useful in the case of multiword expressions.

An alternative to the entry view could be called a contextual view of word identity. Taking cues from the Firthean tradition, this view would attribute a word's identity to the contexts of that word's uses (Firth 1957). From the philosophical literature, this would conform with the idea Wittgenstein distilled in the slogan "meaning is use" (1953). Along these lines, Kilgarriff proposes for lexicography an alternative to the discrete, entry view. He suggests that a word sense, rather than discrete and bounded, "…corresponds to a cluster of citations for a word… [C]itations are clustered together where they exhibit similar patterning and meaning" (1997:92). Thus, the more useful view of word senses is that they are "…abstractions over clusters of word usages" (p. 108).[11] I suggest that here lies a key to a tractable approach for helping learners with multiword expressions. After all, what is a multiword expression if not an abstraction over clusters of word uses; in other words, a patterning? The difference between the learner and the proficient language user encountering the string *run a fever* or *get out of here* or *make up (your) mind* in a text is that the learner does not see the string as a token of a pattern, as an instance of an abstraction. The learners who do not yet treat these strings as expressions have most likely not had sufficient salient encounters in their input to distill the disparate instances and recognize them as tokens of a type.

From this perspective we can construe a role for lexical knowledge sources in aiding learners with lexical chunks as providing the opportunity to make this abstraction from the limited encounters with the relevant tokens in the input. Below I elucidate this role made possible by a contextual approach and describe

---

10. Pustejovsky's work on the generative lexicon (1995) describes a computationally tractable approach to capturing the semantic relatedness among various senses of polysemous words and the fact that context can coerce sense extensions or modulations without resorting to simple discrete lists of senses. This knowledge-rich approach poses scalability challenges that make it currently impractical for the sorts of applications for learners that I am interested in here.

11. Kilgarriff defines a usage as "a particular occurrence of the word in a context" (1993:65).

a practical implementation for helping learners learn lexical chunks.[12] As background, I first turn to a third limitation of traditional dictionary representations that stands in the way of this implementation: besides being centralized and static, they are passive.

6.   Lexical representations as passive

Current lexical resources intended for end-users, whether they are machine-readable or paper, are useless unless the user recognizes a need for the information and initiates a query. This property of dictionaries has consequences. It means that a learner must recognize a particular gap in knowledge before such a dictionary can help address that gap. But some of the most persistent gaps in our second language knowledge are persistent precisely because we are unaware that they exist. In fact, I have already suggested that this is a central problem that multiword expressions pose for the text-oriented foreign language learner that I described above. As mentioned there, one reason that these expressions are challenging for learners whose primary input comes as text is that there is no indication in text that a particular string of words constitutes a chunk. In this respect, unknown chunks can be harder for a learner to recognize as unknown than, for example, unknown words. When I encounter an unfamiliar word in a text, the form itself strikes me as unfamiliar. I readily detect this as a gap in my lexical knowledge, and this is the first step that leads dictionary users to look something up (de Bot et al. 1997). Multiword expressions, however, can fly below radar in this respect, since many of them are made of familiar words combined in deceptively familiar ways.

---

12. I have been contrasting an entry view of word identity with a contextual view, suggesting that stand-alone dictionaries are modeled upon the entry view. Here I should point out that one of the most important developments in lexicography in recent decades has been the pioneering work of John Sinclair (as scholar and as editor-in-chief of COBUILD) in incorporating a contextual view of word identity within the tight confines of the traditional dictionary format. With respect to lexical knowledge discovery, Sinclair gave the machine-readable corpus a central role as knowledge source. In terms of lexical knowledge representation, COBUILD created a new notion of the dictionary definition, not simply describing a word meaning, but rather embedding the word's contextual traits within the very prose of the definition itself, for example, instantiating its collocations, selectional restrictions and its semantic prosody. I would also like to add that during the writing of this chapter I received news of Professor Sinclair's passing. We have lost a true pioneer. His contributions are profound and deservedly well-known. I know that I am only one of numerous EFL educators who dared to suggest that my students use English-English dictionaries only after Professor Sinclair's COBUILD editions appeared. And certainly, anyone trying to envision a next generation of lexical resources can do so only by standing on his shoulders.

Bishop (2004) investigated this possibility experimentally and found evidence that this is the case; subjects looked up unknown formulaic sequences significantly less frequently than unknown words when neither had been highlighted in the text. Bishop attributed this to the subjects' failure to recognize the multiword expression as an unfamiliar whole (p. 239). This property of multiword expressions is worth illustrating in some detail.

The close parallel between the following two sentences belies a less apparent phraseological difference between the strings *the matter* and *the problem*.

(1) a. What's <u>the matter</u> with the car?
     b. What's <u>the problem</u> with the car?

There is a difference and proficient English users grasp it. Yet from (1) it is easy to understand what Bishop (2004: 229) and others point out as the learner's difficulty in acquiring multiword expressions from input: the forms do not indicate which sequences are compositional and rule-generated and which are idiomatic wholes. The difference in the case of (1) becomes apparent only in contrast to other variations, for example, in potential answers to the question in (1):

(2) a. There's nothing <u>the matter</u> (with the car).
     b. *There's nothing <u>the problem</u> (with the car).

The contrast in (2) suggests that *the matter* is behaving idiomatically, that is, like a multiword expression rather than a rule-generated noun phrase. Specifically, while it looks like a typical noun phrase (say, like *the problem*), (2) shows that its distribution does not match that of a typical noun phrase. In fact, both in its semantics and its syntactic distribution, *the matter* here resembles instead a bare adjective: the adjective *wrong* in this case:

What's <u>wrong</u> with the car? There's nothing <u>wrong</u> (with the car).

The point here is that none of these distinctive features of *the matter* as an idiomatic chunk are apparent from an encounter with, say, (1a).

Recall that this example is intended to illustrate the consequences of the passive nature of dictionaries, be they paper or digital. In order to be of use, they require that the user take the initiative to consult them, and a typical scenario where this happens is when the user recognizes something in their input as unfamiliar. As the examples show, however, unlike unfamiliar words, unfamiliar multiword expressions encountered in text can seem deceptively familiar, sequences of words camouflaged within other sequences of words, some contiguous (*from the point of view of*) and some not (*take X into Y's own hands*), some of them chunks only when embedded within a particular larger string but not elsewhere (*the matter* in

What's the matter with him? but not in *They discussed the matter with him*), and rarely with an indication of their boundaries in these strings.

This challenge that foreign language learners face when encountering lexical chunks in text can be taken as a challenge to lexicographers as well. Whether the lexical resource is paper or digital, whether the look up requires just a mouse-click on the text or flipping through hundreds of paper pages, multiword expressions pose a two-fold problem. First, as I have already noted, a passive dictionary will not help a learner who does not recognize the input as unknown. The noun *matter* is one of the most frequent 400 words of English and it looks like any other definite noun phrase when it occurs in *the matter*. Why look anything up here? Second, even if a learner were to look something up here, a traditional entry-driven dictionary would be of limited value for a substantial number of the hundreds of thousands of multiword expressions. Imagine the unlikely case of a learner deciding to look up *matter* encountered in the string *What's the matter with the car? Collins COBUILD English Dictionary for Advanced Learners*, for example, will provide 26 definitions of the noun *matter* to choose from. One of them is a match (the 5th of the 26). In the case of massive numbers of other multiword expressions, there will be no relevant dictionary entry at all. Consider just a few: *the look on X's face*; *X went out of X's way to V*; *for the first time in X's Y* (e.g., *for the first time in her career*); Y *take X into Y's own hands* (e.g., *He took the law into his own hands*). And those lexical chunks that do appear in dictionaries often challenge the usefulness of the notion of headword. The chunk *point of view* can be found under the headword *point* but not under *view* in COBUILD, for example. These aspects of multiword expressions strain the conventions of representation in traditional lexicography, in particular here, the fact that these resources require the learner to know both when to consult them and how.

7.   **An illustration: Collocator**

In this section I sketch an existing tool that my colleagues and I have designed to implement an alternative to both traditional lexical knowledge representations and the entry view of words. To describe this implementation, I need to return to the picture of a digital world where both the text as well as the lexical knowledge sources are machine readable. Earlier I pointed out that this creates the possibility that a user can directly look up an unknown word in the text by simply clicking on it to access the relevant entry as a pop-up from the digital dictionary. I noted too that, despite the convenience, this still assumes a passive lexical resource which waits for the user to select a target word and initiate a look up of it. In the case of multiword expressions, one of the several limitations of passive resources that I pointed out is that they provide no way of overcoming the paradox that hinders text-oriented learners: learners encountering an unknown multiword expression in text may very well not recognize it as such; yet without this recognition the learner will not initiate a query and will thus miss an opportunity to learn it from the encounter.

The application I want to describe here exploits a similar setting – digital text and digital knowledge source – but it is designed to recognize actively for the user those portions of the text that are worth querying. This, of course, would constitute harassment of the user if it targeted individual words (What user wants pop-ups popping up above unselected words in their reading?). Rather, the tool is designed to detect multiword expressions in textual input and thereby help overcome the paradox that multiword expressions pose there for learners. In this case, the tool, called Collocator, detects collocations (Wible et al. 2004; Wible et al. 2006).[13]

Recall the promise of a contextual view of words as an alternative to the entry view of dictionary representation. Word senses are seen on this alternative view as clusters of usages. In fact, I borrowed Kilgarriff's contextual characterization of word meaning as a useful characterization of multiword expressions: they constitute clusters or patterns of word usages. Active detection of inconspicuous tokens of these patterns for the learner in text is Collocator's first step in bootstrapping out of the paradox. A further requirement for detecting a pattern is repeated exposure to tokens of it. A pattern, after all, is an abstraction of something recurrent. Thus, a second function of Collocator is to provide repeated exposure to ample instances of a detected multiword expression in a variety of contexts.

8.   Lexical knowledge discovery

I have discussed knowledge representation extensively yet said almost nothing so far about knowledge discovery, the other task of lexicography. Here I sketch how Collocator extracts the collocations it detects on the user's webpages. Using a 20-million word portion of British National Corpus (BNC), our algorithm applies mutual information (MI) measures to pairs of words that appear within a five-word window of each other in the running text of that corpus. The MI threshold score can be raised or lowered to adjust the recall and precision of the

---

13. Collocator has been developed in a collaboration between myself and members of Chin-Hwa Kuo's CAN laboratory at Tamkang University, particularly Nai-Lung Tsao. A more detailed description of its functionality and knowledge discovery techniques are given in Wible, Kuo, and Tsao (2004) and Wible et al. (2006).

searches.[14] Results are then stored and referenced as the collocational knowledge base of Collocator.

For the tool to detect and display collocations occurring in a webpage that the user is viewing, the user activates Collocator on that page by clicking an icon on the browser's toolbar. Note that this is not the same as a passive resource that requires a user to submit a specific query. To activate the Collocator, a user need not select any target words or collocations. This is because our working assumption is that learners may well be unaware of which word combinations encountered constitute multiword expressions (specifically collocations in the case of the Collocator tool). Accordingly, it is crucial to the tool's design philosophy that it not require the user to target a specific collocation for query. Instead, at the user's request Collocator actively searches the current webpage to detect occurrences of collocations there. This means that the tool can uncover collocations in the text which the user would be unable to recognize as collocations unaided. Results can be displayed on a dropdown menu from the browser toolbar. Each collocation detected in that webpage is listed on that menu as a pair of words (in base form), for example *seek…help*. Two options are given for each pair on the list: (1) highlight within the webpage the token of the collocation that Collocator detected there, and (2) show more examples of that collocation from BNC, thus providing the repeated exposure that reveals the pattern to be in fact a pattern.

Here it is worth pointing out certain novel challenges that must be addressed if a tool is to actively detect multiword expressions in real time. To frame this family of challenges I compare such a tool with a traditional stand-alone dictionary and the sort of lexical knowledge discovery involved in both. Unlike simple lexemes, collocations and other multiword expressions cannot be detected reliably by simple string matching (that is, by the identification of a fixed string of characters between white spaces). The main reason these expressions resist detection by string matching is that the words in a collocation or other multiword expression need not be adjacent to each other. For example, *spend time* could occur as simply *spend time*, but also as *spend a lot of time*, *spend more time*, *spend the greatest portion of time*, and so on. String matching is not up to the task of detecting all of these various tokens as instances of the same collocation.

Notice that a traditional static and passive resource need not perform under these conditions. Lexicographers can carefully deliberate over the choice of example sentences to include in a dictionary entry; whether a sentence that a user encounters in his or her reading is also an instance of this word usage need be of no concern to the dictionary writer. That responsibility lies with the user. With an

14. The tool is not confined to a specific statistical measure for discovering collocations. We are currently comparing results among a variety of word association measures.

active tool like Collocator, however, this responsibility shifts from the user to the tool itself. Collocator not only stores collocations in its knowledge base, but must determine case by case whether those collocations occur in the text that the user is reading. If we take this task as a sort of lexical knowledge discovery, then it is a kind of discovery that traditionally lexicographers have not had to address. In detecting cases of *spend time*, for example, Collocator must discriminate between the true positive *spend increasing amounts of their time* and the non-instance *spend so much and have time to enjoy it*. Automatically detecting collocations in real time for the user also involves finer distinctions than this. For example, in the case of *take place*, there is more than one collocation that could constitute a true positive. *Take place* is a collocation and it means 'occur'. In addition, however, non-adjacent cases of *take...place* could be either non-instances that the tool should pass over (as in *take this to your place*) or a true positive of a different collocation which the tool should detect (as in *take the teacher's place* or *take the place of*, meaning 'replace'). There is a variety of possible computational approaches to this task, for example, involving pattern matching or syntactic parsing (See Wible, Kuo, Tsao & Hung (2006) for some work on this).

Digital environments raise the possibility that our lexical resources for learners can be active and dynamic rather than passive and static. My point here has been to sketch how the nature of multiword expressions on the one hand and the goal of making the learners' resources active and dynamic on the other raises the bar for lexicographers and opens a range of novel yet tractable research issues.

9.   Learning multiword expressions and the nature of the World Wide Web

The World Wide Web is a massive archive of digital documents that can be linked to each other thanks to the Internet underlying the Web and to the capacity of the Web's mark-up conventions to create these links among documents. The Web is easily the largest collection of documents in history. Some estimates put the number of distinct websites as of February 2007 at over 100 million and the number of webpages at just under 30 billion.[15] Yet unlike any other large, respectable collection of documents, the Web stores its documents in a way that has no relation to what those documents are about. Think of an imaginary library that shelves books according to a lottery run by the acquisitions librarian. There is no Dewey

---

15. I found this information by following FAQ links on the World Wide Web Consortium's website at http://www.w3.org/WWW/, which led to these estimates at http://www.boutell.com/newfaq/misc/.

Decimal-like system or ontology that assigns a location or address to a webpage according to its content. This chaos is arguably the main reason such attention (and money) is lavished on the navigation level of the Web, its search engines like Google (Battelle 2005).

Turning to language learning, there are roughly two ways of construing the Web as a language learning environment. First, the Web can be used as a location for storing and publishing content designed explicitly for language learning. Content of this sort would include online language lessons or activities perhaps within online course websites and this possibly within a larger Learning (Activity) Management System (LMS or LAMS). It would also include online learner dictionaries or other reference sources intended for language learners or teachers. To benefit from these sorts of content, however, users must find them (locate their Web address and go there) and remember where they found them or bookmark them if they intend to return. Achieving the critical mass of user traffic or social convergence on a website that is needed to make its content widely useful is becoming more daunting with each new million websites that are created monthly.[16]

Language learning on the Web along the lines of this first approach has some strikes against it with respect to learning or teaching multiword expressions. First, since the number of these expressions is so vast and they fit so poorly into the static representations that centralized learning content would require, any attempt to author content for learning lexical chunks would meet a bottleneck almost immediately if attempted on a large scale or merely scratch the surface of the relevant domain if attempted on a small scale.

A second way of viewing the Web as a source for language learning is to see it as a massive archive of pre-existing content that has not been designed for the purpose of language learning and teaching but which learners and teachers can exploit for that purpose. The line of reasoning I have been following throughout this chapter comports better with this second view of the Web as a resource for learning multiword expressions. We have exploited this approach, for example, with the Collocator by creating a tool that piggy-backs on the navigational level of the Web, following users in their unrestricted browsing of its existing content. In doing so, however, we have imposed on ourselves some novel challenges. Since our tools are intended to work in real time on whatever texts the user chooses to browse, those tools need to be more robust than resources intended, say, to help experienced lexicographers find patterns in corpus data for inclusion in traditional dictionaries. And scaling this approach up to work on longer lexical chunks

---

16. Based on the Netcraft Web Server Survey, the number of existing websites increased by over 19 million in the last six months of 2006 (http://news.netcraft.com/archives/web_server_survey.html).

presents substantial but tractable issues that constitute a current research program for us (Wible, Kuo, Tsao & Hung 2006).

10.   Conclusion

Digital environments offer fertile ground for acquiring multiword expressions and for creating well-motivated resources for fostering this acquisition process. Criteria for designing such resources should go beyond concerns for convenience of look up. Ideally, these criteria will extend to alternative ways of conceiving of the situated user in these environments, of the precise difficulties that multiword expressions present for them there, the new sorts of lexical knowledge that this requires, and novel means of both discovering it and representing it to learners.

Acknowledgements

Research reported in this chapter was supported by Taiwan's National Science Council, grant #NSC93-2524-S-032-005.

References

Battelle, J. (2005). *The search: How Google and its rivals rewrote the rules of business and transformed our culture*. London: Portfolio.

Bishop, H. (2004). The effect of typographic salience on the look up and comprehension of unknown formulaic sequences. In Schmitt, N. (ed.) *Formulaic sequences: Acquisition, processing, and use*, 227–240. Amsterdam: John Benjamins.

Boguraev, B. & T. Briscoe (eds.) (1989). *Computational lexicography for natural language processing*. London: Longman.

Bolinger, D. (1976). Meaning and memory. *Forum Linguisticum, 1*, 1–14.

Bolinger, D. (1977). Idioms have relations. *Forum Linguisticum, 2*, 157–169.

Bybee, J. (1998). The emergent lexicon. *Chicago Linguistics Society 34*, 421–35.

Chen, H.-J. (2007). *Effects of input in the acquisition of formulaic sequences by EFL learners in Taiwan*. PhD dissertation, Tamkang University, Taiwan.

de Bot, K., T.S. Paribakht & M. Wesche (1997). Towards a lexical processing model for the study of second language vocabulary acquisition. *Studies in Second Language Acquisition, 19*, 309–29.

Fellbaum, C. (ed.) (1998). *WordNet: An electronic lexical database*. Cambridge MA: The MIT Press.

Firth, J.R. (1957). *Papers in Linguistics 1934–1951*. London: Oxford University Press.

Hanks, P. (2003). Lexicography. In Mitkov, R. (ed.) *Handbook of computational linguistics*, 48–69. Oxford: Oxford University Press.

Jackendoff, R. (1995). The boundaries of the lexicon. In Everaert, M., E.-J. van der Linden, A. Schenk & R. Schreuder (eds.) *Idioms: Structural and psychological perspectives,* 133–165. Hillsdale NJ: Lawrence Erlbaum Associates.

Kilgariff, A. (1993). Dictionary word sense distinctions: An enquiry into their nature. *Computers and the Humanities, 26,* 365–387.

Kilgariff, A. (1997). 'I don't believe in word senses'. *Computers and the Humanities, 13,* 91–113.

Liu, A. L.-E. (2002). A corpus-based lexical semantic investigation of verb-noun miscollocations in Taiwan learners' English. MA thesis. Tamkang University, Taiwan.

Miller, G. (1998). Nouns in WordNet. In Fellbaum, C. (ed.) *WordNet: An electronic lexical database,* 23–26. Cambridge MA: The MIT Press.

Nattinger, J. R. & DeCarrico, J. S. (1992). *Lexical phrases and language teaching.* Oxford: Oxford University Press.

Pustejovsky, J. (1995). *The generative lexicon.* Cambridge MA: The MIT Press.

Robinson, M. (1980). *Housekeeping.* New York, NY: Farrar, Straus, Giroux.

Schmitt, N. & R. Carter (2004). Formulaic sequences in action: An introduction. In Schmitt, N. (ed.) *Formulaic sequences: Acquisition, processing, and use,* 1–22. Amsterdam: John Benjamins.

Walker, D., A. Zampolli & N. Calzolari (eds.) (1995). *Automating the lexicon: Research and practice in a multilingual environment.* Oxford: Oxford University Press.

Wang, W.-J. (2005). The effects of degrees of explicitness of automated feedback on English learners' acquisition of collocations. MA thesis, Tamkang University. Taiwan.

Weinert, R. (1995). The role of formulaic language in second language acquisition: A review. *Applied Linguistics, 16*(2), 180–205.

Wible, D. (2005). *Language learning and language technology: Toward foundations for interdisciplinary collaboration.* Taipei: Crane.

Wible, D., C.-H. Kuo, M.C. Chen, N.-L. Tsao & T.-F. Hung (2006). A ubiquitous agent for unrestricted vocabulary learning in noisy digital environments. *Lecture Notes on Computer Science, 4053,* 503–12.

Wible, D., C.-H. Kuo, N.-L. Tsao & T.-F. Hung (2006). A computational approach to the discovery and representation of lexical chunks. *Proceedings of TALN 2006,* 868–875.

Wible, D., C.-H. Kuo, N.-L. Tsao (2004). Contextualizing language learning in the digital wild: Tools and a framework. *Proceedings of IEEE International Conference on Advanced Learning Technologies.* Joensuu, Finland.

Wittgenstein, L. (1953). *Philosophical investigations.* London: Macmillan.

Wray, A. (2002). *Formulaic language and the lexicon.* Cambridge: Cambridge University Press.

Zernik, U (1991). *Lexical acquisition: Using on-line resources to build a lexicon.* Hillsdale, NJ: Lawrence Erlbaum Associates.

Recording and exploiting phraseological units

Phraseology in learners' dictionaries

What, where and how?

Dirk Siepmann

This chapter raises the question as to whether learners' dictionaries adequately represent routine formulae in terms of coverage and generativity. Most monolingual learners' dictionaries are found to concentrate rather too narrowly on traditional non-compositional idioms, while severely neglecting routine formulae which are semantically fully transparent (cf. Siepmann 2005b), thereby failing to conform to semantically-oriented definitions of collocation (e.g. Hausmann 2003; Mel'cuk 2003).

1.   Introduction

The constant growth of machine-held corpora has provided us with increasing evidence of the essentially phraseological nature of language (Sinclair 1991; Feilke 1996; Altenberg 1998; Wray 2002). Stemming from this, there has been growing recognition that both in first and second language acquisition, phraseological competence is at the centre of linguistic competence rather than at the periphery. Lexical approaches to foreign language teaching in particular (Lewis 2000; Segermann 2003) have stressed the importance of raising students' awareness of conventionalized expressions while at the same time drawing attention to their re-analysability for productive purposes.

This raises the question as to whether learners' dictionaries adequately represent phraseology in terms of both coverage and generativity. The present chapter is an account of a number of empirical investigations into this question, focussing on semantically fully transparent routine formulae. Most monolingual learners' dictionaries are found to concentrate rather too narrowly on traditional non-compositional idioms (e.g. *carry the can*) and collocations (as defined in the semantically-based approach to collocation; e.g. *confirmed bachelor*), while severely neglecting routine formulae which are semantically fully transparent (cf.

Siepmann 2005b). As a result, they fail to conform to semantically-oriented definitions of collocation (e.g. Hausmann 2003; Mel'čuk 2003).

After a brief discussion of various approaches to defining collocation in Section 2, Section 3 presents the results of a few spot checks into coverage of these
items in learners' dictionaries. Section 4 reviews evidence from a growing literature which shows that learners are either not aware of semantically transparent
items or fail to use them adequately. Section 5 argues that this situation could be
remedied by providing learners with onomasiological rather than semasiological
dictionaries.

2. Definitions of collocation

This is not the place for a detailed discussion of various definitions of collocation
(see Herbst 1996; Hausmann 2003; Siepmann 2005b). Suffice it to say that the
subject of collocation has been approached from three main angles:

- Semantically-based approaches (e.g. Benson 1986; Mel'čuk 1998; González-
  Rey 2002; Hausmann 2003) assume that collocations are typically made up of
  two constituents which differ in their semantic status: a semantically autonomous base such as *compliment* combines with a semantically dependent collocate such as *pay*, such that the collocate takes on a specific meaning ('offer')
  contingent on the base. In many cases this distinction of semantic status allows semanticists to differentiate between collocations and free combinations
  (semantically autonomous + semantically autonomous: *he likes money*) on
  the one hand, and collocations and phraseology (i.e. semantically irregular
  items) on the other.
- The frequency-oriented approach looks at statistically significant co-occurrences of two or more words. It is therefore alone in providing a workable
  heuristic for discovering the entire class of co-occurrences, but its exclusive
  reliance on automatic statistical analysis has sometimes led to the inclusion
  of chance co-occurrences such as 'hotel at', 'either hotel' (Kjellmer 1994) or
  'nature because' (Sinclair 1995) and to an insufficient consideration of lexico-
  grammatical and semantic-pragmatic factors. As noted by Klotz (2000: 83),
  for example, a purely formal analysis of collocations such as *catch + ball* is
  insufficient to disambiguate the verb, which can be variously paraphrased as
  'grab' or 'hit'.
- A third, more recent approach to phrasemes and collocations (Feilke 1996,
  2003) might be termed 'pragmatic', since it claims that the structural irregu-
  larities and non-compositionality underlying such expressions are diachron-

ically and functionally subordinate to pragmatic regularities which determine the relationship between the situational context and linguistic forms. In this view, collocation can best be explained via recourse to contextualisation theory (Fillmore 1976). In other words, idiomaticity is independent of particular syntactic-semantic configurations; its *raison d'être* is a conventional restriction on usage established by speakers. The proverb *he who laughs last laughs best* is a case in point. It is syntactically irregular by today's standards and would therefore normally be regarded as a prime example of a phraseological item. However, its German equivalent *wer zuletzt lacht, lacht am besten*, although not irregular, is still idiomatic and usually receives only one of several possible interpretations (thus, it does not mean, for example, 'the person who is the last to laugh has the most pleasant laugh'). This approach, however, runs into difficulties when it comes to explaining a large number of co-occurrences operating at the level of semantic features (cf. Siepmann 2005b: 424–430), such as long-distance collocations of the type *turning to ... we find / we note*.

The problems attendant upon these three approaches can be resolved in all-encompassing approaches to language theory (Hoey 2005) and lexicography (Siepmann 2005b) which take collocation as their starting point. In keeping with neurological evidence on the structure of the brain (Lamb 1999), such approaches assume that, in speakers' minds, lexical items become progressively loaded with all sorts of information about their typical grammatical, lexical, semantic and pragmatic contexts of use. In Hoey's terms, words and other units may be 'primed' for lexical and grammatical collocation as well as for semantic-pragmatic association.

The present chapter focuses on lexical items of regular syntactic-semantic composition whose co-occurrence is statistically significant; nevertheless these would be classified as free combinations under the semantic approach to collocation. Typical examples of such 'fully transparent' collocations are English *I've got [liquid, crumbs, etc.] all over my [item of clothing, body, body part]* or French *regarde où tu vas* (*watch where you put your feet, watch where you are going*). For one thing, these items are clearly not idioms, since they are immediately comprehensible to anyone who is familiar with their basic constituents. For another, it is evident that the 'literal' meaning of a lexical realisation of the first example sentence, such as *I've got grease all over my shirt*, could only be construed as referring to a shirt entirely smeared with grease, but, of course, this is not what the sentence means to a native speaker, who will take it to mean that only part of the shirt's surface has been stained. Thirdly, the same meaning could be expressed quite differently in another language such as German: *I've got grease all over my shirt -> ich habe mein Hemd mit Fett beschmiert / mein Hemd ist voller Fett / mein Hemd ist ganz fettig*. Similar observations can be made for the second example, where the interlingual equivalents clearly show that the phrase is idiomatically constrained. The standard German translation uses two entirely different and more specific verbs: *pass auf, wo du hintrittst.*

Interestingly, then, what is a seemingly free combination in one language may translate as a collocation, thus revealing its conventionality: *den Rock enger machen* (seemingly free) –> *take in the skirt* (collocation) (Siepmann 2005b: 420).

3.   Coverage of semantically transparent items in encoding dictionaries

A number of market-leading monolingual learners' dictionaries and bilingual encoding dictionaries were tested on their coverage of fully transparent collocations. The major finding is that semantically transparent items are still largely ignored

Table 1. Fully transparent spoken-language collocations in four major learners' dictionaries

Multi-word marker	Oxford Advanced Learner's Dictionary (2005)	Cambridge International Dictionary of English (2001)	Collins Cobuild English Dictionary (2001)	Longman Dictionary of Contemporary English (2003)
1. my thoughts (thinking, feelings, point, sentiments etc.) exactly	–	–	–	–
2. I'll get it (e.g. phone)	–	–	–	–
3. don't ask	SUB-ENTRY	–	–	SUB-ENTRY
4. too much to ask	–	–	–	–
5. It's got to mean something	–	–	–	–
6. Once a N, always a N	SUB-ENTRY	–	–	SUB-ENTRY
7. are you busy?	–	–	–	–
8. I know a NP when I see one	– (example in sense division 7)	–	–	–
9. even if I say so/it myself	–	–	–	–
10. have you seen the time? (= is that the time, look at the time)	–	–	–	–

by these dictionaries, which in many other respects are superb accomplishments of corpus-based lexicography. Let us now consider the results in some detail.

3.1 Spoken English

The first spot check concerned ten items randomly selected from a corpus comprising spoken material (transcripts of American and British radio programmes, parliamentary proceedings, etc.) and fiction. The items included what would traditionally be deemed fixed expressions, such as *don't ask* and colligations of the type *my* NP *exactly*, where the noun phrase slot allows a number of variants (e.g. *feelings*, *sentiments* or *thoughts*). The results can be seen in Table 1.

Although the spot check may not reflect a representative selection, the results appear to suggest that there is still rather patchy coverage of semantically transparent multi-word units in the four big learners' dictionaries, and that there would not have been much point in including further items in the search. There are only two items which have been given sub-entry status in the most recent re-editions of the *Longman Dictionary of Contemporary English* and the *Oxford Advanced Learner's Dictionary*.

3.2 Written English

A similar picture emerges from an investigation into fully transparent items typical of written language. The results can be seen in Table 2.

The items chosen here are recurrent multi-word units, most of which are peculiar to academic writing. Since these multi-word units serve the pragmatic function of signalling the coherence relations between two pieces of text, Siepmann (2005a) refers to them as 'multi-word discourse markers' or 'second-level discourse markers', where the word *level* refers to frequency levels, in order to set less frequent second-level markers apart from the more common first-level discourse markers such as *nevertheless* or *however*.

Here too it is evident that semantically transparent multi-word markers, which constitute semantic units in their own right, are not usually given entry status. There is only one exception to this, in that Longman records the summary marker *to sum up*.

There are also a few examples of the use of multi-word markers in the dictionaries in question. In OALD 7 (2005), for example, the items *to sum up* and *simply put* have been highlighted in an illustrative sentence. CCED 3 (2001) provides some guidance on multi-word markers based on the verb *put*, but fails to point

Table 2. Fully transparent written-language collocations in four major learners' dictionaries

Multi-word marker	OALD (2005)	CIDE (2001)	CCED (2001)	LDOCE (2003)
1. We may guess that	–	–	–	–
2. to sum up	– (highlighted in example)	–	– (in example)	ENTRY
3. to use ADJ/poss N term	–	–	–	– (in example: *to use the technical term*)
4. similarly with	–	–	–	–
5. it is different with	–	–	–	–
6. this brings us/me to NP	–		–	ENTRY
7. simply put (stated) / put simply	– (highlighted in example)	–	– ('you can use ex- pressions like *to put it simply* before say- ing something ...')	–
8. to recap(itulate)	–	–	– (*to recap briefly* in example)	–
9. for complete- ness / for the sake of completeness	– (in example)	–	–	– (in example)
10. note that	– (spoken use in example)		– (spoken use in example, sense division 10)	–

out the wide variety of possible patterns (*simply put, simply stated, stated simply, to put it simply*, etc.).

The situation with the full-size bilingual dictionaries is very similar. Among other things, the English-French and English-German sections of five dictionar- ies were tested for coverage of the same multi-word markers (see Table 3).

The results speak for themselves: today's bilingual dictionaries are still a long way from giving such markers adequate treatment, and there is no significant dif- ference in coverage between language pairs. With three correct renderings out of ten and another not far out, the *Oxford Hachette French Dictionary* shapes up best among all the dictionaries examined. The *Collins German Dictionary* also has two workable equivalents to offer. All other dictionaries have two acceptable transla- tions at the most.

Table 3. Fully transparent written-language collocations in five major bilingual dictionaries

Multi-word marker	Le Robert & Collins Senior (1993)	Oxford Ha-chette French Dictionary (2001)	Collins German Dictionary (1997)	Langen-scheidts Handwörter-buch Englisch (1995)	Muret-Sanders Großwörter-buch Eng-lisch (1979)
1. we may guess that	–	–	–	–	–
2. to sum up	en résumé / pour récapituler	pour récapituler / en résumé	zusammen-fassend / ?als Resümee	–	
3. to use X's term / in X's words	–	pour reprendre l'expression de	mit Goethe gesprochen, um mit Goethe zu sprechen	–	mit den Worten (gen)
4. similarly with	–	–	–	–	–
5. it is different with	–	–	–	–	–
6. this brings us/me to NP	–	ceci m'amène à la question de	–	–	–
7. simply put (stated)	–	–	–	–	
8. to recap(itulate)	–	–	–	–	
9. for complete-ness / for the sake of com-pleteness	–	–	–	–	–
10. note that	–	–		–	–

As far as the other translation direction is concerned (see Table 4), a cursory glance at some of the target-language renditions shows that uni-directional trans-lations rather than target-language corpus enquiries have served as the source of data.

A case in point is the translation of *es ist zu vermuten, dass* by *it may be sup-posed that* in *The Collins German Dictionary*. Close reading of authentic texts shows renderings such as the following to be either more common or more in keeping with modern style: *it is fair/reasonable to assume that, it is a reasonable assumption that, it is easy to suppose that.*

A redeeming feature of *The Collins German Dictionary* and *Le Robert & Col-lins Senior* is that their essay writing sections contain a fair number of multi-word markers. Of those not found in the above spot check, four (*in s.o.'s words; to sum*

Table 4. Fully transparent collocations in five major bilingual dictionaries

Multi-word marker	Langenscheidts Handwörter- buch Franzö- sisch (1995)	Pons Groß- wörterbuch Französisch (1996)	Collins German Dictionary (1999)	Langen- scheidts Handwörter- buch Englisch (1995)	Muret-Sanders Großwörter- buch Englisch (1979)
1. es ist / steht zu vermuten, dass	–	–	it may be supposed that (?), we may assume / pre- sume that	–	it is to be presumed that (?) / it must be assumed that (?)
2. halten wir fest:	–	–	–	–	–
3. vieles spricht dafür, dass / es spricht vieles dafür, dass	–	–	there is every reason to be- lieve that (?)	–	many facts in- dicate that (?)
4. gleiches gilt für	–	–	the same goes for	the same applies to (F goes for)	the same holds good for
5. anders verhält es sich mit	–	–	–	–	–
6. womit wir bei (NP) wären	–	–	–	–	–
7. vereinfacht gesprochen / ge-sagt	–	-	–	–	–
8. zur Erinner- ung:	–	–	–	–	–
9. der Vollstän- digkeit halber	pour compléter (quelque chose)	pour être complet, pour ne rien laisser de côté	to complete the picture	for the sake of completeness	for the sake of completeness, to complete things / the whole (?)
10. man beachte, dass (here in the sense of 'es ist bemerkenswert, dass')	–	–	–	–	–

up; to recap; es steht zu vermuten, dass) can be found in this part of the *The Collins German Dictionary.*

The empirical investigations reported above suggest that collocations of regular syntactic-semantic composition have suffered comparative neglect in general learners' dictionaries. By contrast, the majority of collocations which fall within the scope of the semantically-oriented approach (see Section 2) can be found in these reference works.

One may then wonder why the former type of word sequences still goes largely unrecorded in learners' dictionaries. One reason is to do with the evolution of linguistics itself. Since the pervasiveness of collocations of regular syntactic-semantic composition has only just begun to be described in the linguistic research literature, dictionary makers cannot be expected to have a clear policy on the inclusion of such items; they may continue to be viewed as rule-based strings of words with little or no individual meaning or function. Their central importance for non-native writers and translators is still being largely overlooked.

As far as monolingual dictionaries are concerned, another closely related reason may be that the lexicographic teams which put together these dictionaries usually consist of native speakers of English only, many of whom may have little experience of foreign languages. This group must find it particularly difficult to notice the idiomaticity of semantically transparent items, since this idiomaticity becomes much clearer from the contrastive perspective of the foreign-born learner.

A third reason which probably applies only to the spoken language is that spoken corpora are still fairly small and that many of the items under discussion may not occur frequently enough in such corpora to attract the attention of the lexicographer or to show up in the results produced by the corpus-enquiry software. This is especially true of variable colligations such as *my* NP *exactly* where the frequency of one particular lexicalisation of the pattern is fairly low.

4.   Semantically transparent collocations in learner language

This section will briefly review the available evidence on learners' use of phraseology, focussing on the use of written-language collocations of regular syntactic-semantic composition. It can be reasonably hypothesized that there is a link between the patchy or inadequate treatment of such collocations in semasiological learners' dictionaries (see also Section 5) on the one hand, and language teachers' and students' low awareness of them on the other.

Succinctly stated, corpus-based analyses of the phraseological competence of foreign learners (e.g. Bahns 1997; Cobb 2003; De Cock 2003; Granger 1998;

Howarth 1996; Nesselhauf 2005; Paquot this volume; Siepmann 2005a) have shown that

- learners use fewer phrases more often;
- they have lexical 'teddy bears' for particular pragmatic functions which they use much more frequently than other phrases of similar frequency in native discourse; many of these are found in textbooks (*in my opinion, for example,* etc.);
- they have a disproportionate preference for one-word markers such as *however* over multi-word markers fulfilling similar pragmatic functions such as *that said*;
- there are collocational errors that can be traced back to overgeneralization in the L2 (a learner who creates the miscollocation *perform a project* may have formed this by mixing up –> *perform a task, carry out a task/project*) or to L1 influence.

Siepmann (2005a) carried out a contrastive interlanguage analysis of the use of multi-word markers by advanced German writers of English and found that this compared unfavourably with that of native writers in both quantitative and qualitative terms. Quantitatively speaking, a fairly consistent pattern of over- and under-use emerged in the texts by German natives. Frequency counts indicated that their writing was heavily skewed in favour of lexicalised first-level markers. To take a simple example, German writers tended to prefer the lexicalised first-level marker *for example* to more complex, syntactically-integrated markers common in native academic prose, such as *an example is provided by*. Where German writers chose to use second-level markers, they tended to use the commonest of these with much greater frequency than natives and fought shy of structures which lacked a direct equivalent in their mother tongue.

Qualitatively speaking, the analysis revealed a number of recurrent error types across different categories of multi-word markers. Many of these errors concern complex points of usage such as semantic prosody and verb valency. Here is an example from the work of a German writer of English: "[…]discuss themes within the norms for "Ausländerliteratur" tend to be published, which in turn silences differences and severely limits the writers' personal development. <u>Not surprising that</u> the title of Engin's third publication, 'Nur der Hauch vom Paradies', is also the same as Tekinay's novel" (Siepmann 2005a: 266).

The author of this excerpt has shorn the inferrer *it is not surprising that* of the introductory *it* and the verb, an error which may be due to confusion with *no/small wonder that* where such ellipsis is available.

It is fair to suppose that many errors stem from the word-based methodology which still has currency in the vocabulary sections of EFL/ESL textbooks. This methodology induces the non-native speaker to learn separate items which may become paired in rather haphazard fashion; in sharp contrast, native speakers have at their disposal formulaic pairings which have become loosened (cf. Wray 2002).

5.   Lexicographic treatment of fully transparent collocations: Suggestions for improvement

It should be clear from the above that there is an acute need to provide teachers and students with dictionaries which give due attention to syntactically and semantically compositional collocations such as speech formulae or multi-word markers. This is the subject of the present section, which will make suggestions for improving current lexicographic practice. Issues of selection and classification will be discussed first before moving on to issues of place of entry and description.

5.1   Selection

Ideally, selection should be preceded by inventorying. The problem here is that we do not yet have megacorpora from which all semantically transparent collocations can be extracted automatically. The spoken and academic sections of corpora like the *British National Corpus* or the *Bank of English* are not large enough to provide a complete picture.

Dictionary makers should therefore assemble very large, 'opportunistic' corpora by tapping Internet sources which provide material that is lexically close to spoken or academic language. Fan fiction, e-mails and weblogs, for example, are usually close to spoken language, and there are numerous academic journals on the Internet from which academic texts can be downloaded. My own experience suggests that a corpus should contain at least 150 million words of a particular domain (e.g. road traffic, geography, the human body) to allow the extraction of the majority of semantically transparent collocations typical of that domain.

If such corpora are not available, lexicographers will have to fall back on traditional methods; they will have to alternate pen-and-paper analysis with computer-driven enquiries in an iterative cycle. After a large inventory has been set up manually, the Internet (or specific sections thereof) can be queried to determine the frequency of each inventoried item. It can then be decided which items to include in the dictionary by defining an arbitrary frequency threshold.

5.2   Classification

If we now turn to classification systems, we find that the conceptual arrangement of semantically transparent collocations has at least two advantages over alphabetical arrangement (for a detailed discussion, see Siepmann 2006). Firstly, from the lexicographer's standpoint, synonymy can be handled in a clear and space-saving manner. Secondly, from the user's standpoint, the acquisition of new language material becomes considerably easier; this is because conceptual arrangement accords more closely with the ways in which items are stored in the mental lexicon or phrasicon. Thus, imagine a German learner of English who is searching for a suitable equivalent of the German phrase *ich bin ganz ihrer Meinung* in a monolingual dictionary. Since access to the dictionary's composite meaning units (i.e. collocations) can only be had via the alphabetical list of simple meaning units (i.e. entry words), the learner will probably turn to the entry for the direct translational equivalent of the German noun *Meinung*. However, this search is unlikely to yield useful results since workable equivalents can only be found at the entries for *agree* (*I couldn't agree more*) or *think* (*that's just what I think*), but not at *opinion*.

Let us consider two examples of current practice which illustrate the way in which multi-word markers are normally treated in alphabetical learners' dictionaries. In *Dictionnaire du français* (Rey-Debove 1999), which offers a sprinkling of such markers, the exemplifier *les exemples ne manquent pas* is found as the second example under sub-entry 4:

> 4. UN EXEMPLE: ce qui prouve, illustre ce que l'on veut démontrer. *Voilà un exemple de sa bêtise. Les exemples ne manquent pas. Le professeur demande de donner des exemples de fleurs.* –> **spécimen**. *Un dictionnaire contient des exemples,* des phrases qui sont citées pour illustrer l'emploi d'un mot et mieux comprendre sa définition.

The multi-word marker in question has been entered as an example sentence followed by a full stop. This implies that the phrase can stand on its own, so that its textual function of introducing a series of examples is obscured, thus leading at least the foreign-born user astray. Here are a few contextualized examples:

> De la plus petite à la plus grande commune, les exemples ne manquent pas : Arolsheim, Climbourg, Eckwiller, Hellwihr, Illfelden, Melsbourg, Nordwiller, Preschwiller et même Querbruck.

> Les exemples ne manquent pas. Citons en particulier Bartosch et Alexieff.

The situation is more or less the same in *Collins Cobuild English Dictionary* (CCED), where the digression marker *it should be noted in passing that* appears as an example under a sub-entry at *passing*, thus:

> In passing, it should be noted that ...

Besides lacking context, this example is unfortunate in presenting a marked version of the digression marker in which the adverbial in passing has been fronted. Also, there is no mention of the pragmatic function of the marker in academic text, although Cobuild dictionaries normally offer a specific pointer to pragmatics. Lastly, there is no mention of synonymous collocations such as *it should be mentioned / observed in passing that*; the productive potential of the pattern is not highlighted or discussed.

Examples of such inadequate treatment could be multiplied. What they show is that, as far as semantically transparent collocations such as multi-word markers are concerned, the main value of the monolingual dictionary is in decoding. Unlike individual words, most multi-word units will be difficult to locate for non-native speakers if they do not already know them; if they want to encode a 'composite' meaning, they will therefore turn to the bilingual dictionary, but, as seen above, may not find it covered there either.

In summary, then, it is fair to say that the monolingual alphabetical dictionary is severely limited in its encoding function, since the specific meanings attached to a large number of phraseological units cannot normally be accessed by the learner. To give another example of this, a French learner who is searching for a suitable English equivalent of a French expression such as *dans ces conditions* will be tempted to look at the entry for English *condition*, but will not be able to guess that a close textual equivalent can be found at the entry for *mind* (*with this in mind*). Of course, this assumes that the entry gives a reliable description of the use of this item in academic discourse, something that the following entry for *with this in mind* falls far short of (CCED, s.v. *mind*):

---

mind /maɪnd/ **minds**
(...)

---

19 If you do something **with** a particular thing **in mind**, you do it with that thing as your aim or as the reason or basis for your action. *These families need support. With this in mind a group of 35 specialists met last week.*

This entry fails to do justice to the specific pragmatic functions of *with this in mind* in academic or journalistic text. A more detailed and more reliable entry might provide the following additional information (Siepmann 2005a: 321):

---

mind /ma͟ɪnd/ **minds**

(...)

---

20 You use **with this in mind** to move from one part of a text to another. The first part usually provides the background to what you are about to say in the next part. *Obviously, errors alone don't constitute sublime writing for Longinus. His point, rather, is that error-free writing is more often the product of petty rather than sublime aspirations. <u>With this in mind</u>, it becomes possible to argue that the magnitude of Freud's error is perhaps evidence of the sublime quality of his writing...*

PHR with cl
PRAGMATICS
= *against this background*; *that said*; *on this basis*

More specifically, you can use **with this in mind** in three slightly different modes:

19.1 You can use with this in mind to introduce a topic shift while at the same time reminding your readers that they must remember the background information you have just provided. In this mode, you can combine **with this in mind** with such transitional devices as **let us turn to, let us revisit, I now come to**, etc. *If the subject matter exists, it must be true. Therefore, every utterance is true since it *names* its subject matter. The relation between these two problems should be evident. If we can resolve how it is possible to speak of negated or non-existent referents, then problem of falsehood should become manageable. <u>With this in mind</u>, let us turn to Pelletier's and Denyer's treatment of the problems.*

19.2 You can use **with this in mind** to refer back to a restriction which readers have to remember in order to form a proper understanding of what you are about to say. *Direct comparisons holding entry-date and/or age of immigrants are inappropriate because the female immigrant's husband is, on average, several years older than the male immigrant. <u>With this in mind</u>, the comparisons do not indicate any major difference.*

19.3 You can use **with this in mind** to draw a conclusion from what you have just said. In this case, what you have just said provides the basis for what you are about to say. In this mode, you can combine **with this in mind** with such phrases as **we can understand** or **I venture to suggest**. *Data on language is considered one of the strongest indicators for determining just how traditional or modern a tribe might be. <u>With this in mind</u>, we will note, for example, that the Navajos are probably the most traditional tribe of all, followed by the Pimas.*

It follows from the above that the only way to enable foreign learners to use semantically transparent collocations productively is via bilingual semasiological or, even better, via bilingual onomasiological dictionaries. The principal reason why the onomasiological approach is superior to the semasiological approach is not difficult to find. As communicators, we do not start from lists of individual words which we then go on to combine in a suitable fashion. It is not 'atomised single units, but concepts and processes' (Götze 1999: 11) that are represented in our brain. The concepts we wish to convey and the communicative choices we make are normally expressed either by collocations or, less commonly, by individual words. Collocations are inextricably linked with, and often restricted to, a particular topic area or situation type through what may be described as neuronal assemblies, that is, the repeated association of lexical units or semantic-pragmatic features with a situational or syntagmatic context. Therefore the learner gains considerable advantage from focussing on collocational choices within a particular subject area.

An onomasiological dictionary allows us to solve the problem of separating different meaning units which would normally be allocated to the same article in a semasiological dictionary. An example of this is the French collocation *donner + exemple*, which can be used in three different types of situation with two different meanings:

1. a situation where the speaker/writer wishes to cite another author: *Miller (1995) donne un exemple de ...*
2. a situation where the speaker/writer introduces an example of his or her own: *pour donner un exemple, je vais vous donner un exemple*
3. a situation where the speaker/writer gives an actual example: *l'Arabie Saoudite donne un exemple d'Etat islamique moderne* (= 'is an example')

A second advantage is that the onomasiological approach allows us to bring together synonymous or semantically related expressions at the same place in the

Table 5. Classification of collocations in an onomasiological learners' dictionary

Synonymic or semantically related collocations	Topic Area: Situation Type
encore nommé / autrement appelé / qu'on appelle aussi	Discourse Markers: Reformulation
don't say a word / don't make a sound / be quiet / hush / quiet, please / shut up / wrap up / belt up / put a sock in it	Noise: Telling people to be quiet
Freizeit-N, Gelegenheits-N, Hobby-N	Hobbies: Describing amateurs
when the right moment has come, in due course, at the appropriate juncture, at the appropriate moment, when the time has come	Timing: Right moment

dictionary. This will enable learners to grasp the generativity of these patterns (for examples, see Table 5).

6. Conclusion

This chapter has attempted to point the way beyond traditional monolingual semasiological learner lexicography and on to new horizons. Three crucial points have been made: First, foreign language learners' use of fully transparent collocations is neither quantitatively nor qualitatively adequate. Frequently, their view of language is still based on the individual word as the only meaning unit. Secondly, greater attention needs to be paid to collocational meaning units in language learning and dictionary making. So far, however, there has been a fairly severe neglect of fully transparent collocations in learners' dictionaries. Finally, the ideal repository for such units would seem to be the onomasiological rather than the semasiological dictionary, since the bilingual onomasiological dictionary enables learners to locate units that they are not yet aware of and to use these productively. The next important step in learner lexicography will therefore be to create thematic learners' dictionaries which categorize vocabulary by subject area and which offer a degree of microstructural completeness similar to that of semasiological learners' dictionaries. Such bilingual pedagogic thesauri are currently being developed as part of the Bilexicon project (cf. Siepmann 2006).

References

1. Dictionaries

Atkins, B. T., E. Carpenter & F; Morcellet (eds.) (1993). *Collins Robert French-English English-French dictionary. Unabridged.* (3rd edn). Glasgow: HarperCollins. (CR)

Corréard, M. (ed.) (1994). *Oxford/Hachette French dictionary. French-English/English-French,* Oxford: Oxford University Press. (OH)

Crowther, J., S. Dignen & D. Lea (eds.) (2002). *Oxford collocations dictionary for students of English.* Oxford: Oxford University Press. (OC)

Cambridge international dictionary of English (2nd edn 2001). Cambridge: Cambridge University Press. (CIDE)

Collins Cobuild English dictionary for advanced learners (3rd edn 2001). Glasgow: HarperCollins. (CCED)

Knight, L.S. (ed.) (1999). *Collins German-English English-German dictionary. Unabridged* (4th edn). Glasgow: HarperCollins. (CG)

Langenscheidt-Redaktion (1979). *Muret-Sanders Großwörterbuch Englisch.* Berlin: Langenscheidt.

Langenscheidt-Redaktion (1995). *Langenscheidts Handwörterbuch Englisch*. Berlin: Langenscheidt. (LHE)

Langenscheidt-Redaktion (1995). *Langenscheidts Handwörterbuch Französisch*. Berlin: Langenscheidt. (LHF)

Longman dictionary of contemporary English (4th edn 2003). London: Longman.

Oxford advanced learner's dictionary (7th edn 2005). Oxford: Oxford University Press. (OALD)

Procter, P. (ed.) (2001). *Cambridge international dictionary of English on CD-ROM*. Cambridge: Cambridge University Press. (CIDE)

Rey-Debove, J. (ed.) (1999). *Dictionnaire du français. Référence. Apprentissage*. Paris: Le Robert/ Clé International. (DDF)

Schnorr, V. (ed.) (1996). *PONS Großwörterbuch Französisch*. Stuttgart: Klett. (PGF)

2. Other literature

Altenberg, B. (1998). On the phraseology of spoken English: The evidence of recurrent word-combinations'. In Cowie, A.P., *Phraseology. Theory, analysis, and applications*, 101–124. Oxford: Oxford University Press.

Bahns, J. (1997). *Kollokationen und Wortschatzarbeit im Englischunterricht*. Tübingen: Narr.

Benson, M., E. Benson & R. Ilson (eds.) (1986). *The BBI combinatory dictionary of English*. Amsterdam: John Benjamins.

Cobb, T. (2003). Analyzing late interlanguage with learner corpora: Quebec replications of three European studies. *Canadian Modern Language Review, 59* (3), 393–423.

De Cock, S. (2003). Recurrent sequences of words in native speaker and advanced learner spoken and written English. PhD dissertation, Université catholique de Louvain.

Feilke, H. (1996). *Sprache als soziale Gestalt*. Frankfurt: Suhrkamp.

Feilke, H. (2003). 'Kontext – Zeichen – Kompetenz. Wortverbindungen unter sprachtheoretischem Aspekt'. In Steyer, K. (ed.), *Wortverbindungen – mehr oder weniger fest*, 41–64.

Fillmore, C.J. (1976). Pragmatics and the description of discourse. In Schmidt, S.J. (ed.) *Pragmatik/Pragmatics II. Grundlegung einer expliziten Pragmatik*, 83–104. Munich: Fink.

González-Rey, I. (2002). *La phraséologie du français*. Toulouse: Presses Universitaires du Mirail.

Götze, L. (1999). Der Zweitspracherwerb aus der Sicht der Hirnforschung. *Deutsch als Fremdsprache* 1: 10–16.

Granger, S. (ed.) (1998). *Learner English on computer*. London: Longman.

Herbst, T. (1996). What are collocations: Sandy beaches or false teeth? *English Studies, 77* (4), 379–393.

Hoey, M. (2005). *Lexical priming. A new theory of words and language*. London: Routledge.

Howarth, P.A. (1996). *Phraseology in English academic writing*. Tübingen: Niemeyer.

Kjellmer, G. (1994). *A dictionary of English collocations*. (3 Vols.) Oxford: Clarendon.

Klotz, M. (2000). *Grammatik und Lexis. Studien zur Syntagmatik englischer Verben*. Tübingen: Stauffenburg.

Lamb, S.M. (1999). *Pathways of the brain: The neurocognitive basis of language*. Amsterdam: John Benjamins.

Lewis, M. (2000). *Teaching collocation*. Hove: Language Teaching Publications.

Mel'čuk, I. (1998). Collocations and lexical functions. In Cowie, A. (ed.) *Phraseology. Theory, analysis and applications*, 23–53. Oxford: Clarendon Press.

Mel'čuk, I. (2003). Les collocations: définition, rôle et utilité. In Grossmann, F. & A. Tutin (eds.) *Les collocations: analyse et traitement* [Travaux et recherches en linguistique appliquée Série E, No 1], 23–32.

Nesselhauf, N. (2005). *Collocations in a learner corpus*. Amsterdam: John Benjamins.

Segermann, K. (2003). Wortschatz und Grammatik im Dienst der Kommunikation. *Praxis des neusprachlichen Unterrichts 50* (4), 340–350.

Siepmann, D. (2005a). *Discourse markers across languages. A contrastive study of second-level discourse markers in native and non-native text with implications for general and pedagogic lexicography*. London: Routledge.

Siepmann, D. (2005b). 'Collocation, colligation and encoding dictionaries. Part I: Lexicological aspects', *International Journal of Lexicography, 18* (4), 409–443.

Siepmann, D. (2006). 'Collocation, colligation and encoding dictionaries. Part II: Lexicographical aspects', *International Journal of Lexicography, 19* (1), 1–39.

Sinclair, J.M. (1991). *Corpus, concordance, collocation*. Oxford: Oxford University Press.

Sinclair, J.M. (1995). *Collins Cobuild English collocations on CD-ROM*. London: Harper Collins.

Wray A. (2002). *Formulaic language and the lexicon*. Cambridge: Cambridge University Press.

Compilation, formalisation and presentation of bilingual phraseology

Problems and possible solutions

Mojca Pecman

The present chapter explores the many problems that occur in processing bilingual phraseology and strives to offer concrete solutions. The methodological framework and reflection are based on empirical research into English-French phraseology for academic and scientific purposes. The ultimate goal is to offer French academics and scientists a tool for easy access to English routine formulae in that specific genre. After discussing a series of lexicographical issues related to the compilation, formalisation and presentation of bilingual collocations, we illustrate a model we have developed for retrieving English-French general scientific phraseology. The model is based on the semantic component of the language and involves linking every multiword unit to a conceptual condensed representation of its dominant meaning. Ultimately, we demonstrate the ways in which this model could usefully be used to design a flexible electronic dictionary of bilingual phraseology. The unique feature of such a tool would be that it would offer potential users a flexible approach to collocations: one semasiological, allowing them to access the data from their form and one onomasiological, providing an access key to the same data from their meaning.

1. Introduction

The lexicographical difficulties in dealing with phraseology from a contrastive viewpoint have often been raised but up until now have seldom explicitly been addressed. In the present chapter, we attempt to illustrate the various difficulties that are encountered in studies on bilingual phraseology and the solutions that may be adopted. Our observations are based on empirical research into English-French phraseology for academic and scientific purposes (Pecman 2004). The choice of field was motivated by the desire to offer French academics and scientists a tool for easy access to English routine formulas in that specific genre. As a response to bilingual phraseology processing difficulties, we illustrate a model we have developed for compiling, formalising and presenting bilingual multi-word units. Ultimately, we demonstrate the ways in which this model could usefully be used to design a flexible electronic dictionary of bilingual phraseology. As such, the present chapter draws on the well-founded assumption that linguistic studies in lexical combinatorics should yield concrete results which should help non-native speakers in their second language productions and subsequently in acquiring phraseological proficiency in a non-native language.

2.   Lexicographical issues in bilingual phraseology

Research in bilingual phraseology has lagged seriously behind research in monolingual phraseology, particularly regarding lexicographical matters. There are very few extensive in-depth studies on lexicographical issues in contrastive phraseology: the works by Heid & Freibott (1991) and Fontenelle (1994 and 1997) include insightful debates rarely found on the question. Similarly, while the number of monolingual phraseological dictionaries is constantly growing (cf. Cowie & Mackin 1975; Cowie et al. 1983; Benson M. et al. 1997; Hill & Lewis 1997; Mel'čuk et al. 1999; Zinglé 2003), bilingual phraseological dictionaries, if not collections of proverbs and sayings, are still a curiosity (cf. Kunin 1984; Ilgenfritz et al. 1989; Benson M. & Benson E. 1993).

Corpus researchers are becoming reasonably familiar with the methodologies for extracting bilingual phraseology: these comprise automatic, semi-automatic and manual extraction; extraction from parallel corpora, comparable corpora and monolingual corpora (cf. Maniez 2001; Kraif 2002; Pecman 2004: 164–188; Omazić & Pecman 2006). However, there is as yet no clear picture of how such data can be efficiently compiled, formalised or presented. In order to investigate these complex but necessary steps in processing bilingual phraseology, the following sections offer an overview of major difficulties encountered in bilingual lexicography and raise a challenging, yet in our opinion legitimate question: are bilingual phraseological dictionaries necessary?

2.1   Difficulties in processing bilingual phraseology

A number of the difficulties encountered in processing bilingual phraseology are generic: i.e. they constitute regular obstacles to the description of lexical items and building of lexicons, whether we are dealing with monolingual or bilingual data, monolexical or multi-word units. To mention the most significant ones, the pursuit of lexicographical projects is generally hampered by difficulties due to the following factors:

a.   definition of the target users' needs

The linguistic contents of dictionaries and their general macrostructure are steadily adapted to take the specific needs of target users into consideration. Thus defining the target users' needs is an essential part of a dictionary-making process. In phraseology, this process is all the more difficult as combinatorial dictionaries are relatively new tools and dictionary users do not always possess the necessary interpretative skills to use such a type of dictionary effectively.

b.   evolution of the language

Just like monolexical items, multi-word units are subjected to change through time, which can affect their meaning or structure. In the case of collocations, the change can also affect the span of paradigmatic variation within a collocational framework. For example, the collocational paradigm *[to open up/offer/provide]* *new possibilities/a new [door/route] to sth* has recently recorded an extension: *[to open up/offer/provide] a new avenue for sth*.

c.   design and assignment of different specifications

Whether we consider monolexical or multi-word units, dictionaries often include a variety of information on lexical items. To indicate a lexical item in a particular language variety or context, lexicographers have to design a series of specifications, such as domain specifications (e.g. bio., bot., geog., info., astrol.), register specifications (e.g. colloq., obsol., liter., poet., fig.), usage specifications (e.g. inv., AE., BE.) or specifications which allow the extraction of the unit out of its context (e.g. sth, sb, sb's.). The efficient design of lexicographical specifications and their assignment to lexical items relies on a thorough lexical analysis of data (for further details on annotation and notation of collocations, see Pecman 2005a).

d.   variety of linguistic information to be encoded

Like monolexical units, multi-word units can be described according to a variety of characteristics such as grammatical structure, language function, meaning, etc. This process is all the more difficult as multi-word units constitute complex lexical items. For example, they can reveal a variety of syntactic structures (e.g. v.-n.: *to pay attention*, adj.-n.: *tremendous amount*, n.-adj.: *pitch black*, n-prep.-n.: *peace of mind*, adv.-adj.: *properly dressed*, adj.-prep.-n.: *ill at ease*, etc.) and play different functions in the language (e.g. *at hand* can be used either as an adverbial – *use whatever ingredients are at hand, retribution is at hand, victory seemed at hand* – or as a noun complement, *the book at hand, information at hand, lodging at hand*).

e. complexity of the semantic content of lexical items which is often not easy to render

Defining the meaning of lexical items, whether monolexical or polylexical, is a very complex task. This process is particularly complicated as multi-word units can display different semantic behaviour. Some accept compositional interpretation (e.g. *to cross sb's mind, old wives' tale, kill joy*), while others display a tendency for a non-compositional interpretation (e.g. *to kick the bucket, to spill the beans, red herring*), but many multi-word units can accept both types of interpretation (e.g. *to slip through sb's fingers, black sheep, to fall to pieces*). In the case of a compositional interpretation, the meaning of a multiword unit is derived from its structure and the meanings of its constituent parts.

f. polysemy in particular

Just like monolexical items, multi-word units can have different meanings. In contrastive linguistics, this can lead to different translations in the target language (e.g. *en conséquence* used as a comment clause is translated in English by *as a result* or *as a consequence*; used as an adverb, it is translated by *accordingly* and used as an adjective, it is equivalent to *corresponding*).

g. synonymy

Polysemy, synonymy and related distribution rules have the same impact on multi-word units as on monolexical units. As a consequence, a collocation in a source language can have several synonymous correspondences in a target language and vice versa (e.g. *to sharpen a contrast → renforcer le contraste* or *accentuer le contraste, de plus en plus → more and more* or *increasingly*). Furthermore, the establishing of each pair of equivalents can give rise to a different translational technique (see below). The direction of translation, that is to say the choice of a source language and a target language, can also change the disposition of the data (e.g. *more and more* is generally translated into French by *de plus en plus* but *de plus en plus* leads in English more frequently to the monolexical unit *increasingly* than to the multi-word unit *more and more*). Bilingual dictionaries are thus more useful if they are directed toward the target language (on unidirectional and bi-directional dictionaries, see Hannay 2003).

h.   stylistic variation

This obstacle is closely related to language development. The phraseological lexicon is not only subject to modification for the purpose of naming new realities
like lexical items but also for the purpose of describing a variety of situations by
creating original expressions, often achieved through word play (e.g. *Baghdad is
Bush's blue dress* (politics & journalism), *L'appétit vient en mangeant, la pizza vient
en l'appelant.* (advertising)). In this instance, modified phraseological items obey
the poetic function of language as defined by Jakobson (1963:218). In the case of
word formation, the creation gives rise to neologisms which can with time become
conventional items, while in the case of set phrases, the nonce items are, although
grammatically perfectly acceptable, often a question of one-off creation. A modified phraseological item is seldom integrated into a common core lexicon (on stylistic variation and conceptual blending in phraseology, see Omazić 2005).

i.   illustration of the usage of lexical items by appropriate example(s)

The role of examples in dictionaries is central. They help to identify both the
meaning and behaviour of lexical items. As multiword units often have a complex
grammatical structure, it is important to offer a precise indication on their potential realisations (e.g. *en collaboration avec* → *in collaboration with*, ex. *en collaboration avec l'équipe <X>* → *in collaboration with <X> team, en collaboration avec [le
groupe/l'équipe] de* → *in collaboration with a [group/team] of/from, lancer un projet
en collaboration avec <qn>* → *to initiate a (collaborative) project with <sb>*).

j.   design of a general methodology for article construction capable of covering
     a variety of data

In phraseological lexicography, the microstructure of a dictionary is difficult to
devise as multi-word units can display different properties. It is probably impossible to devise a unique model for processing different types of multi-word data:
collocations, colligations, collocational frameworks, idiomatic expressions, idioms, etc. Nevertheless, all these units share the same fundamental feature: they
behave as continuous or discontinuous sequences of words and appear to be prefabricated, that is, stored and retrieved whole from memory at the time of use,
rather than being subjected to generation or analysis by the language grammar
(cf. Wray & Perkins 2000:1).

    As to the obstacles which are more specific to bilingual phraseology process-
ing, they are mainly caused by the complexity of establishing the equivalences between lexical items belonging to different languages. In this instance, the processing of bilingual phraseology has much to draw from the construction of classical
bilingual dictionaries and from the various studies on translational difficulties

(e.g. Vinay & Darbelnet (1958), Chuquet & Paillard (1989), Paillard (2000), Poirier (2003)). The major obstacles we can observe are due to the following factors:

k.   categorial discrepancies

An equivalent of a collocation in a source language is not necessarily a collocation in a target language (e.g. *jeter un coup d'oeil* → *to glance, passer l'aspirateur* → *to hoover, froncer les sourcils* → *to frown; to blow one's nose* → *se moucher, free and easy* → *décontracté*).

l.   variety of translational techniques

If, however, the equivalent items are to be found in both languages in a multi-word form, there are at least three possible translational techniques:

i.   a collocation can be a trivial lexical correspondence, that is to say allow the word for word translation (e.g. *prendre une douche* → *to take a shower, la fin justifie les moyens* → *the end justifies the means, les hauts et les bas* → *ups and downs*),

ii.   only the base can be translated literally while the collocator has to be selected accordingly, that is in the context of the base (e.g. *to sharpen a pen* → *tailler un crayon, to sharpen a knife* → *aiguiser un couteau, to sharpen a picture* → *affiner une image, to sharpen a contrast* → *renforcer/accentuer le contraste*),

iii. none of the collocational elements can be translated literally, which leads to a more or less different collocational configuration in a target language (e.g. *to be fast asleep* → *dormir à poings fermés, be that as it may* → *quoi qu'il en soit, all in all* → *somme toute*).

m.   register differences

Another difficulty concerns the discrepancies in register between bilingual collocational pairs. Notwithstanding the existence of equivalences across languages, the related items do not necessarily belong to the same register (e.g. *du même coup* (colloquial) → *by the same token* (formal), *at the same time* (neutral); *du coup* (colloquial) → *thus* (formal), *hence* (formal)).

n.   absence of phraseological units in a target language

An additional difficulty arises from the absence of phraseological units in a target language. Some languages express certain ideas through the use of phraseological units, while other languages may simply avoid such constructions (e.g. *[l'objectif/ le but] visé* is a common combination in French which emphasises the inherent meaning of the words *but* and *objectif* through the use of a conventional collocator: *visé*. The English language is far more synthetic in this case and proposes no collocations. Instead, the speakers have to resort to the use of monolexical items: *goal* or *aim*).

o. frequency differences

The last but not least of the difficulties is based in statistics: although equivalent, phraseological units may not have the same usage frequency in their respective languages (e.g. the phrase *Pierre, Paul, Jacques* has higher frequency usage in French than its English counterpart which seems to be less popular: *every Tom, Dick and Harry*).

Although this list makes no claim to comprehensiveness, we have identified no less than fifteen impeding obstacles to bilingual phraseology processing for lexicographical purposes. All of these obstacles should be taken into account during the compilation and formalisation of phraseological data and the models we develop should be designed so that they can be overcome.

2.2 Are bilingual phraseological dictionaries necessary?

At first sight, any attempt to cast a doubt on the very utility of phraseological dictionaries may seem exaggerated. However, it is essential not only to define the feasibility of bilingual phraseological dictionaries but also to determine to what extent it is worthwhile creating them alongside traditional bilingual dictionaries. The issue is then: are bilingual phraseological dictionaries necessary or should we simply strive to improve traditional bilingual dictionaries by systematically adding phraseological information to existing entries?

This claim is most likely to be true for processing general language and it is to a large extent the very method lexicographers employ as they try to define the scope of the different meanings of a specific word, specifically since the advent of corpus linguistics, which has emphasised the role of context in word defining. As Szende (2000: 70) points out, "the difference between equivalent lexical items belonging to different languages is to be found on the combinatorial rather than on semantic level of language". Putting emphasis on combinatorics could thus help us to resolve the "underlying paradox which makes the work of a lexicographer particularly difficult: the lexicographer is supposed to provide the clear-cut separations of meaning while these very often are not easily justifiable" (Szende 2000: 80). In other words, combinatorics could provide the justification for separating out meanings.

Presently, the phraseological information included in traditional bilingual dictionaries is often missing or at best incomplete and presented in a disorderly fashion. In this respect, lexicographers and phraseologists should unite to develop an effective method for systematic and homogeneous inclusion of combinatorial properties of words into already existing dictionaries. Nevertheless, a brief analysis of a number of bilingual and monolingual dictionaries which target language learners (cf. *Oxford-Hachette Dictionary* 1994–1996, *Le trésor de la langue française informatisé* 2002 and its section "syntax" (coded SYNT), *Grand Robert & Collins Electronique* 2004, *Longman Dictionary of Contemporary English* 2005) points to the fact that this claim is increasingly being taken into account in lexicography. The role of corpora in dictionary making, of the context in discovering the new usages and the frequency of words is of paramount importance and has been already discussed by a number of authors (Atkins 1994–1996; Grundy 1996; Maljaei 2000).

On the other hand, the design of bilingual phraseological dictionaries of sublanguages is in our opinion fully justifiable. There are at least three major reasons behind this claim:

i.   within a specific domain, words often have specific usages which are not necessarily found in general language, hence the specific combinatorial properties;

ii. sub-languages have highly developed style conventions, and phraseological information can undeniably be of great help in the process of mastering language conventions within a specific field of knowledge;

iii. related fields of knowledge seem to share the same phraseological features, which further emphasises the need to separate phraseological knowledge from domain specific knowledge expressed through terminologies. In many works on phraseology (cf. Gouadec 1993: 178; Gledhill 2000: 26),[1] we find observations which lead us to conclude that there is an underlying difference between these two types of items, based essentially on the cross-disciplinary nature of phraseological units in comparison with terminology, which is far more domain-specific. Indeed, domain-specific complex sequences (like the following, which belong to chemistry: *to remove/substract an atom/molecule, atom/molecule removal/subtraction* → *retirer/soustraire un atome/une molécule, retrait/soustraction d'un atome/d'une molécule...*) are generally rare.

---

1. During the process of formalisation of phraseological units, or what he calls « chaînes de caractères remarquables », Gouadec notices that, contrary to what is observed for terminologies, the label specifying the field of knowledge is very often left unexploited. Similarly, in his phraseological analysis of a specific scientific discourse (related to the domain of cancer research), Gledhill is compelled to introduce the notion of « generic collocation » in order to distinguish all those word combinations which seem to have a more general usage from those restricted to one single domain.

Non-domain-specific complex sequences, on the other hand, (such as *to discredit a theory → infirmer une théorie, to invalidate a hypothesis → démentir une hypothèse, to consolidate a hypothesis → corroborer une hypothèse…*) are very common. Other specialised languages (e.g. journalistic, political) may display similar behaviour although these sublanguages seem to be characterised by a higher degree of stylistic variation.

In comparison with the phraseology of general language, the specialised fields of knowledge seem to be characterised by far more easily identifiable idiosyncrasies, hence the importance of recording their phraseology in the form of an autonomous database or dictionary.

3.   Semantically oriented modelling of bilingual phraseology

This section illustrates the model we have developed for processing bilingual phraseology within a research project carried out at the University of Nice (Pecman 2004, 2005b). The goal of the project is to bridge the gap between discourse analysis and foreign language learning.

3.1   Compilation and formalisation of bilingual phraseology

In order to be able to investigate scientific phraseology from a contrastive point of view, we have designed a parallel corpus containing 82,800 words. The textual sources are scientific articles, abstracts, activities reports, communications, etc. and are taken from three related domains: physics, chemistry and biology. The corpus was set up so as to be able to observe the phraseological properties of English for Academic Purposes (EAP) and English for Science and Technology (EST). In the context of the English language, only a decade ago there were very few linguists, namely Howarth (1996) and Granger (1998), working on the phraseology of this sub-language, but recently the cross-disciplinary formulaic sequences have attracted more interest (cf. Pecman 2004; Simpson 2004; Tutin 2004; Kübler 2005). In France, this specific genre analysis gave rise to the study of what Phal (1971) previously called "Vocabulaire Général d'Orientation Scientifique" (V.G.O.S.). However, the approach to V.G.O.S. is purely lexical and does not give insights into the phraseology of scientific discourse. We refer to this sublanguage using the term General Scientific Language (GSL) (Pecman 2004: 124–147, 2005b).

The parallel corpus was used for the compilation of bilingual phraseological units (i.e. translation units) with no restriction on whether the equivalents behaved as trivial lexical correspondences or as lexical mismatches. The major criteria on which the extraction of multiword units was based were their frequency in each of the three domains and their re-usability during the writing process. The corpus was searched both manually and automatically, thus combining the advantages of machine retrieval and an intuition-based data capture. The machine processing was carried out using Ztext (Zinglé 1998). The lexical items obtained from these two compilation procedures were put together and stored in a bilingual phraseological database. The lexical resources were then revised and, when needed, corrected with the help of a number of traditional monolingual and collocational dictionaries (cf. *Le Nouveau Petit Robert* 1993, *Le trésor de la langue française informatisé* 2002; *The BBI Dictionary of English Word Combinations* by Benson M. et al. 1997, *Oxford Collocations Dictionary for students of English* 2002, *Selected English Collocations* by Hill & Lewis 1997). Combining the data in this way allowed the incongruences which have appeared in the lists to be bypassed. These incongruences are due to the fact that the corpus is a collection of texts and not a collection of already made databases, dictionaries or lexicons. Such a compilation procedure meets both of the requirements which underline our research: the requirement for a descriptive analysis conducted with the purpose of outlining the major phraseological characteristics of scientific discourse and the requirement for a prescriptive analysis conducted with the purpose of designing a tool for assisted scientific writing. At this stage of corpus processing, the database contained some 2,000 translation units. Nevertheless, this number is not definitive as we are currently continuing to update our data. In order to increase the reusability of our resources for dictionary making, we have recently embarked on an additional data collection from comparable corpora. This supplementary technique should allow us to make up for the insufficiencies that parallel corpora suffer, namely the high number of mistranslations, paraphrasing, etc.

The next step consisted in the formalisation of the collected resources (Pecman 2005a). A number of labels were assigned to each translation unit providing information, namely on the sentential context from which the units were extracted, on the bibliographical reference of the source text, on the scientific field the source text belonged to, on the syntactic function of each unit in the discourse and on the meaning of the unit.

3.2   A unit of meaning as an access point to the foreign language lexicon

The semantic categorisation of multiword units is part of a project to construct a dictionary that offers a flexible approach to resources. Such a dictionary should offer, besides the usual alphabetical access to data, the possibility of accessing lexical resources through semantic queries.

Altogether, 125 semantic categories have been identified so far. In order to give an overview of the semantic organisation of general scientific discourse, we have carried out a conceptual analysis which has led to the construction of an ontology devoted to this specific discourse community (Pecman 2004: 285–315). In the future, we plan to make use of the GSL ontology for further data collection from textual corpora by avoiding retrieval from the whole corpus. Instead, the procedure will involve identifying and describing the ways the concepts listed in GSL ontology are lexicalized within scientific discourse.

Decomposing and recomposing a meaning is unquestionably a risky task. Nevertheless, the meaning is the main pathway for transferring linguistic items from one language to another. As Sterkenburg (2003: 130) points out: "It is of course a perilous undertaking to put meanings into a structure, as language users can have different intuitions about the exact meaning of a word. Every attempt to describe the relationship within the lexicon structurally can therefore be seen by users at a certain point to be an arbitrary attempt to group semantically related words, to form semantic clusters. Nevertheless we cannot ignore the fact that within every language community there is such a thing as a common denominator where meaning is concerned."

Expanding on this idea, we illustrate a model which exploits the semantic component of a language and consists in linking every multiword unit to a condensed conceptual representation of its dominant meaning, more precisely to its hyperonymic synonym. The aim of the model is to offer potential users a flexible approach to collocations: one that is semasiological, allowing them to access data from their form, and another that is onomasiological, providing an access key to the same data from their meaning. In the former case, a multiword unit like *it is widely accepted that* can thus be located through its lexical constituents *widely* and *accept* and consulted together with other multiword units with which it has one constituent in common (i.e. *to accept sth fully/readily, to accept a criterion/condition, to accept a transformation/modification*, etc.). In the latter case, the same multiword unit can also be accessed through its hyperonymic synonym, in this instance coded as |QUOTATION|, and found in an entry together with other units of similar meaning (i.e. *it is commonly/generally/universally/widely accepted that, it is widely/well known that, it [is/has been] (often) asserted/noted/recognised/believed/claimed/argued that*, etc.). Each of these access points is meant to offer a pathway to French equivalents and vice versa, in this particular case to, or starting from, the following units: *il est commun de penser que, il est communément/généralement/unanimement admis que, on admet que, on a longtemps pensé/cru que, on a souvent dit que*, etc. The access to concepts is provided via lexical units which act as indexes and actually represent semantically related words (in this instance:

quotation, quote, citation, allusion, reference, source, opinion, view, point of view, viewpoint, assumption and *position*).

4.   Presentation of bilingual phraseology

Storing bilingual phraseology within an electronic database offers multiple choices for retrieving phraseological units through queries. Consequently, an electronic phraseological database constitutes an adequate workbench for working towards a more useful presentation of phraseological items within dictionaries. Specifically, the retrieval of multiword units according to their meaning offers a valuable list of semantically related set phrases which facilitate observation of the ways a specific notion is expressed in a specific field of knowledge at the lexicon-syntax level. It is thus easy to find out the combinatorial profile of semantically related words in this particular discourse. The query result appears in the form of a list of phraseological clusters (see Figure 1). This material can then be rearranged in order to clearly show the way clusters are built, with emphasis on left and right context of the node word, and the role of units in discourse.

4.1   Designing of conceptual frameworks

Although collocational frameworks are generally defined as grammatical or lexical collocations with a variable lexical 'slot', there is no widespread consensus about how these complex lexical schemes should be presented. In this section, we explore the two most common types of presentation, linear and graphic.

We first investigated the more traditional mode for presenting lexical data, which is a linear configuration (see Figure 1).

Organizing data graphically is another step in our effort to find the suitable mode for presenting bilingual phraseology. It is inspired by the works of Altenberg (1998: 106) but it is also very similar to the concept of "grammaire locale" developed within the project « Dictionnaires Electroniques du LADL[2] (DELA) » (cf. Gross 1997), which is together with Mel'čuk's model of Lexical Functions (Mel'čuk et al. 1995) one of the most comprehensive syntax-based lexicons of the French language available to date.

Such a presentation accounts for the non-superposition of combinatorial properties between languages and clearly shows the collocational structure of

---

2. "Laboratoire d'Automatique Documentaire et Linguistique (LADL)" of the Marne-la-Vallée University.

Phr.

être [communément/généralement/unanimement] admis :

    to be widely accepted

être bien connu :

    to be well known

il est [communément/généralement/unanimement] admis que :

    it is widely accepted that <prop>

on a longtemps [pensé/cru] que :

    it has been (often) [asserted/believed/noted/argued/claimed/recognised] that <prop>

on a souvent dit que, il est commun de penser que :

    it is (often) [asserted/believed/noted/argued/claimed/recognised] that <prop>

on admet que <prop> :

    it is well known that <prop>

Qual.

[généralement/communément] admis :

    widely accepted

Prép.

selon <qn> :

    according to <sb>, in <sb's> words

Figure 1. Linear presentation of the collocational framework of the concept of |quotation|

each language. The final stage in our reflection leads us to consider the possibility of exploiting our formalised data for the design of a multifunctional electronic dictionary.

4.2   Presentation within a multifunctional electronic dictionary

The unique feature of a multifunctional electronic dictionary is its dual approach to lexical resources: semasiological and onomasiological. This idea is a logical extension of Fontenelle's (1994: 55) reasoning which emphasises the importance of providing users with several access keys (base, collocator, lexical function, translation…) which would make the collocational information more easily accessible than in the traditional collocational dictionaries such as *The BBI Dictionary of English Word Combinations*.

If we refer to common classification of dictionaries, the multifunctional electronic dictionary can be classed at the same time in the group of production-

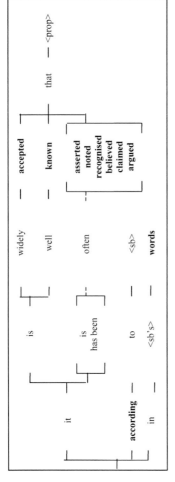

Figure 2. Graphic presentation of the collocational framework of the concept of |QUOTATION| in English

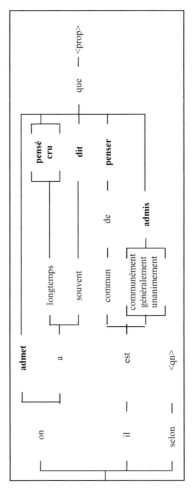

Figure 3. Graphic presentation of the collocational framework of the concept of |QUOTATION| in French

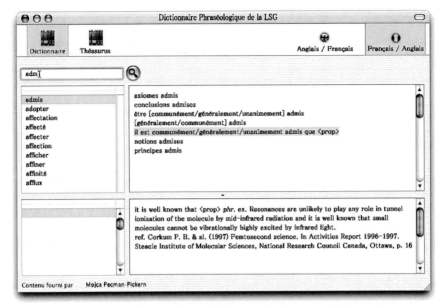

Figure 4. A model for the design of a multifunctional electronic dictionary (a screenshot showing semasiological access to phraseological data)

orientated dictionaries, dynamic dictionaries and reverse dictionaries. According to Hannay (2003:145) "the user of a production-orientated dictionary seeks to discover the expression she needs in another language than her own for expressing a given idea in a given context, and may well at the same time wish to establish how she should use the expression in question". The structure of our multifunctional electronic dictionary meets that requirement. Like every other electronic dictionary, it is also a dynamic dictionary as it allows the complex structure of the language to be reflected and offers multiple access keys to data (Cartier 2000). It is also a type of reverse dictionary because it provides users with the opportunity to access information from the meaning (Sterkenburg 2003).

The following models illustrate what such a dictionary would be like: Figure 4 shows a panel providing semasiological access to phraseological data and Figure 5 onomasiological access.

In comparison with the model of Lexical Functions developed by Mel'čuk (Mel'čuk et al. 1995) which has received due acknowledgment from lexicographers worldwide and has recently led to the development of an effective simplified version of a combinatorial dictionary (cf. the database DiCo) which is partly accessible through the Internet[3] (cf. DicoInfo, the vocabulary of informatics and

---

3. http://olst.ling.umontreal.ca/dicoinfo

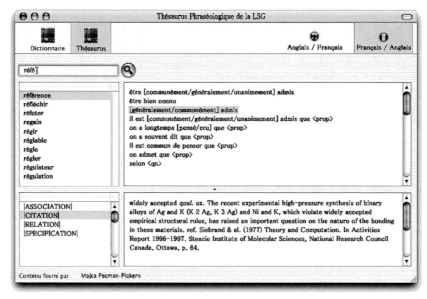

Figure 5. A model for the design of a multifunctional electronic dictionary (a screenshot showing onomasiological access to phraseological data)

Internet), this is quite a different approach to phraseology. Yet in our opinion, its advantage lies in its ability to cover a large amount of data, rather than using a far-reaching and all-embracing description of the combinatorial properties of lexical units which, because of time constraints, leads to a smaller number of considered units. In the last version of the *Dictionnaire explicatif et combinatoire du français contemporain: recherches lexico-sémantiques IV*, (Mel'čuk et al. 1999) there are 180 entries in total while DiCo contains 500 entries.

5. Conclusion

The advantage of the model presented above is its ability to take into account not only the static, frozen properties of collocational units but also their variational capacities, using a cluster representation developed around semantically related nodes. One of the major characteristics of academic phraseology is the overwhelming use of those units which can vary in wording to some extent. Completely frozen lexical clusters are rare in scientific prose. Such a high degree of paradigmatic variation within a single phraseological frame has encouraged us to focus our study primarily on the category of what Renouf & Sinclair (1991) have called *collocational frameworks* or, to employ the terminology of Granger

(1998:154), a "category of *sentence-builders*, phrases which function as macro-organizers in the text". Besides, this type of phraseology is far more complicated to process than any other type of idiomatic expression because of its dynamic aspect, which cannot easily be rendered through static alphabetical lists. Furthermore, the major difficulty in processing collocational frameworks is due to the fact that it is very difficult to state all the possible combinations within a given frame. Recording all the allowed combinations, and automatically all the forbidden ones (i.e. the combinatorial restrictions), implies nothing less than decomposing the mechanism of the economy of language, as put forth by Martinet (1964:168–169) and which is the very principle behind the functioning of the language as an exponential system (Pinker 1999:7). Gross (1996:79; Clas & Gross 1997) has tried to get over this obstacle by putting forward the theory of object class capable of rendering the collocational paradigm not only for single lexemes (e.g. *démarrer la voiture* → *to start a car*) but for a series of lexemes (e.g. *démarrer <transports routiers>* → *to start a <vehicle>*).

In this respect, the procedure for compiling, formalising and presenting the phraseological resources illustrated above allows the major difficulties in processing bilingual phraseology to be bypassed by organising the data semantically and by offering flexible access to the data. Furthermore, the model we have developed takes into account all the necessary steps in the processing of phraseological items, from corpus retrieval to data exploitation in a user-friendly format within a dictionary. This type of analytical model for compiling, formalizing and presenting phraseological resources can thus used be with effect to create tools destined to help non-native speakers to express themselves in a second language.

References

Altenberg, B. (1998). On the phraseology of spoken English: The evidence of recurrent word-combinations. In Cowie, A. P. (ed.) *Phraseology: Theory, analysis, and applications*, 101–122. Oxford: Oxford University Press.

Atkins, B.T.S. (1994–1996). A corpus based dictionary. In *Informations générales. Dictionnaire Hachette-Oxford*. Version 1.1. Oxford: Oxford University Press/Paris: Hachette Livre.

Benson, M. & E. Benson (1993). *Russian-English dictionary of verbal collocations*. Amsterdam: John Benjamins.

Benson, M., E. Benson & R. Ilson (1997). *The BBI dictionary of English word combinations*. (2nd edn). Amsterdam: John Benjamins.

Cartier, E. (2000). Eléments pour une modélisation des dictionnaires électroniques. In Szende, T. (ed.) *Dictionnaires bilingues: Méthodes et contenus*, 135–152. Paris: Honoré Champion.

Chuquet, H. & M. Paillard (1989). *Approche linguistique des problèmes de traduction: Anglais-français*. Paris/Gap: Ophrys.

Clas, A. & G. Gross (1997). Synonymie, polysémie et classes d'objets. *Meta 42* (1): 147–154.

Cowie, A. P. & R. Mackin (1975). *Oxford dictionary of current idiomatic English.* (Vol. 1). Oxford: Oxford University Press.

Cowie, A. P., R. Mackin & I. R. McCaig (1983). *Oxford dictionary of current idiomatic English.* (Vol. 2). Oxford: Oxford University Press.

Fontenelle, T. (1994). Towards the construction of a collocational database for translation students. *Meta 39* (1): 47–56.

Fontenelle, T. (1997). *Turning a bilingual dictionary into a lexical-semantic database* [Lexicographica Series Maior 79]. Tübingen: Niemeyer.

Gledhill, C.J. (2000). *Collocations in science writing* [Language in Performance 22]. Tübingen: Narr.

Gouadec, D. (1993). Nature et traitement des entités phraséologiques. In *Actes de la deuxième Université d'automne en terminologie. Terminologie et Phraséologie: Acteurs et aménageurs. Rennes 2. 20–25 sept. 1993*, 167–193. Paris: La Maison du Dictionnaire.

Grand Robert & Collins electronique français-anglais/anglais-français (2004). Version 1.1. Paris: Dictionnaires Le Robert.

Granger, S. (1998). Prefabricated patterns in advanced EFL writing: Collocations and formulae. In Cowie, A. P. (ed.) *Phraseology: Theory, analysis, and applications*, 145–160. Oxford: Oxford University Press.

Gross, G. (1996). *Les expressions figées en français: Noms composés et autres locutions.* Paris/Gap: Ophrys.

Gross, M. (1997). The construction of local grammars. In Roche, E. & Y. Schabès (eds.) *Finite-state language processing*, 329–354.Cambridge, MA: The MIT Press.

Grundy, V. (1996). L'utilisation d'un corpus dans la rédaction du dictionnaire bilingue. In Béjoin, H. & Ph. Thoiron (eds.) *Les dictionnaires bilingues*, 127–149. Louvain-la-Neuve: Aupelf-Urf/Duculot.

Hannay, M. (2003). Special types of dictionaries. In Sterkenburg, P. van (ed.) *A practical guide to lexicography*, 145–153. Amsterdam: John Benjamins.

Heid, U. & G. Freibott (1991). Collocations dans une base de données terminologique et lexicale. *Meta 36* (1), 77–91.

Hill, J. & M. Lewis (eds.) (1997). *Dictionary of selected collocations.* Based on the original work of Kozlowska, C. D. & H. Dzierzanovska. Hove: Language Teaching Publications.

Howarth, P. A. (1996). *Phraseology in English academic writing: Some implications for language learning and dictionary making*, Tübingen: Niemeyer.

Ilgenfritz, P., N. Stephan-Gabinel & G. Schneider (1989). *Langenscheidts Kontextwörterbuch Französisch-Deutsch.* Berlin: Langenscheidt.

Jakobson, R. (1963). *Essais de linguistique générale: Les fondations du langage.* Paris: Les Editions de Minuit.

Kraif, O. (2002). Méthodes de filtrage pour l'extraction d'un lexique bilingue à partir d'un corpus aligné. *Lexicometrica.* Numéro spécial.

Kübler, N. (2005). Phraséologie verbale transdisciplinaire et spécifique: Essai de classification en sciences de la terre. In Cosme, C., C. Gouverneur, F. Meunier & M. Paquot (eds.) PHRASEOLOGY 2005. The many faces of phraseology. An interdisciplinary conference. 13–15 Oct. 2005, 223–225. Université de Louvain. Louvain-la-Neuve. Belgique.

Kunin, A. V. (1984). *English-Russian phraseological dictionary.* (4th edn). Moskva: Russkij Jazyk.

Le nouveau petit Robert. Dictionnaire alphabétique et analogique de la langue française (1993). Nouv. éd. du Petit Robert de Paul Robert. Paris: Dictionnaires Le Robert.

Le trésor de la langue française informatisé (TLFI) (2002). (Version 4). Analyse et Traitement Informatique de la Langue Française (A.T.I.L.F.).

Longman dictionary of contemporary English (2005). (4th edn). Harlow: Pearson/Longman ESL.

Maljaei, S. (2000). Perspective d'une nouvelle lexicographie bilingue. In Szende, T. (ed.) *Dictionnaires bilingues. Méthodes et contenus*, 107–115. Paris: Honoré Champion.

Maniez, F. (2001). Extraction d'une phraséologie bilingue en langue de spécialité: Corpus parallèles et corpus comparables. *Meta 46* (3), 552–563.

Martinet A. (1964) *Eléments de linguistique générale*. Paris: A. Colin.

Mel'čuk, I. A., A. Clas & A. Polguère (1995). *Introduction à la lexicologie explicative et combinatoire*. Louvain-la-Neuve: Duculot.

Mel'čuk, I. A., N. Arbatchewsky-Jumarie, L. Iordanskaja, S. Mantha & A. Polguère (1999). *Dictionnaire explicatif et combinatoire du français contemporain: Recherches lexico-sémantiques IV*. Montréal: Les Presses de l'Université de Montréal.

Omazić, M. (2005). Cognitive linguistic theories in phraseology. Jezikoslovlje 6 (1), 37–56.

Omazić, M. & M. Pecman (2006). Le rôle des corpus en phraséologie: Apports et limites méthodologiques. In Vergely, P. (ed.) Actes des Journées d'études Doctorants et jeunes chercheurs. Rôle et place des corpus en linguistique. 1–2 juillet 2005, Université de Toulouse Le Mirail. Toulouse: Ch.F.-P.

Oxford collocations dictionary for students of English (2002). Oxford: Oxford University Press.

Oxford-Hachette dictionary (1994–1996). Français-Anglais, Anglais-Français. (Version 1.1). Oxford: Oxford University Press/Paris: Hachette Livre.

Paillard, M. (2000). *Lexicologie contrastive anglais-français: Formation des mots et construction du sens*. Gap/Paris: Ophrys.

Pecman, M. (2004). Phraséologie contrastive anglais-français: Analyse et traitement en vue de l'aide à la rédaction scientifique. Thèse de doctorat. 9 déc. 2004. Dir. H. Zinglé. Université de Nice Sophia-Antipolis.

Pecman, M. (2005a). Systemizing the notation and the annotation of collocations. Jezikoslovlje 6 (1), 79–93.

Pecman, M. (2005b). Les apports possibles de la phraséologie à la didactique des langues étrangères. Apprentissage des Langues et Systèmes d´Information et de Communication (ALSIC), 8 (1), 109–122.

Phal, A. (1971). *Vocabulaire général d'orientation scientifique (V.G.O.S.): Part du lexique commun dans l'expression scientifique*. Paris: CREDIF.

Pinker, S. (1999). *Words and rules. The ingredients of language*. New York, NY: Basic Books.

Poirier, E. (2003). Conséquences didactiques et théoriques du caractère conventionnel et arbitraire de la traduction des unités phraséologiques. *Meta 48* (3), 402–410.

Renouf, A. & J.M. Sinclair (1991). Collocational frameworks in English. In Aijmer, K. & B. Altenberg (eds.) *English corpus linguistics*, 128–143. London: Longman.

Simpson, R. (2004). Stylistic features of academic speech: The role of formulaic expressions. In Upton, T. & U. Connor (eds.) *Discourse in the professions: Perspectives from corpus linguistics*, 233–250. Amsterdam/Philadelphia: John Benjamins.

Sterkenburg, P. van (2003). Onomasiological specifications and a concise history of onomasiological dictionaries. In Sterkenburg, P. van (ed.) *A Practical Guide to Lexicography*, 127–143. Amsterdam: John Benjamins.

Szende, T. (2000). L'information sémantique en lexicologie bilingue. In Szende, T. (ed.) *Dictionnaires bilingues. Méthodes et contenus*, 69–81. Paris: Honoré Champion.

Tutin, A. (2004). Pour une modélisation dynamique des collocations dans les textes. In *Actes d'Euralex, Lorient, 6–10 juillet 2004*.

Vinay, J.-P. & J. Darbelnet (1958). *Stylistique comparée du français et de l'anglais*. (Nouv. éd. rev. et corr). Paris: Didier.

Wray, A. & M. R. Perkins (2000) The functions of formulaic language: An integrated model. *Language & Communication 20* (1), 1–28.

Zinglé, H (1998). ZTEXT: Un outil pour l'analyse de corpus. *Travaux du LILLA* 3. Publications de la Faculté des Lettres, Arts et Sciences Humaines de l'Université de Nice-Sophia Antipolis, 69–78.

Zinglé, H. (2003). *Dictionnaire combinatoire du français: Expressions, locutions et constructions*. Paris: La Maison du Dictionnaire.

The phraseological patterns of high-frequency verbs in advanced English for general purposes

A corpus-driven approach to EFL textbook analysis

Céline Gouverneur

This chapter sets out to give an account of the treatment of the two high-frequency verbs *make* and *take* in three series of English for General Purposes (EGP) textbooks at the intermediate and advanced levels. The focus is on the delexicalised (and hence more phraseological) uses of these verbs, which, recent corpus studies have shown, represent a stumbling block to native-like proficiency. The principles underlying the selection and presentation of the *make* and *take* phraseological patterns are investigated through a quantitative and qualitative analysis of a new corpus of textbook material, the TeMa corpus. The methodology used proved particularly effective in shedding light on issues which cannot be tackled in traditional page-by-page textbook research. Two main observations emerged from the comparisons made across levels on the one hand, and across textbooks on the other. First, there were striking discrepancies between the treatment of the phraseological patterns of *make* and *take* at the intermediate and advanced levels. Secondly, the three textbook series display great consistency in terms of pedagogical choices. Overall, the results obtained provide conclusive evidence of the need for redefining the principles underlying the selection and presentation of phraseological units in EGP textbooks.

1. Introduction

Recent studies have revealed that high-frequency verbs, which have long been regarded as "easy" verbs, are actually a rather treacherous area of language learning. Far from being simple, they represent a major hurdle for learners, who have difficulty coping with them not so much receptively but rather productively, in spoken as well as written English (Lennon 1996; Ringbom 1998) even at more advanced levels of proficiency. Compared to native speakers, learners not only tend to mainly overuse these verbs (Altenberg & Granger 2001; Kaszubski 2000) but they also misuse them to a great extent (Nesselhauf 2004). Whilst the core meanings of the verbs usually seem to be mastered, their delexicalised uses, occurring mainly in phraseological patterns, have been shown to remain a stumbling block to native-like proficiency.

The study presented in this chapter has two main objectives. Its primary goal is to cast light on the current treatment of phraseology in English for General Purposes (EGP) textbooks. To achieve this aim, the phraseological patterns of two high-frequency verbs *make* and *take* are examined in three EGP textbooks, at intermediate and advanced level. *Make* and *take*, which rank among the ten most frequent verb lemmas in English (see Leech et al. 2001) are prototypical examples of so-called 'easy' verbs, hence the special focus on these two verbs in this study. The second aim is to test a new methodology developed especially for textbook analysis, namely the automatic querying of a pedagogically annotated corpus of textbook material, the TeMa corpus.

Assessing textbook design and content is a relatively new research interest (Nitta & Gardner 2005; Reda 2003; Römer 2005; Vellenga 2004). Although textbook research has become more prominent in applied linguistics, accounts of the current treatment of phraseology in ELT material are rare. The handful of studies available have nevertheless demonstrated that although phraseology has become more prominent in ELT materials, there is still room for substantial improvement (Biber et al. 2004; Koprowski 2005, Meunier & Gouverneur 2007). As far as high-frequency verbs are concerned, there is a small body of research which casts doubt on their treatment in even recently published coursebooks. In their pioneering article on the lexical syllabus, Sinclair & Renouf state that delexicalised verbs are 'a major feature which is not currently taught in textbooks' (1988: 153). In a more recent study, O'Dell notes that "coursebooks traditionally have focused on the narrow lexical meaning of the words while paying scant attention to the more delexicalised uses" (1997: 263). In her in-depth analysis of the use of verb-noun collocations by German advanced learners of English, Nesselhauf points out that the number of years of classroom teaching has no influence on learners' mastery of verb-noun collocations, and concludes that "collocations … do not seem to be taught in a way that leads to their acquisition …" (2004: 238). In view of such criticism, one could wonder whether learners' deficiencies in the production of the phraseological patterns of simple verbs might be teaching-induced or, more precisely, material-induced. In other words, could the content and design of teaching material be, to some extent at least, responsible for the learners' weaknesses?

In this chapter I attempt to answer this question through a thorough investigation of the treatment of *make* and *take* in three EFL textbooks at the intermediate and advanced levels. I examine the design of the textbooks as defined by Littlejohn, namely the thinking underlying the materials (1997: 193), in terms of selection and presentation of the lexical content.

2.   Selection, sequencing and presentation of vocabulary content

The task of designing the vocabulary content of a language syllabus is based on a set of well-defined principles. The first necessary step is the careful selection of the lexical content to be learned. Frequency, range, coverage, learnability and usefulness are some of the key factors which most commonly determine this selection (Koprowski 2005; Nation 2001; O'Dell 1997; Sinclair & Renouf 1988; Waring 2001). Authors of new generation textbooks seem to be aware of the importance of offering learners "high frequency, useful vocabulary" (Cutting Edge, back cover, 2003), "general, useful lexis" (Inside Out, back cover, 2001), or "lexis and spoken language" (New Headway, back cover, 2003).[1]

Another decisive factor in the selection is the level of proficiency targeted by the course. Sequencing the lexical content of a language syllabus involves deciding what vocabulary should be taught at what level. Many authors argue that words with high frequency, range, coverage and learnability should be taught first (Nation 2001; Waring 2001), so that a starting or core vocabulary would contain the 2,000 most frequent English words. No such consensus has been achieved regarding what constitutes a more advanced vocabulary. Whilst some authors are in favour of extending the breadth of vocabulary to the lower frequency words, others argue that vocabulary improvement should not be seen only in quantitative terms but also in qualitative terms, and strongly advise to focus on depth of vocabulary knowledge. In an article on high-frequency verbs, Lennon stresses the necessity to "flesh out the incomplete or skeleton entries" (1996: 23) which advanced learners may have in their vocabulary knowledge. Again, recent textbook research provides some hints as to what is actually done in practice. Koprowski's (2005) study raises clear doubts about the procedure adopted by materials designers in the selection of the lexical phrases included in three contemporary textbooks. As for sequencing, Reda (2003: 260) argues that, although the vocabulary of an advanced syllabus should – in principle – be different to the vocabulary addressed at intermediate level or at least deal with it differently, "English for general purposes is basic English, and … perhaps surprisingly, it remains so in intermediate and upper levels in some widely used coursebooks".

---

1. For details, see Meunier & Gouverneur (2007)

Once the lexical content has been carefully selected, the next step is to introduce it into the language course through a number of teaching techniques and learning activities. Vocabulary learning can be direct (or explicit) or indirect (or implicit), form-focused or meaning-focused. Nation (2001: 388) outlines a number of principles for teaching vocabulary and insists that it should be presented from four angles: meaning-focused input, language-focused learning, meaning-focused output and fluency development.

In this chapter, I will attempt to identify the selection, sequencing and presentation principles underlying the lexical syllabus of the three textbooks through an in-depth analysis of the vocabulary exercises presented in the books, or to use Nation's terms (2001), of the language-focused learning strand of the course. In doing this, I shall attempt to answer the following questions: (1) How many instances of the verb lemmas *make* and *take* do the textbooks contain? (2) What meanings and patterns are included, and what proportion of these meanings and patterns are phraseological? (3) What are the different types of learning activities encountered? (4) What aspect of the pattern is focused on? (5) To what extent and how is acquisition favoured? (6) Do the three textbooks bear some similarities in the meanings and patterns they contain? Comparisons will be drawn both across textbooks and across levels and particularly striking and relevant results will be discussed. After a presentation of the TeMa corpus (Section 3), the methodology used to extract and classify phraseological patterns will be discussed in Section 4. The pedagogical exploitation of the corpus will be the topic of the last section.

3.   The TeMa corpus

The data used for the analysis is based on a corpus of **Te**xtbook **Ma**terial called *TeMa*. The TeMa corpus contains the pedagogical material of 10 advanced-level and 7 intermediate-level EGP coursebooks. The textbooks used for the compilation of TeMa have been selected among recent best sellers on the ELT market, with a similar number coming from each of the leading ELT materials publishers. The three series examined more closely in the present study are *Cutting Edge*, *Inside Out* and *New Headway*. TeMa is divided into subcorpora corresponding to various components: the first subdivision is made on the basis of textbook series, level, student's book and workbook; each subcorpus is then further subdivided into the following types of pedagogical material: texts, tapescripts, vocabulary exercises and exercise guidelines. The corpus then undergoes the first stage of the tagging process, whereby each subcorpus is assigned a one-to-four digit identification number (illustrated in Figure 1).

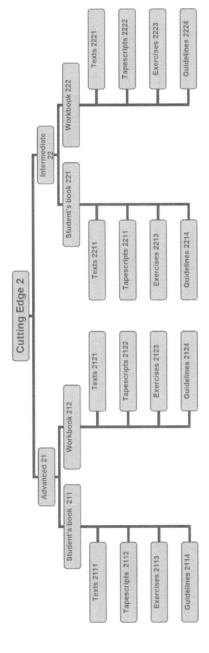

Figure 1. Cutting Edge subcorpus – annotation and breakdown

Each textbook series was first given a code number. *Cutting Edge*, for instance, was assigned number 2. A second number (1 or 2) was then added to indicate level: thus, *Cutting Edge* advanced was 21 and *Cutting Edge* intermediate was 22. A third digit indicated whether the material was from the student's book or the workbook (1 and 2 respectively). The final digit in the four digit code indicated whether the material was texts (1), tapescripts (2), vocabulary exercises (3) or exercise guidelines (4).

The TeMa corpus is innovative in a number of ways.[2] First, with over 700,000 words of textbook material, it is one of the largest pedagogic corpora ever created (see Anping 2005; Biber et al. 2002 or Römer 2004 for other examples of textbook corpora). Secondly, and more importantly, the aspect that singles out TeMa from other types of textbook corpora is the special kind of annotation that was applied to the subcorpus containing the vocabulary exercises. The purpose of the annotation is to label the learning activities the learner has to engage in and the lexical items focused on. In order to tag the corpus pedagogically, a list of over 80 codes was drawn up. These codes refer either to pedagogical tasks (such as 'complete' or 'match', see below) or to pedagogical statuses (such as 'answers' or 'words in a box'). This second type of tagging is illustrated in Figure 2.

<CEIWB-U1-P9-E8>

2223 (BC) collect#$

2223 (BC) make#$

2223 (BC) do#$

2223 (BC) go#$

2223 (CB) My brother 2223 (AB) goes# fishing every weekend, but he never catches anything!$

2223 (CB) Don't disturb your mother – she's 2223 (AB) doing# a crossword.$

2223 (CB) Christina 2223 (AB) makes# all her own clothes, and she always looks fantastic.$

2223 (CB) My uncle says he 2223 (AB) collects# antiques because it's a good way of investing money.$

Figure 2. Vocabulary exercise coding

---

2. For a detailed description of the TeMa corpus and the various ways in which it can be used, see Meunier and Gouverneur (forthcoming)

Each exercise is preceded by a precise reference. The example presented in Figure 2, i.e. <CEIWB-U1-P9-E8>, is taken from **Cutting Edge Intermediate WorkBook** – **Unit 1** – **Page 9** – **Exercise 8**. The four-digit tag before each word or sentence (2223 in this case) refers to the corpus which the exercise comes from (see Figure 1). The two-letter tags between brackets (BC) indicate the status of the four lexical items presented. (BC) is used when the words are presented in a box (B) and should be used to complete (C) sentences. This was coded 'box to complete' (BC). The (AB) tag in the last sentence of Figure 2, refers to the status of the lexical item *collect*, namely an answer from a box, hence (AB). The introductory tag in front of each exercise line gives information on the pedagogical task to be carried out. In this example, (CB) means 'complete the sentence with words from a box'. Each sentence ends with a dollar sign ($) and within the sentences, the elements focused on (e.g. answers, highlighted elements etc.) are followed by a hash (#). These additional signs make it easier to spot the beginning and the end of sentences as well as the exact lexical items being practised.

So far textbook research has mainly been carried out manually, very often using page by page analysis (see for instance Vellenga 2004). In this respect, the TeMa corpus is particularly innovative since the annotation procedure allows for automatic query of the corpus (see Meunier & Gouverneur forthcoming).

Table 1 is a breakdown of the twelve subcorpora used in this study: the vocabulary exercise subcorpus of the intermediate and advanced student's books and workbooks of *Cutting Edge*, *Inside Out* and *New Headway*.

Table 1. Exercise subcorpus breakdown

Corpus used for the analysis	Words: 72,566	%
Cutting Edge	**24,078**	**33%**
2113	5,869	
2123	6,242	
2213	5,794	
2223	6,173	
Inside Out	**26,629**	**37%**
3113	7,109	
3123	8,158	
3213	5,747	
3223	5,615	
New Headway	**21,859**	**30%**
6113	5,582	
6123	10,851	
6213	3,321	
6223	2,105	

As shown in Table 1, the words are equally distributed between the three textbooks, with each one providing about 30 % of the total number of words.

4. Methodology: Extracting and classifying phraseological patterns

The study focuses on the phraseological patterns of *make* and *take*. These patterns were identified and defined in two phases. The first step involved extracting all the instances of the lemmas *make* and *take* in the twelve vocabulary exercise subcorpora. This was done automatically. Running concordances in WordSmith Tools3 yielded the following results (cf. Table 2): out of the total 72,566 words of the exercises, there were 298 occurrences of *make* and 241 occurrences of *take*, which corresponds to a relative frequency of 41 *make* and 33 *take* per 10,000 words. The instances appear to be unevenly distributed between the two levels, with almost twice as many instances of *make* and *take* in the intermediate exercises compared to the advanced exercises, as shown in Table 2 (see figures in bold). These results should however be interpreted with extreme caution as they provide initial quantitative evidence but no qualitative information on the use and treatment of the verbs.

Table 3 displays the distribution of the *make* and *take* occurrences across textbooks without level distinction.[3]

The overall picture that emerges is that the *make* and *take* lemmas are equally distributed among the three textbooks, each containing about one third of the occurrences, with slightly fewer in *New Headway*.

Table 2. *Make* and *take* lemmas distribution across levels

Corpus	Words	Make lemmas	/ 10,000	Take lemmas	/ 10,000
All exercises	72,566	298	41	241	33
Advanced	43,780	150	**34**	111	**25**
Intermediate	28,786	148	**51,5**	130	**45**

Table 3. Proportions of *make* and *take* lemmas across textbooks

Textbook	Make	Take
Cutting Edge	37%	36%
Inside Out	36%	35%
New Headway	27%	29%
Total	100%	100%

---

3. No level distinction proved relevant at this stage.

Table 4. *Make* meanings and patterns

Meanings and patterns	Examples
1. Create, produce	*the company also makes products that ... (6111)*
	2213 (B) *made in Japan*
2. Causative uses	*It made me feel quite worried for you.* (3121)
	3213 (MQT) *make#* 3213 (MA) *someone angry#$*
3. Do / perform	*It is very easy to make mistakes in your letters...* (3121)
	3223 (AE) *make a lot of noise#...*
4. Earn	*I stand to make a lot of money if it's accepted.* (6123)
	6223 (A) *make profit#$*
5. Delexical uses	*... you're not very good at making decisions about your own life...* (3211)
	6223 (A) *make a complaint*
6. Phrasal verbs	*they need someone to make up the number for football* (2121)
	It took two days for them to make up. (3223)
7. Other uses	*She makes perhaps 26 miles per hour* (6111)
	I do hope you can make it (3211)
	3223 (MQ) *make#$*

After extracting all the instances of *make* and *take* in the twelve subcorpora, the second step consisted in sorting them into their various meanings and patterns in order to identify the phraseological patterns. This classification was carried out manually. The meanings were defined on the basis of previous studies (see for instance Altenberg & Granger 2001) and the senses presented in three commonly used learners' dictionaries.[4]

Tables 4 and 5 contain the meanings and patterns that were identified for each verb.[5]

The verb + object pattern appeared to be the most prominent syntactic pattern and was therefore selected as the pattern to be examined, both on the basis of its frequency and also on the basis of Nesselhauf's recent study on learners' misuse of high-frequency verbs, which has shown that the verb-object structure is the most problematic pattern for common verbs in advanced learner production

---

4. The dictionaries used are: *Macmillan English Dictionary, Cambridge Advanced Learner Dictionary* and *Longman Dictionary of Contemporary English*.

5. The meanings distinguished in the exercises are similar to the meanings distinguished in the texts. Therefore, in order to be exhaustive, the examples are taken both from the exercises and from the texts.

Table 5. *Take* meanings and patterns

Meanings and patterns	Examples
1. Move	*A taxi took it from West London to Gatwick Airport (2211)*
	6213 (MQE) *Can you take us to the airport?#$*
2. Eat or drink	*… and they probably take drugs too… (3221)*
	6213 (CB) *do you take milk in your tea?*
3. Phrasal verbs	*…you suggest to everyone that they take off their ties… (2221)*
	2223 (MQ) *You really take# 2223 (MA) after your father#*
4. Need	*… after finally taking the time to read them… (2221)*
	… it usually takes about a year to get used to it… (6211)
5. Delexical uses	*the unions finally decided to take action… (6123)*
6. Think of in a certain way	*Take it easy, relax… (2113)*
	The doctor told me to 3223 (AB) take# things easy.
7. Accept	*Staff will be available to take your enquiry the following times. (3221)*
	6213 (BC) *take your call#$*
8. Transport	*We took the ferry from Calais… (6123)*
	2213 (BU) *take a train#$*
9. Other uses	3223 (BC) *take#$*

(Nesselhauf 2004). We decided to examine restricted collocations, as defined by Cowie (1998), i.e. word combinations in which some substitution is possible, but with some arbitrary limitations on substitution; in which at least one element has a non-literal meaning, and at least one element is used in its literal sense; and the whole combination is transparent. The phraseological patterns of *make* and *take* examined in the following sections are thus verb-noun restricted collocations.

The various senses of *make* and *take* were thus grouped into larger categories according to the working definition. For *make*, the delexical uses, 'earn' and 'do/perform' senses were included in the restricted collocations category. Other major meanings and patterns were kept in distinct groups, and those for which there were only one or two examples were all put into an "Other" class. The phrasal verbs were deliberately kept in a separate category, since they represent a particular kind of phraseology, which is not dealt with in this study. After the classification five senses remained for *make*: 'produce', 'causative', 'phrasal verbs', 'restricted collocations' and 'other'. For *take*, the 'restricted collocations' category includes the delexical uses and the 'need', 'accept' and 'transport' senses.

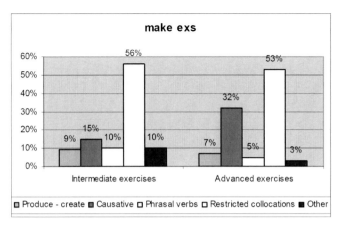

Figure 3. Proportions of *make* meanings and patterns across levels

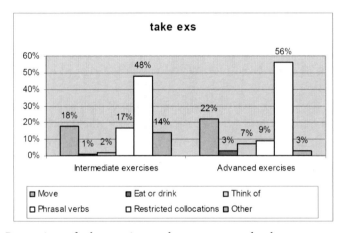

Figure 4. Proportions of *take* meanings and patterns across levels

The first issue addressed in the analysis has to do with the selection of *make* and *take* patterns included in the exercises. The proportions of meanings and patterns included at each level are given in Figures 3 and 4.

The two graphs show that, without textbook distinction, the restricted collocations are the most frequent type of use in the exercises at both levels, with almost half of the total number of instances. The relatively high proportion of the 'other' category is due to the large number of isolated words, for instance in boxes. As far as the distribution across textbooks is concerned, the picture is similar, with each series containing at least 50% of collocations.

These encouraging figures attest the strong presence of the phraseological patterns of *make* and *take* in the textbooks. Materials writers seem to have taken special care to include a significant number of phraseological uses in the exercises. A word of caution is however required here as the percentages only indicate that the phraseological patterns *appear* in the exercises but do not give any further details on whether or not those patterns are exploited pedagogically, and if so, how they are treated.

5.   Pedagogical exploitation

5.1   Exercise focus

In order to gain deeper insight into the actual treatment of *make* and *take* in the textbooks, all the instances of restricted collocations were categorised according to whether they were the explicit focus of the exercise or not. Three degrees of focus were established: direct focus, indirect focus and no focus at all. The pedagogical codes beside the verb-object collocations (e.g. AE, B, H) were used to identify the type of focus. In the direct focus option, the verb, the object or the whole expression are practised clearly and intentionally, as in [*3113(A)make# a wish*], where the learner has to produce *make* to complete the expression with *wish*. If the focus is indirect, then the pattern is not the direct focus of the exercise but is included in a sequence which is the focus of the task and which is short enough for the learner to notice the pattern. In [*6113(DQ)no progress can be made# 6113(DA)everything is at a standstill#$*],[6] for instance, the aim of

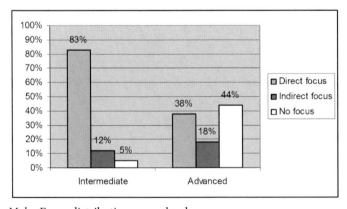

Figure 5. *Make*: Focus distribution across levels

---

6.   The two tags (DQ) and (DA) refer to the question part and the answer part of a 'define' exercise (D).

Table 6. Types of focus distribution across textbooks

	Direct focus		No focus		Indirect focus	
	Interm.	Adv.	Interm.	Adv.	Interm.	Adv.
Cutting Edge	77%	39%	0%	45%	23%	16%
Inside Out	83%	35%	9%	55%	8%	10%
New Headway	87%	38%	9%	40%	4%	22%

the exercise is to find a synonym for the expression containing *make* (and not to learn the pattern *make progress*), but the expression is so short that the learner's attention is inevitably drawn to the pattern. There is no focus at all when the phraseological pattern is part of the general context and no attention is drawn to it, as in [*2113(CB)Have you ever 2113(H)sought spiritual advice# before making a big decision?$*]. In this case, the focus of the exercise is on *to seek spiritual advice* and not on *to make a big decision*.

The degree of focus varies significantly according to proficiency level, as illustrated for *make* in Figure 5.

While the phraseological patterns of *make* are the objects of direct focus in 83% of all the exercises at intermediate level, only 38% of the advanced exercises directly focus on those patterns. Figure 5 shows that, despite encouraging preliminary results as to the number of phraseological patterns in the exercises at both levels (see Figures 3 and 4), careful observation of the tags and coding helps refine these results. Even though the restricted collocations of *make* and *take* do appear in substantial proportions in all exercises, they are actually studied only in intermediate textbooks. They are then relegated to the background context and are no longer dealt with explicitly in upper-level coursebooks. The percentages in Table 6 reveal that the three textbooks all follow the same trend, i.e. noticeable decrease of direct focus on phraseological patterns at advanced level (average of only 37%), with a high percentage of no focus at all (average of about 45%) and an average of 16% of indirect focus.

This lack of direct focus on restricted collocations at the advanced level might well be one of the reasons why more proficient learners have so many problems dealing with high-frequency verbs. Instead of fleshing out the knowledge they acquire in the early stages of language learning, as Lennon advises (1996), textbooks tend to insist on high-frequency verbs at the intermediate level and play down their importance at higher levels because they are considered mastered or acquired. This is most regrettable, since, as learner corpus evidence has demonstrated, this is far from being the case.

5.2   Learning activities

This section explores the learning activities, i.e. what learners are required to do in the vocabulary exercises. Only the activities with direct focus on the phraseological pattern are considered. Here again, the use of tags both speeded up and simplified the process of automatic identification of the exercises.

The analysis of all the vocabulary exercises in the three textbooks at both levels revealed eight different types of activities, which can be grouped into four larger categories: 'complete' 'match', 'replace', and 'understand'. The 'complete' category, tagged (C), refers to exercises in which learners have to fill in blanks in sentences. Learners are expected either to provide the answer from scratch (C), or to choose from a number of possibilities provided in a box (CB), in a previous exercise (CE) or from a multiple choice included in the sentence (CZ). Matching exercises (M) involve matching the beginning and the end of an expression or the meaning of a word or an expression and the form corresponding to this meaning. The third type of exercise, 'replace' (R), refers to exercises where learners have to replace one element highlighted in a sentence either with one element that is not given (R) or with one element to be chosen from a box (RB). In the 'Understand' (U) category, learners have to prove they understand a particular word or expression.

Table 7 displays the proportions of the various exercises at the two levels.[7] No verb or textbook distinction proved relevant here. A first noticeable feature is the relatively high degree of continuity in the learning activities from one level to the other. This is attested by the prevalence of 'complete' category in both intermediate

Table 7. Learning activities for *make* and *take* across levels

Learning activities	Intermediate	Advanced
Complete (C)	23%	18%
Compl. Box (CB)	22%	25%
Compl. Ex (CE)	15%	7%
Compl. Mult. Ch. (CZ)	3%	9%
Match (M)	18%	17%
Replace (R)	1%	7%
Replace box (RB)	0%	4%
Understand (U)	12%	0%

7.   The total proportions do not reach 100% (respectively 94% and 87%). The reason for this is that some of the occurrences of *make* and *take* do not correspond to tasks but to answers or words in a box and are therefore not taken into account in this table.

and advanced exercises: 63% and 59% respectively. Matching exercises were also found at both levels in similar proportions (17% and 18%). Alongside this partial consistency, Table 7 reveals three striking discrepancies between levels. First, intermediate textbooks ask learners to go back to previous exercises (CE) in order to find the answers to the exercise they are working on twice as often as advanced textbooks do (15% to 7%). The second difference has to do with the proportion of 'understand' activities: 12% in intermediate exercises and 0% in advanced exercises. The third discrepancy lies in the proportions of the 'replace' category: 1% in intermediate exercises and 7% in advanced exercises. These are purely quantitative observations, but aside from their primary descriptive power, the figures presented in Table 7 can also be used to shed light on the mental processes triggered in the learning activities at the various stages of learning, since, by definition, learning activities can be expected to activate particular cognitive processes that favour learning and acquisition.

Nation (2001) describes three key processes involved in vocabulary acquisition: noticing,[8] retrieval and generative use. *Noticing* occurs when attention is given to a lexical item, i.e. when the learner is made aware that this item exists as a "useful language item" (2001:63). This is the case when learners look up words in a dictionary, guess meaning from context, deliberately study a word, or have a word explained to them. The second important process is *retrieval*, which may be receptive or productive. Receptive retrieval involves seeing or hearing a word or an expression and having to recall its meaning in listening or reading. Productive retrieval is when a learner wants to communicate a particular meaning and has to recall the appropriate form corresponding to that meaning in speaking or in writing. *Generative use* occurs when previously met words are encountered or used in new contexts. It is closely related to the concepts of recycling and repetition. Generative use, like retrieval, may also be receptive, when a word is met in a new reading or listening context, or productive, when a known word is used in a new speaking or writing context.

Given the fact that collocational use is a major problem for advanced learners, and that completing a sentence requires their being able to retrieve and use the pattern appropriately, the prevalence of complete exercises at both levels is very positive. One should nevertheless proceed with caution, since the degree to which productive retrieval is triggered depends on where the answer is to be retrieved from. In this respect, less than 20 % of all the exercises in the advanced textbooks require actual production of the answer (retrieval from the mental lexicon). In all the other cases, learners only have to select the right solution from a

---

8.   For a detailed discussion of the concept of noticing and its role in second language acquisition and learning, see Schmidt 1990, 1992, 1993.

given list of words or expressions, which represents a lower degree of productive retrieval. This apparent lack of cognitive complexity might however be said to be compensated by the large number of multiple choice exercises (CZ), which are three times as frequent in advanced textbooks (9%) as they are in intermediate textbooks (3%). Such exercises constitute repeated input entries and may favour noticing of the words or expressions included in the multiple choice. The fact that such exercises include a number of distractors might also be interpreted as a way of making the 'complete' activities more complex at the advanced level and more appropriate to the learners' proficiency.

The difference in (CE) activities (i.e; Complete – find answer in the previous Exercise) in intermediate (15%) and advanced exercises (7%) implies that there is more recycling and immediate retrieval at the intermediate level. If one assumes that some of the lexical items encountered in one exercise are re-used in new contexts in the surrounding exercises, which is most probable, this would mean that referring the learner to previous exercises encourages generative use, recycling and repetition, three key factors for vocabulary acquisition, which, unfortunately, seem to be lacking at more advanced stages of learning.

Understanding the meaning of a word or an expression is a common activity in the early stages of learning (12%) and is abandoned at later stages (0%). This state of affairs is regrettable, as understanding requires noticing. This is not to say however that noticing is completely absent from advanced exercises. The 'replace' activities, for instance, are quite common in advanced exercises (11%) and almost completely absent in intermediate exercises (1%). In order to be able to perform such tasks, learners have to focus their attention on the word or expression to replace, and thereby notice its form and/or meaning.

All in all, the analysis identified both level-independent and level-specific learning activities. One might assume that the similarities and differences between levels reflect the materials writers' wish to adapt to learners' proficiency levels. Whether the choices are made with full awareness of the learners' developmental stages and of the mental processes triggered by the various exercises is an issue worth addressing in the future (see Gouverneur forthcoming).

5.3   Lexical focus

In her study on the inappropriate use of collocations and their elements, Nesselhauf (2004) claims that the hypothesis according to which the restriction in verb-noun collocations only affects objects must be challenged (2004:68). The verb is also a problem, to the extent that it even represents the most frequently deviant element (2004:71) in learners misuses, followed by the noun. In a considerable

Table 8. Object of focus in the learning activities

Object of focus	Intermediate	Advanced
the verb	**31%**	7%
the object	5%	**41%**
the whole expression	52%	48%
the two parts	12%	4%

number of cases, it is the whole collocation that is incorrect. The main problem is a wrong choice of verb (see Nesselhauf 2004: 73). *Make* and *take* are among the verbs that are not used by learners when they should be (2004: 77) and *make* appears to be the more problematic of the two.

The annotation of the TeMa corpus makes it possible to analyse precisely which element of the collocation is being practised in the exercises with direct focus on the pattern. The focused element can be the verb, as in [*3213(A)made# a mistake*]; the noun, as in [*3113(CE)you'll only make 3113(AE)progress#$*]; the whole expression, as in [*…and we 6223(AE)made a complaint#…*]; or the two parts of a collocation at the same time, in matching exercises for instance, such as in [*3113(MQT)to make# 3113(MA)way for the new*], where the verb and the noun are given equal weight.

Table 8 highlights the marked contrast between the object of focus in intermediate and advanced exercises. Intermediate exercises place more emphasis on providing the verb (31%) than the advanced exercises (7%), which tend to focus on the object (41%). Such practice is in direct contradiction to findings of advanced learner corpus studies. Since the problems are mainly related to the choice of the verb, exercises should arguably focus primarily on studying these verbs and not the nouns they are used with; This was noted by Nesselhauf (2004: 269): "It is regrettable …, that many of the existing exercises for practising collocations focus on the noun …, most often providing the verb and leaving a gap for the noun in gap-filling exercises. What is much more helpful for the learner is exercises providing the noun and asking for the verb". Ideally, practice of the verb, which is characteristic of the early stages of learning, should be reinforced at higher proficiency levels. However, on the positive side, the advanced books place a great deal of emphasis on the whole expression, which means that learners are made aware of the co-occurrence of the two elements of the expression as the constituent parts of a recurrent chunk in the language. However, those exercises do not usually address productive skills.

As for the lexical consistency across the three textbooks, Koprowski (2005: 330) strongly criticized the lack of lexical agreement of three textbooks in the selection

Table 9. Lexical consistency across textbooks

	Make		Take	
	Advanced	Intermediate	Advanced	Intermediate
3 textbooks	7%	15%	0%	0%
2 textbooks	7%	35%	21%	22%
1 textbook	86%	50%	79%	78%

of the lexical phrases they contain. The present study confirms Koprowski's criticism, as shown in Table 9.

Of all the phraseological patterns of *make* in the advanced exercises, only 7% are common to the three textbooks, 7% are common to two textbooks and 86% appear in only one textbook. In the intermediate exercises, 15% of the collocations appear in the three textbooks, 35% appear in two textbooks and 50% in only one textbook. The picture is even more striking for *take*, where not one single collocation is common to the three advanced textbooks, 21% appear in two textbooks and 79% appear in only one textbook. In the intermediate exercises, none appears in the three textbooks, 22% appear in two textbooks and 78% appear in only one textbook.

These results are rather puzzling and question the selection principles adopted by textbook designers. If frequency, range, coverage, learnability and usefulness are widely accepted criteria, what may account for such varied lexical content? One might argue that the lexical items dealt with in the exercises strongly depend on the vocabulary contained in documents and the texts, but this argument has only limited power since many exercises – and particularly those on phraseology- are developed independently of the texts (see Meunier & Gouverneur 2007). This lack of consistency is therefore difficult to understand and justify.

6. Conclusion

This chapter has aimed to shed light on the current treatment of the phraseological patterns of two high-frequency verbs in three commonly used EGP textbooks. Comparisons between levels (intermediate and advanced) and between textbooks through automatic query of a textbook corpus have yielded puzzling results regarding the selection and presentation of the phraseological patterns of *make* and *take*. Discrepancies across levels have been shown to be particularly striking, mainly as far as presentation is concerned. While intermediate textbooks devote many of their vocabulary exercises to the explicit practice of *make* and *take* verb-noun collocations, textbook designers clearly play down their importance in the exercises intended for advanced learners, despite the formidable difficulty these patterns still cause at an advanced level. As far as comparisons of different textbooks of the same level are concerned, the three textbooks have been shown to follow similar trends in the presentation of the phraseological patterns. A serious lack of consistency was identified however in the selection of the patterns, with very few collocations common to the three textbooks.

All in all, the methodology used to analyse the TeMa corpus has been shown to be effective. The innovative pedagogical annotation allowed us to automatically retrieve a wide range of features and, in doing so, to deal with topical issues that cannot as effectively be tackled using the traditional page-by-page textbook research method. The sometimes puzzling results yielded in this analysis have opened up new avenues which are worth investigating further in order to improve the treatment of phraseology in textbooks.

Acknowledgements

I gratefully acknowledge the support of the Communauté française de Belgique, which funded this research within the framework of the 'Action de recherche concertée' project entitled 'Foreign Language Learning: Phraseology and Discourse' (No. 03/08-301).

References

Altenberg, B. & S. Granger (2001). The grammatical and lexical patterning of MAKE in native and non-native student writing. *Applied Linguistics 22* (2), 173–195.

Anping, He (2005). Corpus-based evaluation of ELT textbooks. Paper presented at the joint conference of the AAACL and the ICAME, 12–15 May 2005, University of Michigan.

Biber, D., S. Conrad, R. Reppen, P. Byrd & M. Helt (2002). Speaking and writing in the university: A multidimensional comparison. *TESOL Quarterly 36* (1), 9–48.

Biber, D., S. Conrad & V. Cortes (2004). If you look at...: Lexical bundles in university teaching and textbooks. *Applied Linguistics 25* (3), 371–405.

Walter, E. & K. Woodford (eds) (2005) *Cambridge advanced learner's dictionary.* Cambridge: Cambridge University Press.

Cowie, A. (ed.) (1998). *Phraseology. Theory, analysis, and applications.* Oxford: Oxford University Press.

Gouverneur, C. (forthcoming). Phraseology in instructed foreign language learning: A corpus of textbook material under scrutiny. PhD dissertation, Université Catholique de Louvain.

Kaszubski, P. (2000). Lexical profiling of English (learner) corpora: Can we measure advancement levels? In Lewandowska-Tomaszczyk, B. & J. P. Melia (eds) *PALC'99: Practical applications in language corpora. Papers from the International Conference at the University of Łódź, Poland, 15–18 April*, 1999, 249–86. Frankfurt: Peter Lang.

Koprowski, M. (2005). Investigating the usefulness of lexical phrases in contemporary coursebooks. *ELT Journal 59* (4), 322–332.

Leech, G., P. Rayson & A. Wilson (2001). *Word frequencies in written and spoken English*. Harlow: Longman.

Lennon, P. (1996). Getting 'easy" verbs wrong at the advanced level. *International Review of Applied Linguistics 34* (1), 23–36.

Littlejohn, A. (1997). The analysis of language teaching materials: Inside the Trojan horse. In Schmitt, N. & M. McCarthy (eds) *Vocabulary: Description, acquisition, pedagogy*, 190–216. Oxford: Oxford University Press.

Meunier, F. & C. Gouverneur (2007). The treatment of phraseology in ELT textbooks. In Hidalgo, E., L. Quereda & J. Santana (eds.) *Corpora in the foreign language classroom. Selected papers from the Sixth International Conference on Teaching and Language Corpora (TaLC 6)*. University of Granada, Spain, 4–7 July, 2004, 119–139. Amsterdam: Rodopi.

Meunier, F. & C. Gouverneur (forthcoming). New types of corpora for new educational challenges: Collecting, annotating and exploiting a corpus of textbook material. In Aijmer, K. (ed.) *Corpora and Language Teaching*.

Nation, I.S.P. (2001). *Learning vocabulary in another language*. Cambridge: Cambridge University Press.

Nesselhauf, N. (2004). *Collocations in a learner corpus*. Amsterdam: John Benjamins.

Nitta, R. & S. Gardner (2005). Consciousness-raising and practice in ELT coursebooks. *ELT Journal 59* (1), 3–13.

O'Dell, F. (1997). Incorporating vocabulary into the syllabus. In Schmitt, N. & M. McCarthy (eds.) *Vocabulary: Description, acquisition and pedagogy*, 258–278. Oxford: Oxford University Press.

Reda, G. (2003). English coursebooks: Prototype texts and basic vocabulary norms. *ELT Journal 57* (3), 260–268.

Ringbom, H. (1998). High-frequency verbs in the ICLE Corpus. In Renouf, A. (ed.) *Explorations in corpus linguistics*, 191–200. Amsterdam: Rodopi.

Römer, U. (2004). Comparing real and ideal language learner input: The use of an EFL textbook corpus in corpus linguistics and language teaching. In Aston, G., S. Bernardini and D. Stewart (eds.) *Corpora and language learners*, 151–168. Amsterdam: John Benjamins.

Römer, U. (2005). *Progressives, patterns, pedagogy. A corpus-driven approach to English progressive forms, functions, contexts and didactics*. Amsterdam: John Benjamins.

Rundell, M. & G. Fox (eds) (2002). *Macmillan English dictionary for advanced learners*. Oxford: Macmillan.

Schmidt, R. (1990). The role of consciousness in second language learning. *Applied Linguistics 11*, 129–158.

Schmidt, R. (1992). Psychological mechanisms underlying second language fluency. *Studies in Second Language Acquisition 14*, 357–385.

Schmidt, R. (1993). Awareness and second language acquisition. *Annual Review of Applied Linguistics, 13*, 206–226.

Sinclair, J. & A. Renouf (1988). A lexical syllabus for language learning. In Carter, R. & M. McCarthy (eds.) *Vocabulary and language teaching*, 140–158. Harlow: Longman.

Summers, D. (ed.) (2003) *Longman dictionary of contemporary English*. Harlow: Pearson Education.

Vellenga, H. (2004). Learning pragmatics from ESL & EFL textbooks: How likely? *TESL-EJ 8* (2). Available from http://www.kyoto-su.ac.jp/information/tesl-ej/ej30/a3.html. Last consulted 16.07.07.

Waring, B. (2001). *How should teachers incorporate vocabulary teaching into their classes?* Published online in ELT News. Available online at http://www1.harenet.ne.jp/~waring/papers/eltnews.html Last consulted 16.07.07.

Textbooks

Barker, H., S. Cunningham & P. Moor (2003). *Cutting edge advanced. Teacher's book*. Harlow: Pearson Education.

Comyns Carr, J. & F. Eales (2005). *Cutting edge intermediate workbook*. Harlow: Pearson Education.

Cunningham, S. & P. Moor (2003). *Cutting edge advanced. Student's book*. Harlow: Pearson Education.

Cunningham, S. & P. Moor (2005). *Cutting edge intermediate. Student's book*. Harlow: Pearson Education.

Gomm, H. & J. Hird (2000). *Inside out. Teacher's book intermediate*. Spain: Macmillan Education.

Gomm, H. & J. Hird (2001). *Inside out. Teacher's book advanced*. Spain: Macmillan Education.

Jones, C. & T. Bastow (2001). *Inside out. Student's book advanced*. Spain: Macmillan Education.

Jones, C. (2001). *Inside out. Workbook advanced*. Spain: Macmillan Education.

Kay, S. & J. Vaughan (2000). *Inside out. Student's book intermediate*. Spain: Macmillan Education.

Kerr, P. (2000). *Inside out. Workbook with key intermediate*. Spain: Macmillan Education.

Soars, L. & J. (2003). *New headway advanced. Student's book*. Oxford: Oxford University Press.

Soars, L. & J. (2003). *New headway advanced. Teacher's book*. Oxford: Oxford University Press.

Soars, L. & J. (2003). *New headway advanced. Workbook*. Oxford: Oxford University Press.

Soars, L. & J. (2003). *New headway intermediate. Student's book*. Oxford: Oxford University Press.

Soars, L. & J. (2003). *New headway intermediate. Teacher's book*. Oxford: Oxford University Press.

Soars, L. & J. (2003). *New headway intermediate. Workbook*. Oxford: Oxford University Press.

SECTION IV

Concluding remarks

Phraseology in language learning and teaching

Where to from here?

Sylviane Granger and Fanny Meunier

This concluding section aims to take stock of the work devoted to phraseology in foreign language learning and teaching and to identify major avenues for future theoretical and applied work in the field. A distinction will be made between what is known about phraseology and what still remains to be discovered, with teachers and learners taking centre stage.

Linguistic analysis has amply demonstrated the patterned nature of language, both lexically and grammatically, stressed the pervasiveness of phraseology in oral and written communication, and the difficulties that learners have in mastering native-like phraseology. Psycholinguistic research has also shown that language is, to a great extent, acquired, stored and processed in chunks. It would therefore not seem unreasonable to propose that phraseology should occupy a central and uncontroversial position in instructed second language acquisition (ISLA).[1]

To date however, although phraseology has received more attention, notably via pedagogical lexicography, it would be misleading to claim that there is uncontroversial consensus about its role in pedagogy. Instead, the picture is one of contrasts.

To the layperson, language described in terms of 'phrases' (and not as single words) probably prompts the following images: Berlitz-like phrase books for tourists or businessmen and typically humorous books contrasting idioms in various languages. This said, the Berlitz-like books, initially looked down upon by teaching specialists, nevertheless constituted the first attempts to provide users

---

1. ISLA is used here as a cover term for second language acquisition and foreign language learning, but also for any approach to a non-native language which involves the use of pedagogical material, be it in tutored or self-instructed settings.

with ready-made expressions in the target language. As for idioms, teachers and students alike seem to view them as phraseological teddy bears,[2] probably not so much because they use them very often but because they are very popular for the fascinating cultural window they open onto the target language. For trained teachers, phraseology is often associated with collocations (typically verbs or adjectives plus nouns collocations) or with pragmatically and communicatively useful phrases such as 'how do you do?', 'nice to meet you', or 'what's the weather like today?' Concepts such as word grammar, colligations, collostructions and patterns probably do not rank very highly on teachers' priority lists, which is perfectly understandable given the relative novelty of such concepts. As for learners, they very often consider[3] a foreign language as a mix of grammar and lexis hopefully acquired through the practice of the four skills.

All in all, whilst concepts such as frequency, statistical co-occurrence, variability, idiomaticity, patterns and phraseology are becoming increasingly familiar to researchers addressing linguistically-related issues, they still have a long way to go to reach the classroom, even if only indirectly, and numerous challenges must be faced. One of those challenges is **dealing with learners' attitudes** and **boosting their motivation.** Some may simply not be interested in learning multiword units when they consider that one word only is problematic enough to learn (see Coxhead, this volume); others may be afraid of being accused of plagiarism (ibid.), and yet others may give preponderance to communication rather than accuracy (although one could argue that accuracy and effective communication often go hand in hand). One of the future challenges for teachers will be to help learners become aware of the pervasiveness of phraseology and its potential in promoting fluency in language (e.g. storage and retrieval facilities, improved receptive and productive communicative competence, see Wray and Fitzpatrick, this volume).

A second issue that should be addressed is the **availability of the phraseological information.** Teachers and learners should find the information they are looking for rapidly and easily, and here, the limits of paper and ink seem to have been reached. We believe that the phraseological (r)evolution in language learning and teaching will be electronic or will simply not be. Wible (this volume) has proposed ways of accounting for learners' needs and for empowering both learners and teachers with electronic literacy. In electronic dictionaries, the linear restrictions and unique access key of the paper dimension can be overcome via improved look-up processes and hypertext functionality. As for textbooks, it seems that only sound use of new literacies (online reading, hyperlinks, highlighting of

---

2.   In reference to Hasselgren's (1994) 'lexical teddy bears'

3.   This view of language can be partly teaching-induced.

salient aspects, exhaustive presentation of items, multiplicity of elaboration and rehearsal options) will foster the phraseological enterprise, without undermining other aspects such as focus on grammar or culture. Recourse to new technologies is one practical way of overcoming the thorny paradox that teachers face: because of time pressure, they need to generalize, to take shortcuts, which often involves making a complex reality appear simpler than it actually is; they find it hard to reconcile this need with the atomizing character of a phraseological approach to language, which presents every word as having its own meaning, collocations, colligations, etc depending on the context in which it is used (see Hoey 1998). The point is well made by Cook (2003: 108): "Hardly surprisingly, the description of English which emerges from corpus analysis (...) is dauntingly complex and particular. But this description cannot be presented to students all at once. The issue still remains how to simplify and stage the language presented to learners, and to simplify the rules used to explain it, in a way which will enable them to come gradually closer to native speaker use (if that is their goal)."

But does the pervasiveness of phraseology in language mean, as John Sinclair suggested in the very title of his plenary at the Louvain phraseology conference, that the new motto for ESL and EFL teachers should be: 'The phrase, the whole phrase and nothing but the phrase"? In other words, should the **centrality of the phrase in language** unquestionably lead to the **centrality of the phrase in teaching?** Statements on the importance of phraseology in language description and its potential for teaching abound: Sinclair (ibid) points that "the normal primary carrier of meaning is the phrase and not the word"; Porto (1998) states that lexical phrases are "an ideal unit for teaching" which "prove highly motivating by developing fluency at very early stages and thus promote a sense of achievement", and that lexical phrases are "highly memorable for learners and easy to pick up". It should however be acknowledged that many of the claims made in the literature lack substantiation. Do lexical phrases really prove highly motivating for learners? Are these phrases really easily retrievable and highly accessible? Whilst a few studies are beginning to assess such claims (Coxhead, Wray & Fitzpatrick, this volume; and Eyckmans et al., 2005) and tend to demonstrate that phraseological units may be good candidates for teaching an L2, there is an urgent need for more empirical evidence of the actual impact of a phraseological approach to teaching and learning. The types of phrases that are worth teaching as wholes, the optimal length (if any) of such phrases, or the effects on short and long term retention are but a few of the questions that future research needs to address.

Another challenge that teachers and learners of an L2 face is how to deal with the **lexis-grammar interface**. Many proponents of a lexical/phraseological approach typically tend to present grammar and phraseology as opposed. Porto (1998) suggests that "some patterns which traditionally receive grammatical pedagogic treatment might indeed be best introduced as lexical phrases". She gives the examples of first, second, and third conditionals; passive; reported speech; -ing form; past participle; *will, would,* and *going to,* and adds that "the concept of time <u>may be</u> (our underlining) most efficiently presented through lexis rather than tense". Porto picks up Lewis's idea that learners should explore grammar by themselves and that "[g]rammar is primarily receptive" (Lewis 1993: 149). A radically different view however is expressed by Lowe (2006), who claims that proposing a new and original way of teaching grammar does not guarantee its success:

> some post-modernists are arguing for a new way of teaching grammar, by not teaching it as such but by letting it emerge. They argue for drawing the learners' attention to grammar in text holistically (...) [J]ust because this procedure is new and original, does it make it more efficient in learning terms than what went before, which as the pre-parceling of grammar into learnable 'grammar items' or 'grammar units'?

Our view of phraseology in language learning and teaching is in accordance with Lowe's. Whilst we strongly believe in putting more emphasis on phrases in second/foreign language learning, we would consider it wrong to equate this emphasis with an absence of focus on grammar. Together with Harwood (2002: 153), we want to "simply call for the teaching of lexis to come higher up the agenda". We also believe in **principled eclecticism** (as proposed by Meunier, in press) to help meet the needs of various types of learners thanks to the inclusion of more analytical, functional, data-driven or cognitive approaches in language learning. Options should also be provided for more refined collostructional analyses and extra corpus examples. We are of course well aware that it is not because something is frequent in the language that is necessarily worth teaching. What is taught should make sense to the learners, be useful for them and be adapted both to their areas of interests and to their level. We thus call for a harmonious combination of technology (corpora, statistical measures, etc.), common sense and teachers' experience in selecting relevant units for teaching.

Another challenge that must be addressed in the future is the danger of **extrapolating from L1 and second language learning to foreign language learning**. Here again, Lowe (2006) offers insightful comments and states that whilst it:

> can hardly be doubted now that L1 learners, children that is, engage some kind of in-built predisposition to 'grow' their language in an immersion environment through an unconscious internal process of meaning-mapping, chunking, and approximation, utilising the ever-present parental feedback [...] it can be doubted [...] that the majority of L2 learners will benefit from being expected to operate the same process – i.e. a process of absorbing language unconsciously – as the primary process in the L2 classroom.

Instructed settings are typically considered as input-poor environments and the advantages of input-rich L1 and second language environments must be compensated by different learning and teaching strategies such as increased awareness raising activities, more focus on form or forms, and more explicit and sometimes even intrusive approaches to learning. Given the limited number of hours devoted to foreign language teaching in schools, it would be utopian to expect grammar and phraseology to somehow take care of themselves. We therefore urgently need to identify the best ways to teach them using the various methodologies and data at our disposal (corpus data, cognitive approaches, elicitation techniques) and to promote interdisciplinary research into phraseology (see Granger & Meunier in press, for an overview of the many faces of phraseology).

The next (dual) challenge lies in the hands of corpus linguists and NLP specialists: first, promoting constant **refinement of statistical measures and automatic procedures** to help uncover frequent multiword units that might be worth teaching, and secondly, creating **ready-made and user-friendly interfaces** to enable learners and teachers to access multiword units from a variety of genres and text types. Recent corpus-based research has demonstrated that the field of phraseology is wider than was previously thought and that compositional prefabricated units are more frequent and useful than the colourful, non-compositional idioms that are often focused on in teaching (cf. Siepmann this volume; Paquot 2007; De Cock 2004). Further research is needed to refine the methods and measures used to uncover relevant units and make them accessible to learners.

A final challenge lies in addressing the acute need for **pre- and in-service teacher training**. Awareness of phraseology in the wide sense should be promoted. Vocabulary teaching today is still too often exclusively word-based. Teachers (and particularly non-native teachers) should be made aware of the phraseological view of language and of the exercises and tools that research on phraseology has promoted, as they will undoubtedly help foster both teacher and learner empowerment.

Phraseology is a key factor in improving learners' reading and listening comprehension, alongside fluency and accuracy in production. However, its role in language learning largely remains to be explored and substantiated and it should therefore not be presented as the be-all and end-all of language teaching. Teachers have to do a "delicate balancing act" (Harwood 2002) which consists in exposing learners to a wide range of lexical strings while at the same time ensuring that they are not overloaded with them and are also able to abstract key concepts and useful rules of grammar. What is needed are teaching and learning practices which are informed by evidence from descriptive and theoretical linguistic analyses, second language acquisition research, psycholinguistics findings, and which are validated and assessed in the classroom.

References

Cook, G. (2003). The uses of reality: A reply to Ronald Carter. In B. Seidlhofer (ed.) *Controversies in applied linguistics*, 104–111. Oxford: Oxford University Press.

De Cock, S. (2004). Preferred sequences of words in NS and NNS speech. *Belgian Journal of English Language and Literatures (BELL)*, New Series 2, 225–246.

Eyckmans, J., Kappel, J., Stengers, H., Demecheleer, M. & Boers, F. (2005) Formulaic sequences and perceived oral proficiency. Putting a lexical approach to the test. In Cosme C., C. Gouverneur, F. Meunier & M. Paquot (eds) (2005) *Proceedings of the phraseology 2005 conference, 13–15, October 2005, Louvain-la-Neuve*, 117–119. Louvain-la-Neuve: Université catholique de Louvain.

Granger, S. & Meunier, F. (eds.) (in press). *Phraseology: An interdisciplinary perspective*. Amsterdam: John Benjamins.

Harwood, N. (2002). Taking a lexical approach to teaching: Principles and problems. *International Journal of Applied Linguistics*, 12 (2), 139–155.

Hasselgren, A. (1994). Lexical teddy bears and advanced learners: A study into the ways Norwegian students cope with English vocabulary. *International Journal of Applied Linguistics*, 4, 237–260.

Lewis, M. (1993). *The lexical approach. The state of ELT and a way forward*. London: Language Teaching Publications.

Lowe, C. (2006). An appraisal of modern current trends in ELT: Ten articles. *IH Journal of Education and Development 20*. Available from http://www.ihworld.com/ihjournal/

Meunier, F. (in press). Corpora, cognition and pedagogical grammars: An account of convergences and divergences. In De Knop, S. & T. De Rycker (eds.) *Cognitive approaches to pedagogical grammar*. Berlin. Mouton de Gruyter.

Paquot, M. (2007). Towards a productively-oriented academic word list. In J. Walinski, K. Kredens & S. Gozdz-Roszkowski (eds) *Corpora and ICT in language studies. PALC 2005* [Lodz Studies in Language 13], 127–140. Frankfurt: Peter Lang.

Porto, M. (1998). Lexical phrases and language teaching. *Forum* 36 (3). Available from http://exchanges.state.gov/forum/vols/vol36/no3/p22.htm

Author index

Subject index